Dance, Music and Cultures of Decolonisation in the Indian Diaspora

Dance, Music and Cultures of Decolonisation in the Indian Diaspora provides fascinating examples of dance and music projects across the Indian Diaspora to highlight that decolonisation is a creative process, as well as a historical and political one.

The book analyses creative processes in decolonising projects, illustrating how dance and music across the Indian Diaspora articulate socio-political aspirations in the wake of thinkers such as Gandhi and Ambedkar. It presents a wide range of examples: post-apartheid practices and experiences in a South African dance company, contestations over national identity politics in Trinidadian music competitions, essentialist and assimilationist strategies in a British dance competition, the new musical creativity of second-generation British-Tamil performers, Indian classical dance projects of reform and British multiculturalism, feminist intercultural performances in Australia, and performance re-enactments of museum exhibits that critically examine the past. Key topics under discussion include postcolonial contestations, decolonising scholarship, dialogic pedagogies, and intellectual responsibility. The book critically reflects on decolonising aims around respect, equality, and the colonial past's redress as expressed through performing arts projects.

Presenting richly detailed case studies that underline the need to examine creative processes in the cultures of decolonisation, *Dance, Music and Cultures of Decolonisation in the Indian Diaspora* will be of great interest to scholars of South Asian Studies, Diaspora Studies, Performing Arts Studies and Anthropology.

The chapters were originally published as a special issue of *South Asian Diaspora*.

Tina K. Ramnarine is a musician, anthropologist and global cultural explorer. She has published widely, including *Beautiful Cosmos: Performance and Belonging in the Caribbean Diaspora* (2007), *Musical Performance in the Diaspora* (Routledge, 2007) and *Global Perspectives on Orchestras: Collective Creativity and Social Agency* (2018).

Dance, Music and Cultures of Decolonisation in the Indian Diaspora

Edited by
Tina K. Ramnarine

LONDON AND NEW YORK

First published 2020
by Routledge
2 Park Square, Milton Park, Abingdon, Oxon, OX14 4RN

and by Routledge
52 Vanderbilt Avenue, New York, NY 10017

Routledge is an imprint of the Taylor & Francis Group, an informa business

First issued in paperback 2021

© 2020 Taylor & Francis

All rights reserved. No part of this book may be reprinted or reproduced or utilised in any form or by any electronic, mechanical, or other means, now known or hereafter invented, including photocopying and recording, or in any information storage or retrieval system, without permission in writing from the publishers.

Trademark notice: Product or corporate names may be trademarks or registered trademarks, and are used only for identification and explanation without intent to infringe.

British Library Cataloguing-in-Publication Data
A catalogue record for this book is available from the British Library

ISBN13: 978-0-367-81975-0 (hbk)
ISBN13: 978-1-03-208410-7 (pbk)

Typeset in Minion Pro
by codeMantra

Publisher's Note
The publisher accepts responsibility for any inconsistencies that may have arisen during the conversion of this book from journal articles to book chapters, namely the inclusion of journal terminology.

Disclaimer
Every effort has been made to contact copyright holders for their permission to reprint material in this book. The publishers would be grateful to hear from any copyright holder who is not here acknowledged and will undertake to rectify any errors or omissions in future editions of this book.

Contents

	Citation Information	vi
	Notes on Contributors	viii
1	Dance, music and cultures of decolonisation in the Indian Diaspora: towards a pluralist reading *Tina K. Ramnarine*	1
2	Dancing the rainbow nation as it bleeds: the *Surialanga Dance Company* in post-apartheid South Africa *Smitha Radhakrishnan*	18
3	Music competitions, public pedagogy and decolonisation in Trinidad and Tobago *Christopher L. Ballengee*	36
4	The *BBC Young Dancer* and the decolonising imagination *Magdalen Gorringe*	53
5	Decolonising Indian classical dance? Projects of reform, classical to contemporary *Sitara Thobani*	69
6	Gender, new creativity and Carnatic music in London *Jasmine Hornabrook*	83
7	Decolonising moves: gestures of reciprocity as feminist intercultural performance *Priya Srinivasan*	99
8	Decolonising human exhibits: dance, re-enactment and historical fiction *Prarthana Purkayastha*	113
	Index	129

Citation Information

The chapters in this book were originally published in *South Asian Diaspora*, volume 11, issue 2 (2019). When citing this material, please use the original page numbering for each article, as follows:

Chapter 1
Dance, music and cultures of decolonisation in the Indian Diaspora: towards a pluralist reading
Tina K. Ramnarine
South Asian Diaspora, volume 11, issue 2 (2019) pp. 109–125

Chapter 2
Dancing the rainbow nation as it bleeds: the Surialanga Dance Company *in post-apartheid South Africa*
Smitha Radhakrishnan
South Asian Diaspora, volume 11, issue 2 (2019) pp. 127–144

Chapter 3
Music competitions, public pedagogy and decolonisation in Trinidad and Tobago
Christopher L. Ballengee
South Asian Diaspora, volume 11, issue 2 (2019) pp. 145–161

Chapter 4
The BBC Young Dancer *and the decolonising imagination*
Magdalen Gorringe
South Asian Diaspora, volume 11, issue 2 (2019) pp. 163–178

Chapter 5
Decolonising Indian classical dance? Projects of reform, classical to contemporary
Sitara Thobani
South Asian Diaspora, volume 11, issue 2 (2019) pp. 179–192

Chapter 6
Gender, new creativity and Carnatic music in London
Jasmine Hornabrook
South Asian Diaspora, volume 11, issue 2 (2019) pp. 193–208

Chapter 7
Decolonising moves: gestures of reciprocity as feminist intercultural performance
Priya Srinivasan
South Asian Diaspora, volume 11, issue 2 (2019) pp. 209–222

Chapter 8
Decolonising human exhibits: dance, re-enactment and historical fiction
Prarthana Purkayastha
South Asian Diaspora, volume 11, issue 2 (2019) pp. 223–238

For any permission-related enquiries please visit:
http://www.tandfonline.com/page/help/permissions

Contributors

Christopher L. Ballengee is an Associate Professor of Music at Anne Arundel Community College, Arnold, USA. His research interests include Indian Caribbean musical traditions, world music pedagogy, ethnographic film and theatre sound design. He holds a PhD in ethnomusicology from the University of Florida, Gainesville, USA; Master of Music in ethnomusicology from Bowling Green State University, USA; and a Bachelor of Arts in Music from Lenoir-Rhyne University, Hickory, USA.

Magdalen Gorringe is a doctoral research student at the University of Roehampton, London, UK, researching 'The Professionalisation of Classical Indian Dance Forms in Britain' on a Vice Chancellor's Scholarship. She grew up in India where she started learning Bharatanatyam and is interested in creating routes into the profession for younger classical Indian dancers, as well as in using dance in activism. She is a co-founder of The Natya Project, which seeks to provide professional progression routes for young classical Indian dancers in the UK.

Jasmine Hornabrook is an ethnomusicologist focusing on music, transnational networks and identity in South Asian diasporas. She is interested in how cultural practices facilitate a sense of belonging and identity across nation-state borders. She completed her doctoral research at Goldsmiths, University of London, UK, and examined music and migration in the Sri Lankan Tamil diaspora. She works on the Leverhulme-funded project 'Migrant Memory and the Postcolonial Imagination' in the School of Social Sciences at Loughborough University, UK.

Prarthana Purkayastha is a Senior Lecturer in Dance at Royal Holloway University of London, UK. Her monograph *Indian Modern Dance, Feminism and Transnationalism* (2014, Palgrave Macmillan New World Choreographies series) won the 2015 de la Torre Bueno Prize from the Society of Dance History Scholars and the 2015 Outstanding Publication Award from the Congress on Research in Dance. Her research locates South Asian dance at the intersections of race, gender and nationhood.

Smitha Radhakrishnan is an Associate Professor of Sociology and LuElla LaMer Slaner Associate Professor of Women's Studies at Wellesley College, USA. She is the author of the book *Appropriately Indian: Gender and Culture in a New Transnational Class* (Duke, 2011), as well as numerous articles related to her research on gender, globalisation and development. Outside academic life, she is a lifelong Bharatanatyam practitioner, who currently teaches and performs in Natick, USA.

CONTRIBUTORS

Tina K. Ramnarine is a musician, anthropologist and global cultural explorer. She has published widely on musical performance, politics and arts responses to global challenges. Her publications include the books *Creating Their Own Space: The Development of an Indian-Caribbean Musical Tradition* (2001), *Ilmatar's Inspirations: Nationalism, Globalization, and the Changing Soundscapes of Finnish Folk Music* (2003), *Beautiful Cosmos: Performance and Belonging in the Caribbean Diaspora* (2007), and the edited volumes *Musical Performance in the Diaspora* (2007) and *Global Perspectives on Orchestras: Collective Creativity and Social Agency* (2018). She co-edited *We Mark Your Memory: Writing from the Descendants of Indenture* (2018). She is Professor of Music at Royal Holloway, University of London.

Priya Srinivasan is a dancer, choreographer and scholar. She has a dual career as a researcher at the Alfred Deakin Institute of Citizenship and Globalization based at Deakin University, Australia, and an independent artist. She prioritises decolonisation, making visible minority women's histories. She is the author of the award-winning book *Sweating Saris: Indian Dance as Transnational Labour*, which looks at the connection between decolonisation, citizenship, immigration and dance. Developing two key concepts from her book including the 'unruly spectator' and the 'dancing body as the labouring body', her work brings together a critical feminist praxis in unearthing subaltern women's texts through live bodily performance with visual art and interactive multimedia. Her scholarly and performance work has been presented internationally.

Sitara Thobani is an Assistant Professor in the Residential College in the Arts and Humanities at Michigan State University, East Lansing, USA. She received her DPhil in Social and Cultural Anthropology from the University of Oxford, St. Antony's College, UK. Her research interests focus on art and cultural production in South Asia and the diaspora; the construction of racial, religious and national identities; and representations of India from the 19th century to the present.

Dance, music and cultures of decolonisation in the Indian Diaspora: towards a pluralist reading

Tina K. Ramnarine

ABSTRACT
Decolonisation is a creative process, as well as a historical and political one. This article outlines key issues in researching the creative processes of decolonisation with reference to dance and music in the Indian Diaspora. It begins with Gandhi's 'experiments with truth', which first developed a political reach in the context of Indian indenture within the British Empire but left a fractured legacy in the decolonising era. Their conceptual import frames a discussion on participatory research, dialogic pedagogies and intellectual responsibility. The notion of dialogue contextualises examples of musical collaborations, as well as intellectual exchanges between Gandhi and two of his interlocutors: Ambedkar and Tolstoy. These shift discussion from an oppositional narrative of decolonisation towards more complex views of cultural and intellectual interactions in decolonising processes. The final section introduces the volume's case studies, which collectively encourage a pluralist reading of dance and music in the cultures of decolonisation.

Decolonisation is a creative process, as well as a historical and political one. This article outlines key issues in researching the creative processes of decolonisation with reference to dance and music in the Indian Diaspora, which spreads across Europe, North America, the Pacific, the Gulf countries and elsewhere. The Indian Diaspora is large and diverse. It has been shaped by colonialism, nationalism and neoliberal globalisation.

An important trope in decolonisation processes is the history of colonial labour. The system of Indian indenture was part of this history, and the basis for nineteenth-century patterns of migration that formed what has been called the 'old' Indian Diaspora. The 'new' one emerged from the mid-twentieth century onwards due to later patterns of migrant labour and secondary migrations, including from the Caribbean and East Africa to Europe, Canada and the USA. The categories of 'old' and 'new' are of limited use. The 'old' and 'new' Indian Diasporas are not distinct. Their histories overlap. They are connected by complex transnational and kinship relationships. These include the Diaspora's relations with India: its potential to invest in India and thus secure its place in the global economy, to act internationally in diplomatic ways that foster notions of India's soft power, and to develop cultural and economic flows through its vast transnational networks (Hegde and Sahoo 2017). Despite the strength of India's presence in the imagination of its Diaspora, the Indian Diaspora is also concerned with nationalist politics and (anti-) immigration discourses within the variety of nation states of settlement. Overall, through the range of its connections, the Indian Diaspora articulates interests in reshaping geopolitical relations of power and in forging new alliances, which are characteristic of the decolonising era.

Performing arts practitioners, including dancers and musicians, play a central role in maintaining links between India and its Diaspora, as well as in representing a diverse range of performances on international stages (Ramnarine 2017). While they are interested in the historical and contemporary dynamics of transnational connections, they also challenge ideas about diasporic otherness and national belonging. Dance and music are linked with cultural heritage discourses, the continuity of tradition, and identity politics. They offer generalised representations of India, and specific ones relating to diasporic, regional and historical diversities. In London, for example, there are Punjabi, Gujarati, Tamil and Indian-Caribbean communities, which are identified as part of the larger Indian Diaspora. But, due to historical links, they overlap with other Diasporas, including Caribbean, African and, more generally, South Asian.

Dance and music practitioners promote mutually respectful social engagements in the cultures of decolonisation. They often fall short of realising decolonising political aims around respect, equality and the colonial past's redress. Sometimes their creative processes are celebrated for building artistic bridges and articulating inclusive social and national visions. At other times, they become embroiled with new forms of inequality and violence despite practitioners' decolonising intentions. Both possibilities are investigated in this volume. Contributors examine specific projects and creative processes to show how these work towards both the dismantlement of colonial ways of thinking and the construction of new nationalisms, including inclusive and exclusionary forms of multiculturalism. Moreover, the Indian Diaspora shares some but not all the priorities of other decolonising contexts. There are few discussions on restitution of land or reparation for dispossession, which are prevalent, for example, amongst indigenous communities in Australia and the Americas. Adopting global, but not universal perspectives on decolonisation bring these relations, differences and conversations to the fore, as the scholars of decoloniality, Walter Mignolo and Catherine E. Walsh (2018) note, and they are necessary for future performing arts research too.

Decolonisation remains a horizon of expectation since the colonial past of global modernity is still within living memory. The most urgent decolonising challenges lie in the diverse domains of nationalist modernity, which exhibit ongoing struggles with segregation, stratification and sovereignty. The inextricable relationship between colonial and nationalist modernity leaves intellectuals attempting – as the historian, Partha Chatterjee observed – 'to make sense of a global order of empire without colonies' (2012, 336). Researching the creative processes of decolonisation offers some contributions to making sense of this global order. The task is complicated by a variety of historical, economic and political considerations, not least by the many dimensions of decolonisation, unified only by the historical background of Europe's territorial and economic ambitions over the last five centuries. In addition, although decolonisation raises issues around independent national sovereignty, it often reproduces former structures of colonial power. In his classic study, *The Wretched of the Earth*, the public intellectual and psychiatrist, Frantz Fanon considered the failure of the postcolonial state in terms of neo-colonial politics.

Decolonisation has re-implemented colonial structures in the hands of a national bourgeoisie marked by its 'wave-lengths tuned in to Europe', its 'gang-like' behaviour for short-term profits, its willingness 'to accept the dividends that the former colonial power hands it', its facilitation of the former colonial power's indirect rule, and its 'caricature' of Europe (2001, first published in 1961, 139–141). For Fanon, this kind of national bourgeoisie should be opposed too (ibid, 141).

One of the major figures of Indian independence, Mahatma Gandhi (1869–1948) looms large in the global decolonising imagination. His principle of non-violent confrontation provided a foundation for independence movements across the colonised world and, later on, for civil rights struggles. He wrote about his 'experiments with truth' in his autobiography (2001, first published in 1927), which have encouraged forms of revisionist critical thinking extending into the decolonising era. His experiments were based on lived experiences, self-representations and symbolic political actions. They first developed a political reach in the historical context of Indian indenture, the colonial system of contracted labour that was related to maintaining the trade in sugar, tea, spices and other mass-marketed, global commodities. These were produced labour-intensively within the British Empire. In the post-enslavement era, plantations were sustained by indenture, which shaped the Indian labour histories of South Africa, Fiji, Mauritius and the Caribbean (largely Trinidad and Tobago, Guyana and Suriname during the period 1838–1917). Indenture was at its height when European imperial powers were beginning their more aggressive campaigns for territorial colonial possessions, which the revolutionary Russian leader, Vladimir Ilyich Lenin described as the total seizure of the planet motivated by economic exportation of capital, not just commodities (for further discussion see Chatterjee 2012, 268–271).

Anti-colonial performances within independence movements provide a backdrop for researching contemporary decolonising performance projects. In India, anti-indenture songs protested against British exploitation, which had emerged against the longer histories of north Indian labour migrations and songs of longing for family members departing for work (Kumar 2017). These songs contributed to a broader performing arts repertoire (dance, music and theatre), expressing anti-colonial political sentiments prominent in, for example, nineteenth-century Calcutta (Chatterjee 2012).

Gandhi's experiments with truth are also one kind of anti-colonial performance expression. Reception to these experiments has been mixed. They have left a fractured legacy in the decolonising era. They have been viewed positively as part of a spiritual quest and as a means to overcome inequalities imposed both externally by colonising powers and internally, in India, through the replication of social hierarchies. His experiments with truth aligned with his campaigns for pluralism within nationhood, the value of traditional Indian crafts practices, and workers' rights through modes of civil resistance known as *satyagraha* or truth force (Guha 2018). They were a 'lived philosophy' based on the Russian writer, Leo Tolstoy's notion of compassion; and they were sometimes contradictory because moral principles may guide conduct but they do not determine action (Sorabji 2012). By contrast, critics have questioned the ethical dimensions of his experiments, viewing them as theatrical expressions for political effects, particularly in relation to dalit rights (Roy 2014). In this respect, Gandhi's most significant dialogues were with the politician, Bhimrao Ramji Ambedkar (1891–1956), who adopted satyagraha to insist on political reform in India as a way of ensuring dalit and women's rights, and thereby shaping a more egalitarian society. Gandhi and Ambedkar first met in 1931. Importantly, although they both criticised the perpetuation of untouchability, they held opposing views on the issue of caste (as a hierarchical system within Hinduism) and its validity for the future nation state. Ambedkar rejected Hinduism and turned to Buddhism towards the end of his life because of the caste issue. Their debate – and its consequences: Ambedkar's rejection of and Gandhi's adherence to caste – is of utmost relevance to the contemporary decolonising nation state even though it is complicated by religious frameworks (Roy 2014, Jaffrelot 2005); and it is an example of dialogic action (discussed below).

Paradoxically, caste became obsolete for indentured subjects and their descendants. The voyages across seas and caste irrelevance in plantation life shattered its hold in the making of social relationships. The 'old' Diaspora thus offers models for addressing the internal social inequalities of contemporary Indian life. It yielded one of the fiercest critics of the caste system, the Indian-Trinidadian writer V. S. Naipaul (1932–2018), who called Gandhi's view of the holiness of poverty 'a defect of vision' (2002, first published in 1977, 85–103). This is a way in which the Indian Diaspora (itself undergoing processes of decolonisation) speaks to India about its particular decolonising trajectories, offering commentary tinged by nostalgia, concern and hope for the ancestral state, alongside insights into lived diasporic experiences at the end of Europe's empires. Gandhi's legacy is fractured too because the extent to which he was able to reflect critically on colonial indoctrination with regard to 'racial' hierarchies, especially during his years as a young lawyer in South Africa, is unclear. He simultaneously serves as a model for revising race thinking (e.g. in Nelson Mandela's post-apartheid South Africa) or for re-inscribing it (e.g. in controversies over a Gandhi memorial statue in Ghana in 2016).

It is useful to consider the conceptual import of Gandhi's experiments, which frames the following discussion on participatory research, dialogic pedagogies and intellectual responsibility. Although his experiments remain controversial, they highlight the extent to which decolonisation is not a simple story focused on unravelling the practices of empire with an uncomplicated view of opposition between the coloniser and the colonised. It is an interrogation of a more entangled past. For example, while colonial indoctrination has become a major topic in decolonising pedagogies, one cannot overlook the fact that a figure like Ambedkar benefitted from a colonial education, equipping him for political service in India, because generations of his family had joined the British military. Nevertheless, decolonising politics is preoccupied with looking ahead and its importance lies in its interrogation of future relations within and across postcolonial states. Ultimately, therefore, with reference to dialogues between Gandhi and Tolstoy, this article shifts discussion from an oppositional narrative of decolonisation towards more complex views of cultural and intellectual interactions in decolonising processes.

Participatory research and decolonising scholarship

Performing arts researchers are well placed to analyse the details of creative processes in the cultures of decolonisation by examining specific performance projects that shift away from narratives of coloniser–colonised oppositions, with either pro- or anti-colonial perspectives, towards models of collaboration, dialogue and responsibility. The dance researcher and practitioner, Sitara Thobani, for example, argues that Indian dance in its classical forms 'has become a key aspect of the mutual constitution of not only postcolonial Indian and South Asian diasporic identities, but also of British national identity as multicultural and transnational' (2017, 6). This double configuration is complicated. As Thobani elaborates:

> the India conjured up in these performances recasts British identity as modern, dynamic and cosmopolitan even as it reinscribes Indian and diasporic identities as exotic, feminine and mystical in particularly racialised and gendered ways ... it reinscribes specific forms of coloniality. (ibid)

Such insights are often based on practice; on dancing and performing music. This practical dimension leads to challenging colonial indoctrination, informing pedagogic approaches, and prompting questions about the social impacts of participatory methods. The social impacts of research agendas raise ethical issues and broader questions about intellectual responsibility. Practice itself is a form of critical thought. This means it can be understood not only in terms of performance's representational capacities but also as a contribution to decolonising scholarship, which is itself a body of work concerned with the social agency of intellectual work. Alongside practice, performing arts researchers are influenced by theoretical paradigms in literary theory, postcolonial studies, new imperial histories (reassessments of the past) and analyses of intercultural connections that replace concepts of exotic differences (see Burnard, Mackinlay and Powell 2016, Norton 2018, Ramnarine 2018).

This combination of practice and theory in participatory research (supplemented by reflexivity and ethnography) is at its best a way of studying alongside people, not only turning them into subjects for intellectual enquiry. When performing arts researchers reflect on decolonisation, they often do so from participation in explicitly decolonising projects, which include discourses on multicultural diversity, reparation, and conflicts in identity politics (e.g. Thiong'o 2005, Thobani 2017, and also see Ballengee, Gorringe, and Thobani, in this volume). From this perspective, another useful trajectory for developing performing arts research contributions to decolonising scholarship is theorisation from the global south – a term encompassing the perspectives of those who have been oppressed, marginalised and discriminated against, often in the name of law and constitutional rights (De Sousa Santos 2014). The global south is a set of diverse intellectual approaches that brings thinkers into dialogues in various ways without mediations via former colonial centres.

By emphasising the theoretical dimensions of lived experiences, the global south is aligned with participatory methods in the performing arts disciplines. De Sousa Santos writes about the embodied and experiential knowledge of southern theories: 'Our knowledge flies at low altitude because it is stuck to the body' (2014, 12). Since bodies are the 'squandered knowledge' of the world (ibid), they are diverse, inexhaustible, and turn mono-cultural concepts of diversity into 'complex contemporaneity' (ibid, 13). Performing arts researchers comment on what kind of knowledge is transmitted by performers. Priya Srinivasan, for example, explores the multiple points of view transmitted by Indian dancing bodies in rehearsing and performing formalised gestures. Even the fabric of their costumes, 'weaving and wearing one's own cloth', is part of the story of Indian struggles for independence (2012, xi). While creative considerations often obscure the point that dance is part of the world of work, like productive, agricultural, construction and technological tasks, Indian dancers are part of a transnational labour force in different political economies (ibid). The smallest details of creative practices tell larger stories. Gandhi used cotton as a symbol of self-reliance to confront and reconfigure the economic relationships between Indian and British textile workers. These relationships were also scholarly ones. Notably, Indian dancers were constituted as exhibits in nineteenth-century ethnographic exhibitions that put the world on display and were linked with scientific research. In decolonising scholarship, these dance performances are reenacted to present alternative points of view (see Purkayastha in this volume) – evidence that the knowledge embodied in performance is not, after all, entirely squandered.

De Sousa Santos's notion of complexity can be applied to three key concerns of performing arts research: the dialectic between tradition and innovation, the legacy of encounter and exchange, and collaborative creativities. How do researchers juxtapose traditional performance practices sustained as the brands of cultural heritage and survival on one hand with creative innovations occurring in unfolding decolonising relationships on the other? In part, we do so by considering both historical contexts and political aspirations, as well as by excavating the dynamics of power, protest and revision to think about contemporary decolonising agendas. Given that decolonising scholarship has the potential to disrupt the status quo one might celebrate the fact that it is increasingly prominent. Reconsideration of hitherto conventional disciplinary assumptions has resulted in critiques of historical representations, centre-periphery geographies, ethnographic processes in the making of others, and educational curricula that perpetuate bias in dominant systems of knowledge. With its revisionist, and even revolutionary potential, decolonising scholarship is gaining intellectual currency amongst a new generation of scholars inspired by critical analyses of disciplinary histories and concerned with pluralist forms of knowledge-making, global inequalities and liberation from hegemonic models of exploitation (including imperialist, capitalist and patriarchal).

Dialogic pedagogies and intellectual emancipation

One classic concern in decolonising scholarship is colonial indoctrination, which affects perceptions about social order. The Indian-Trinidadian writer Sam Selvon narrated a story familiar across the decolonising world. He began with childhood memories of seeing an old Indian fish seller. He spoke about the limping Indian man, who was teased because customers had to help him lift his tray of fish. One day he turned up with an assistant, a white man; and Selvon recalled his reaction. He was 'furious with the old Indian for putting the white man in such a humiliating position' and, in retrospect, he asked, 'this gut feeling I had as a child, that the Indian was just a piece of cane trash while the white man was to be honoured and respected – where had it come from?' (1987, 13). Selvon turned to personal memory, drawing on the Jamaican political leader and writer, Marcus Garvey's dictum of intellectual emancipation, to speak about going beyond colonial indoctrination by thinking about divided postcolonial societies and decolonising complicities in the perpetuation of inequalities. In view of such divisions and complicities, researchers need to think carefully about resurgent ethno-nationalisms in decolonising states, including its violent forms, as well as about the limited capacities of multicultural policies to engineer inclusive societies within which individual cultural rights protected. These are pressing issues in contexts of decolonising border crossings, for example across perceived ethnic and cultural divides (see Ballengee and Radhakrishnan, in this volume).

Another classic concern, linked with indoctrination, is English language dominance (and this is of course in relation to British imperialism), which informs much work in literary, historical and postcolonial studies. Chatterjee's discussion on how a colonial education in English produced a new class of Indians eager to set up schools and curricula, which in turn had far-reaching effects on literary nationalism and theatre practice (2012, 224–228), is reproduced in other contexts. Ngũgĩ wa Thiong'o, for example, noted that he was a student of English in Kenya in 1962 and that at that time African literature was produced in languages that reflected the continent's imperial histories (English, French or Portuguese). These languages were assumed to politically mediate 'between African people in the same nation and between nations in Africa ... having a capacity to unite African peoples against divisive tendencies inherent in the multiplicity of African languages within the same geographic state' (2005 [1986], 6–7). Thiong'o was imprisoned in 1977 for his non-English language theatre work, which was based on song and dance forms as 'integral parts of conversation' (ibid, 45). In his cell, he started writing a novel in Gikuyu language, hoping that his students were reading Fanon and Lenin, and motivated by a politics of decolonisation to reconnect with 'the mainstream of the struggles of African people' (ibid, 85). His approach highlights performing arts inscriptions of political ideas on bodies, performing stages and – for music – the artefacts of recording technologies. Thiong'o, like other activists, demanded curricula reform and he called for 'decolonizing the mind' to use the title of one of his most influential books (2005 [1986]).

Decolonising scholarship continues to demand curricula reform. For example, the writer, Maria del Pilar Kaladeen noted that education provided a route out of the sugar plantation for the Indians who remained in Guyana following the abolition of indenture. It was a British education and it led people to migrate again in response to the call to help rebuild post-World War Two Britain. The next generation, however, born in Britain, faced historical amnesia in curriculum design. Indenture has remained one of the hidden histories of nineteenth-century British colonial plantations in the Caribbean and, subsequently, of that most iconic ship, the *Empire Windrush*, which marked a new era of Caribbean migrations to Britain (Kaladeen 2018).

Hidden histories, nevertheless, are a part of lived experiences with pedagogical possibilities. Thus, the French cultural theorist, Jacques Rancière articulated a notion of inclusivity and revolutionary liberation in his book, *The Ignorant Schoolmaster: Five Lessons in Intellectual Emancipation* (1991), written at a time of pedagogical reform in France. He asks us to take equality as a presupposition rather than as a goal, arguing that 'explication is the myth of pedagogy, the parable of a world divided into knowing minds and ignorant ones' (ibid, 6). For him, lived experience is a way of knowing, which means that knowledge is not a one-way transfer from pedagogue to student. His insights are particularly relevant since decolonising approaches are not yet in mainstream education. The difficulties in truly pursuing them might lie in their radical challenges to existing hierarchies. As Rancière comments, the pedagogue might have a problem with emancipation since 'every common person might conceive his human dignity, take the measure of his intellectual capacity, and decide how to use it' (ibid, 17).

Reading scholarship within the frame of decolonisation, whether or not its vocabularies are used, is an emancipatory exercise in Rancière's sense of intellectual emancipation. For example, the music researcher, Gerry Farrell commented on cultural investments in retaining the idea that Indian music is somehow unknowable such that it can continue 'to be rediscovered some 200 years after its first appearance in the academic and popular consciousness of the West' (1997, 9). In his book, *Indian Music and the West* (1997), he described one of the earliest intellectual exchanges about music, which took place in Varanasi, in 1786. This was an exchange between Jiwan Shah and Francis Fowke, who compared the pitches of the Been and the harpsichord. Farrell observed that not only were these musicians unable to assume the validity of the knowledge they generated but also that their exchange took place in a relationship of inequality (ibid, 15), one characterised by intellectual and economic possession, as India came to occupy a central place in British imperial worldviews (ibid, 18).

Both Indian and British scholars began to acknowledge India's cultural heritage in 'a new way' (ibid, 146) in the context of the Indian nationalist independence movement. They understood that Orientalist intellectual perspectives had shaped representations of Indian history. To critique and destabilise these representations they turned to resurgent cultural forms. But musicological debates continued to pose familiar questions about whether Indian music should be notated, whether it should be harmonised and orchestrated, and how the spread of the harmonium might be curtailed (ibid). Farrell argued that it was not until the 1950s that the conflict between tradition and innovation became irrelevant. This was when Ravi Shankar's practices as a sitarist established him as the major representative of Indian music, whose presence on the world stage had 'far-reaching effects on both popular and classical musicians' (ibid, 170). Farrell discussed Shankar's collaborations with *The Beatles*. Shankar also collaborated with the violinist Yehudi Menuhin. Their collaboration illustrates, in a celebratory way, a meeting of equals, of representatives from two classical traditions, far removed from the unequal relations of the earlier musical encounter between Shah and Fowke. The set of albums Shankar and Menuhin released in 1967, 1968 and 1976 was entitled *West Meets East*. Despite the title's evocation of the exotic imaginary, of difference, Menuhin developed a sustained interest in Indian classical music, as well as in yoga; and Shankar, conversely, in the concerto and symphony. Shankar spoke about the 'love and friendship' they shared in playing together in a 1986 documentary film, *A Portrait of the Maestro of the Sitar*. In this film, Menuhin spoke about their collaboration in terms of how he was struck by music-making as 'a consecration', and his belief that the oriental and the occidental were parts of each other.

For Farrell, the 'colonial re-creation of India' was compromised as Indian musicians began to work with jazz musicians, rap artists and orchestras; and it was difficult for him to assess how this work related 'to the wider history of the West's cultural encounter with India' (1997, 230). Two decades after his observations, the concept of the West itself is critiqued and the geopolitical balance of power is changing rapidly. The practices of Indian musicians working with jazz, rap and classical counterparts, amongst others, are part of a global story about music in the twenty first century.

Dialogues are crucial if we are to avoid the conceptual dangers of a binary polarisation between the global south and the global north. Across west and east, south and north, there are many contributions to decolonising epistemological experiments. The educator and philosopher, Paulo Freire argues for a pedagogy that seeks the 'continuing transformation of reality, in behalf of the continuing humanization of men' (2017, first published in 1970, 65). The dialogues between Shankar and Menuhin can be understood within his conceptual frame. Musical dialogues are pedagogical situations in which music, as the object of study, is re-presented to each participant. The re-presentations extend the individual's 'thematic universe' and inaugurate 'the dialogue of education as the practice of freedom' (ibid, 69). In other words, in sharing their practices, the musicians' dialogues hold the potential to dispel the conceptual borders of west and east, for their audiences, as well as for the individuals themselves; and they are crucial to a decolonising project based on freedom rather than oppression. Freire's elaboration on the thematic universe turns to history and its legacies, and to his claim that the fundamental theme of our epoch is domination and its opposite – liberation (ibid, 76); the latter reached through both praxis and reflection, enabling scientific and humanist revolutionary leaders to dismiss the myth of 'the ignorance of the people' (ibid, 107). Oppression persists through anti-dialogical action based on the techniques of divide and rule, manipulation of the masses by dominant elites, and forms of cultural invasion that convince the oppressed of their cultural inferiority (ibid, 114–126).

The dialogues between Shankar and Menuhin are, by contrast, examples of a dialogical theory of action, in which subjects 'meet in cooperation in order to transform the world' (ibid, 140). Their recording projects, labelled provocatively for a contemporary audience, *West Meets East*, are meetings 'to *name* the world in order to transform it' (ibid, emphasis in the original). The antithesis to cultural invasion is cultural synthesis, but the major point concerns the significance of cultural action itself, not the spectrum of possibilities within dialogical action. In this respect, Freire's argument resonates with the central thesis of this volume – that we view decolonisation as being a creative process too. In Freire's words, 'cultural action, as historical action, is an instrument for superseding the dominant alienated and alienating culture. In this sense, every authentic revolution is a cultural revolution' (ibid, 153).

The concepts of cultural invasion, synthesis and alienation demand careful scrutiny. It is essential to bear in mind the ways in which colonies also shape colonial centres. It is essential to think about postcolonial interactions. Britain was shaped profoundly by its imperial experiences. Ships transported gramophone records, as well as people, and the first records of Indian music appeared in Britain in 1899. The composer, Gustav Holst listened to them, and his study of Indian music and its influence on his creative practice have provided examples of colonial cultures shaping musical languages in Britain (Ghuman 2014, 107). Ravi Shankar's recordings of mantras in the 1997 album *Chants of India*, the last one to be produced by George Harrison, contributed to the spread of ritual expression in popular culture, in the language of business, in New Age philosophy and in the psychology of well-being. Today, there is a lively British-Asian musical scene in Britain, especially in cities like London and Birmingham. This scene finds its way into mainstream and institutional contexts, such as the BBC Proms Concerts at the Royal Albert Hall (Ramnarine 2017). These are all examples of dance and music providing alternative vocabularies for interaction, with many practitioners expressing hopes that their dialogues might lead to transformations (also see the chapters in this volume for examples of the different ways in which these are articulated).

Intellectual responsibility, Gandhi and indenture

Decolonising perspectives dominated global intellectual re-assessment of Indian indenture in 2017, largely because that year marked the centenary of its abolition. Indenture was at its height by the time that Gandhi passed his matriculation examinations in 1887 and began making preparations to study law in England the following year. Gandhi, studying in London, 'played' at being an English gentleman, as he wrote in his autobiography (1927). He qualified in 1891, and two years later he relocated to South Africa to practice law. There he encountered Balasundaram. This Tamil man, an indentured labourer, had been beaten by his employer. He sought Gandhi's help, who assisted him with regard to his employment contract. Such were the conditions of Balasundaram's servitude, however, that only the Protector of Indentured Labourers or his employer could release him from the contract. Gandhi managed to ensure that Balasundaram's indenture was transferred to another employer, and he then attracted other cases. Stories about his legal activism circulated around Madras, now Chennai. Gandhi's 'experiments' transformed him from playing the role of an English gentleman to becoming a champion of labour rights within the system of indenture and, later, a prominent voice in the Indian independence movement. These transformations were rooted in using his colonial education to challenge colonial power, albeit his inability to fully confront questions about indoctrination. Balasundaram's role in this history, though less celebrated, is also significant within the frames of Freire's dialogic action and Rancière's dignity in intellectual emancipation.

Gandhi appears in the musical record, in songs performed in Guyana that celebrated his achievements in the Indian independence movement. Scholars from India studied Indian diasporic music. Ved Prakash Vatuk recorded around 900 songs in Guyana, which were sung for ceremonial, religious and festival occasions, accompanied by instruments such as tabla, harmonium, sarangi (a bowed-stringed instrument) and cymbals. Song texts dealt with the recruitment of Indian labour, the voyage to the New World, experiences on the sugar estates and hopes for independence. Vatuk notes that in some song texts, the 'Indian freedom movement is pictured as a marriage party, in which Gandhi is a bridegroom going to marry "Freedom"' (1964, 230). Gandhi themes persisted in post-independence Guyanese songs. For example, songs about Cheddi Jagan, a descendant of indenture, who was elected Chief Minister in 1953 and later became President (1992–1997), likened him to Gandhi (Vatuk 1964, 231–232). When Jagan first won the elections, the British government intervened with military action in fear that the Soviet Union would gain a footing in South America because of Jagan's Marxist views.

Gandhi appears in historical retrievals, which is integral to a decolonising view of the past. In this spirit, a manuscript found in the British Library has been restored and translated from Bhojpuri to English (Mohabir, forthcoming). This book was originally published in 1916, *Damra Phag Bahar* (Holi songs of Demerara): a collection of folk songs compiled in Guyana by Lalbihari Sharma. It is one of the few books written by an Indian indentured subject in the Caribbean. It invokes Gandhi, tangentially, through a tribute to a man called Parmanand, a Punjabi Arya Samaj missionary, who went to Guyana from South Africa where he had lived with Gandhi for a month. After establishing a Hindu school to counter Christian missionary pedagogic influences, Parmanand left Guyana for active involvement in Indian independence politics in the USA. Having eventually returned to the Punjab, he was arrested for his involvement in a pan-Indian revolutionary attempt and sentenced to life imprisonment.

Parmanand's biography takes us away from colonial constructs of Indian migrants as labourers and peasants in indenture histories. Parmanand did not arrive in South Africa or in Guyana as an indentured Indian, as the writer, Gaiutra Bahadur (2018) points out, and even Lalbihari Sharma, who was an indentured labourer, was not the subaltern she expected.

Similarly, when I first began to work on the musical practices linked with indenture histories, a renowned performer of the popular genre chutney, which became the defining example of Indian indenture performance histories and their legacies in the Caribbean, told me: 'long time ago most of the singers used to sing only classical songs' (Sundar Popo, personal interview, 22 July 1996 in Ramnarine 2001, 38). I thought it would be worth accepting this testimony literally and it has been one of the most intriguing historical insights in my research enquiries. It led me to thinking about Wajid Ali Shah's performance legacies, especially his patronage of dance and music. When he was deposed in 1856 by British authorities following the annexation of Awadh (Oude) by the East India Company, he moved with his retinue to Calcutta. His performing arts school was next to the depot from where Indian migrants boarded the ships that transported them to other parts of the British Empire. It is possible that members of his retinue were amongst the migrants (Ramnarine 2001, 130–131). Colonial representations of Wajid Ali Shah have obscured his 'achievements as an early modern cultural figure', who set the precedent for a subsequent cultural nationalist agenda in which dance and music became modern institutionalised disciplines (Chatterjee 2012, 219–220). Decolonising representations of dance and music recuperate these achievements.

Performance projects in the cultures of decolonisation have the capacity to 'irritate Europe' in Frank Schulze-Engler's sense of 'the uneasy relationship between "Europe" and the "postcolonial"'; and this irritation is exacerbated by having to come to terms with European colonial pasts and new cosmopolitanisms (2016, 670). Decolonisation extends beyond the irritation of Europe, however, and it departs from the centre-periphery models that dominated much critical thinking about the relation between imperial homeland and its colonies. It is imperative to understand the irritations that arise in coming to terms with the past within decolonising nation states in both Europe and its former colonies, and then to look beyond irritations to see decolonisation as a global story, however diverse its manifestations, narrating aspirations for equality, and related to other struggles for this cause.

This relation is illustrated by the labour struggles behind decolonising and revolutionary politics, which frame the dialogues between two highly influential thinkers. In 1910, Gandhi established Tolstoy Farm, his site for satyagrahis, the non-violent resisters against the South African regime. The preceding year he had translated, into Gujarati, Tolstoy's 1908 *Letter to a Hindu: The Subjection of India – Its Cause and Cure*. Tolstoy concluded his letter by arguing that the Indians, the English, the French, the Germans, and the Russians did not need constitutions, revolutions, congresses, weapons, schools, art, cinema or gramophones as much as they needed to realise one simple truth, one expressed by all the world's religions: the truth of what love demands from humanity. Tolstoy's Christian concept of non-violence as universal love was linked with Gandhi's practice of non-violence.

Gandhi wrote a letter to Tolstoy on 1 October 1909 informing him about the situation of the Indian indentured labourers in South Africa. On 7 October 1909, Tolstoy replied to Gandhi:

> May God help all your dear brothers and co-workers in the Transvaal. This fight between gentleness and brutality, between humility and love on one side, and conceit and violence on the other, makes itself ever more strongly felt here to us also.

On 8 May 1910, having read Gandhi's book, *Indian Home Rule*, Tolstoy wrote to Gandhi that his treatment of passive resistance (literally truth force) was 'a question of the greatest importance, not only for India but for the whole humanity'. Their correspondence demonstrates mutual respect.[1]

This dialogue opens a window onto the story of Indian indenture, one part of the story of Indian independence, and also part of the story of other struggles – showing us a world that is rethinking the bases of human relations. Colonial rule had to confront its own internal contradictions, especially after the Second World War (Shipway 2008, 11–14). It is also worth pointing out, albeit briefly, the insights to be gained by looking at the effects of colonial rule and the Bolshevik Revolution concurrently (ibid), and to note the extent to which the decolonising world turned to Lenin's writing. This provides one historical frame for understanding decolonising connections between postcolonialism and postsocialism, as well as for considering the dynamics currently developing between India and Russia.

While complex relationships of power in the nineteenth century were choreographed between the British Empire and the Russian Empire, Gandhi and Tolstoy, two individuals living within their different orbits, corresponded about colonial labour and the independence movement. The most ambitious dimension of their correspondence lies in their contemplations of truth, as a spiritual quest for the benefit of humanity. This quest was a moral exercise contributing, alongside political exercises undertaken by figures like Ambedkar, to the twentieth-century's re-conceptualisations of human labour and political rights in the wake of independence and revolutionary movements. Decolonising scholarship in the twenty first century is also a moral exercise; it is premised on intellectual responsibility. It is an experiment in which 'truth' itself comes under scrutiny to consider the epistemologies and dialogic bases of knowledge. Experiments with performing arts aesthetics, together with their dissemination and reception, contribute to decolonising politics in dance and music projects. In this sense, too, we research decolonisation as a creative process.

The articles in this volume

This volume emerged from a conference co-sponsored by the Horniman Museum and Gardens and the Royal Anthropological Institute on the theme: 'South Asia and its Diaspora: Musical Performances in the Cultures of Decolonisation'. The conference was held at the Horniman Museum and Gardens in Forest Hill, London, on 4 November 2017. The call for papers highlighted that the conference would take a broad view of the performing arts and it attracted many submissions on dance, as well as music. The conference was hosted in connection with the Horniman's 2017 summer series, which featured the diversity of South Asian music from traditional to urban electronic experimental projects, as well as its creative resonances with contemporary culture in the UK (hence this volume's geographic focus).

Contributors to this volume collectively investigate the interrelated worlds of performance and scholarship in the cultures of decolonisation. They draw on theoretical discussions by writers such as Frantz Fanon, Walter Mignolo and Paulo Freire. They employ reflexive, participant and ethnographic methodologies. This combination means that the discussions in this volume are located precisely in the nexus between praxis and critical thought, which is essential to developing decolonising perspectives. Through biography, testimony, archive and performance work, the contributors highlight decolonisation as an ongoing process within which it is necessary to consider institutions, governance, interculturalism, race relations, multiculturalism and identity politics.

The first two articles (Radhakrishnan, Ballengee) discuss complex negotiations between creative practices and the postcolonial nation-state's identity politics, which emphasise internal national struggles in decolonising processes. South Africa is shaped by the political legacies of Gandhi and Mandela. Smitha Radhakrishnan's article analyses choreography and pedagogy in the Surialanga Dance Company of Durban, South Africa, in the post-apartheid era. By considering the details of creative processes, including rehearsal and performance, Radhakrishnan discusses how this company has been inspired by Mandela's political vision to represent, or enunciate (to use Mignolo's term) a uniquely South African version of Bharatanatyam, one which incorporates Zulu dancers. As such, it challenges ideas about purity in Indian dance performance with sometimes violent consequences. Thus, the company reveals ways in which colonial ideas persist in post-apartheid South Africa. Radhakrishnan argues that despite threats to its project, this company continues to articulate a powerful social vision.

Likewise, Christopher L. Ballengee discusses the role of the arts in articulating social visions by examining how music both establishes and disrupts postcolonial national identities in Trinidad and Tobago. The state defined national identity and began a programme of nation building that included music competitions to institutionalise expressive forms such as calypso (a vocal genre highlighting topical commentary) and steel pan as national symbols. Ballengee describes how other kinds of musical expressions, such as Indian Trinidadian tassa competitions can be viewed as sites of decolonisation within postcolonial state representations. Multiculturalism becomes a key component in continuing to revise representations of national identity. Decolonisation is an ongoing process of shaping the postcolonial nation state.

The next three articles in this volume concern the British context. The irritation of Europe, previously noted, leads to redefining national identities as explored in Magdalen Gorringe's article, which discusses nostalgia and cultural essentialism in the televised competition, the BBC *Young Dancer*. Gorringe presents it as a demand for radically re-imagining identity constructions, albeit acknowledging its complex surrounding dialogues. In its most optimistic offering, this competition provides a model for navigating between essentialism and assimilation since it includes a South Asian dance category (covering bharatanatyam and kathak), which is situated under the umbrella of British dance. For its practitioners, situating South Asian forms within the category of British dance marks inclusion within national representations of art forms. Gorringe argues that in this way the competition helps us to imagine a decolonised future.

Imagining future possibilities underscores plural affiliations within contemporary transnational performance networks. Another way of thinking about inclusion within national representations is explored by Sitara Thobani, who points out that the dance practices in India that were categorised as classical genres were reconstructed in the heyday of twentieth-century anti-colonial politics. These categories were linked with a nationalist claim to a stable Indian cultural identity. By examining how these categories relate to Indian nationalist politics, Thobani offers a further perspective on identity politics. She builds on critiques of the nationalist reconstruction of Indian classical dance to discuss how this reconstructive project is enacted in the transnational present and how its assumptions are maintained in the multicultural British context. By highlighting different nationalist representations, both Gorringe and Thobani explore some of the complexities of Britain's colonial past and its new cosmopolitans.

Decolonising processes are interlinked with intersectional identity politics, including diaspora and gender. Jasmine Hornabrook's article delves into this topic by focusing on new creative musical projects amongst Tamil second-generation female musicians in Britain, which challenge traditional concepts of femininity. The Tamil Diaspora is the result of long labour histories, including nineteenth-century indenture and the 1940s rebuilding of post-Second World War Britain. It is also the result of migration due to ethnic tensions that erupted in the Sri Lankan Civil War (1983–2009), and it is largely this latter context that informs Hornabrook's analysis. Gender expectations in musical performance alongside constructions of women as tradition bearers in Indian nationalist representations provide the backdrop for Hornabrook's suggestion that the second-generation Tamil female musicians with whom she has developed ethnographic research in London might be seen as undertaking feminist acts.

This topic is explored in the following article too. Priya Srinivasan examines Tamil women's performances in the Australian context, as well as intercultural projects, as feminist praxis. She turns to analytical concepts of neighbouring and gift to think about decolonisation from a place of praxis and intra- or inter- cultural artistic exchange. She suggests that the concept of the neighbour implicitly demands a reciprocal counter-gesture, which enables a deeper understanding of feminist decolonising performance processes. Srinivasan's work as a dancer includes collaborating with the Melbourne-based Carnatic singer, Uthra Vijay. Both have worked with a number of other collaborators. An important collaboration, in the context of Australia, has been with Indigenous Australians. Intercultural projects therefore reference broader decolonising relationships and they point to new emergent histories of encounter.

The final article in this volume combines history, contemporary performance and reflexive commentary to discuss the potential of reenactment in the cultures of decolonisation. Prarthana Purkayastha explores dance performances in historical sources and their reenactments in her own practice. Surveying literature on nineteenth-century colonial exhibitions and world's fairs, Purkayastha highlights the complicity of academic disciplines such as anthropology and ethnology in promoting 'violent forms of pedagogy' (see Chatterjee 2012). Her article focuses on the failed Liberty's 1885 exhibition in London, and especially on *nautch* dancers. By re-imagining their experiences she pursues an experiment in exhuming the memories of dancers who have been forgotten by both British and Indian nationalist histories. Turning to the trope of reenactment, Purkayastha argues that historical fiction as a corporeal methodology might be a viable decolonising strategy for dance studies. As a pedagogue, she notes some of her own strategies for supporting a decolonising orientation in the university classroom, and as a practice-based researcher she reveals some of the ways in which she promotes her ideas about curricula decolonisation in the context of professional disciplinary societies. This volume ends with a view on the importance of pedagogic spaces in offering practitioner-scholars everyday opportunities to reflect on decolonising processes in classroom dialogues.

These case studies span across Australia, the Caribbean, South Africa and the UK to highlight current approaches to researching the creative processes of decolonisation with reference to dance and music in the Indian Diaspora (and embracing the Sri Lankan Tamil Diaspora, which connects with South India). They are located within the intersecting frames of praxis and theoretical engagement, and thus speak to the conceptual pitfalls Santos identifies: the "blindness of theory renders practice invisible or under theorised, whereas the blindness of practice renders theory irrelevant" (2014, 35). They revisit colonial hierarchies in performance representations and offer decolonising commentaries. They examine decolonising aspirations for a future based on establishing more equitable social relationships. Collectively, they offer a pluralist reading of dance and music in the cultures of decolonisation. They affirm the need to research creative processes as the performing arts circulate across transnational spaces in the making and unmaking of power.

Note

1. This correspondence is available at, https://en.wikisource.org/wiki/Correspondence_between_Tolstoy_and_Gandhi (accessed 23 September 2018).

Acknowledgements

I wish to express sincere thanks to Margaret Birley, organiser of the 2017 conference at the Horniman Museum, co-sponsored by the Royal Anthropological Institute, who invited me to give the keynote lecture. I am grateful to Barley Norton for kindly commenting on the ensuing volume as a whole and offering highly useful comments for its conceptual integration. I finalised it thanks to the inspiration I gained as a visiting research scholar at the Centre for the Study of the Indian Diaspora, University of Hyderabad directed by Ajaya K. Sahoo, to whom I am especially grateful for his interest and support at various stages of bringing this volume to fruition.

Disclosure statement

No potential conflict of interest was reported by the author.

References

Bahadur, Gaiutra. 2018. "Rescued from the Footnotes of History: Lal Bihari Sharma's Holi Songs of Demerara." In Los Angeles Review of Books. Accessed September 23, 2018. https://lareviewofbooks.org/article/rescued-from-the-footnotes-of-history-lal-bihari-sharmas-holi-songs-of-demerara/.

Burnard, Pamela, Elizabeth Mackinlay, and Kimberley Powell, eds. 2016. *Routledge International Handbook of Intercultural Arts*. London: Routledge.

Chatterjee, Partha. 2012. *The Black Hole of Empire: History of a Global Practice of Power*. Princeton: Princeton University Press.

De Sousa Santos, Boaventura. 2014. *Epistemologies of the South: Justice against Epistemicide*. London: Routledge.

Discography

Fanon, Frantz. 2001 [1961]. *The Wretched of the Earth*. London: Penguin Classics.

Farrell, Gerry. 1997. *Indian Music and the West*. Oxford: Oxford University Press.

Films

Freire, Paulo. 2017 [first published in 1970]. *Pedagogy of the Oppressed*. Translated by Myra Bergman Ramos. UK: Penguin Books.

Gandhi, M. K. 2001 [first published in English 1927]. *An Autobiography: Or the Story of my Experiments with Truth*. Translated from Gujurati by Mahadev Desai. London: Penguin Books.

Ghuman, Nalini. 2014. *Resonances of the Raj: India in the English Musical Imagination, 1897-1947*. New York: Oxford University Press.

Guha, Ramahandra. 2018. *Gandhi: The Years That Changed the World, 1914-1948*. Penguin, Kindle.

Hegde, Radha S, and Ajaya K Sahoo. 2017. "Introduction." In *Routledge Handbook of the Indian Diaspora*, edited by R. S. Hegde, and A. K. Sahoo, 1–14. London & New York: Routledge.

Jaffrelot, Christophe. 2005. *Dr Ambedkar and Untouchability: Analysing and Fighting Caste*. London: Hurst & Company.

Kaladeen, Maria del Pilar. 2018. "Invisible Passengers." In *Mother Country*, edited by Charlie Brinkhurst-Cuff, 265–275. London: Hachette.

Kumar, Ashutosh. 2017. *Coolies of the Empire: Indentured Indians in the Sugar Colonies, 1830-1920*. Cambridge: Cambridge University Press.

Mignolo, Walter D, and Catherine E. Walsh. 2018. *On Decoloniality: Concepts, Analytics, Praxis*. Durham: Duke University Press.

Mohabir, Rajiv, translator. forthcoming. *I Even Regret Night: Holi Songs of Demerara. By Lalbihari Sharma*. Los Angeles, CA: Kaya Press.

Naipaul, V.S. 2002 [first published in 1977]. *India: A Wounded Civilization*. London: Picador.

Norton, Barley. 2018. "Orchestrating the Nation: Court Orchestras, Nationalism and Agency in Vietnam." In *Global Perspectives on Orchestras: Collective Creativity and Social Agency*, edited by Tina K. Ramnarine, 301–323. New York: Oxford University Press.

Ramnarine, Tina K. 2001. *Creating Their Own Space: The Development of an Indian-Caribbean Musical Tradition*. Barbados, Jamaica, Trinidad and Tobago: University of West Indies Press.

Ramnarine, Tina K. 2017. "Musical Performances in the Indian Diaspora." In *Routledge Handbook of the Indian Diaspora*, edited by R. S. Hegde, and A. Sahoo, 156–169. London & New York: Routledge.

Ramnarine, Tina K. 2018. "Orchestral Connections in the Cultures of Decolonisation: Reflections on UK, Caribbean and Indian Contexts." In *Global Perspectives on Orchestras: Collective Creativity and Social Agency*, edited by T. K. Ramnarine, 324–350. New York: Oxford University Press.

Rancière, Jacques. 1991. *The Ignorant Schoolmaster: Five Lessons in Intellectual Emancipation*. Translated by Kristin Ross. Stanford, CA: Stanford University Press.

Ravi Shankar. 1997. *Chants of India*. Angel Records.

Roy, Arundhati. 2014. "The Doctor and the Saint." In *Annihilation of Caste*, edited by B. R. Ambedkar and critically annotated by S. Anand. London: Verso.

Schulze-Engler, Frank. 2016. "Irritating Europe." In *The Oxford Handbook of Postcolonial Studies*, 669–691. Oxford: Oxford University Press.

Selvon, Sam. 1987. "Three Into one Can't Go – East Indian, Trinidadian, Westindian." In *India in the Caribbean*, edited by David Dabydeen, and Brinsley Samaroo, 13–24. London: Hansib.

Shipway, Martin. 2008. *Decolonization and Its Impact: A Comparative Approach to the End of Colonial Empires*. Malden, MA: Blackwell Publishing.

Sorabji, Richard. 2012. *Gandhi and the Stoics: Modern Experiments on Ancient Values*. Chicago, IL: University of Chicago Press.

Srinivasan, Priya. 2012. *Sweating Saris: Indian Dance as Transnational Labour*. Philadelphia, PA: Temple University Press.

Thiong'o, Ngũgĩ wa. 2005 [first published in 1986]. *Decolonising the Mind: The Politics of Language in African Literature*. Oxford: James Currey.

Thobani, Sitara. 2017. *Indian Classical Dance and the Making of Postcolonial National Identities: Dancing on Empire's Stage*. Abingdon: Routledge.

Tolstoy, Leo. 1908. *Letter to a Hindu: The Subjection of India – Its Cause and Cure*. With an Introduction by M. K. Gandhi (1909). Accessed September 23, 2018. https://www.gutenberg.org/files/7176/7176-h/7176-h.htm.

Vatuk, Ved Prakash. 1964. "Protest Songs of East Indians in British Guiana." *The Journal of American Folklore* 77 (305): 220–235.

Yehudi Menuhin and Ravi Shankar. 1967. *West Meets East*. LP Recording. HMV and EMI's Angel Records imprint. Volume 2 was published in 1968 and volume 3 in 1976.

1986. *Pandit Ravi Shankar: A Portrait of the Maestro of the Sitar*. Documentary film (DVD). Director, Nicolas Klotz. F Productions.

Dancing the rainbow nation as it bleeds: the *Surialanga Dance Company* in post-apartheid South Africa

Smitha Radhakrishnan

ABSTRACT

This article analyzes the work of the Surialanga Dance Company of Durban, South Africa, which debuted at Nelson Mandela's inauguration in 1994. Inspired by Mandela's vision of intercultural harmony and created through sustained engagement with Zulu culture, Surialanga created a uniquely South African version of Indian classical Bharatanatyam that threatens colonial and apartheid constructs of "pure" Indian identity. But the company's powerful decolonial message has become less resonant in a post-apartheid context that continues to be structured by what Ndlovu-Gatsheni has called the "colonial matrix of power," a legacy of colonialism and apartheid that results in a narrow focus on ethnic and racial identities. Drawing both from direct participation and interviews with the director and company members (2001–2008; 2018), this article traces the history of Surialanga's decolonising praxis from Mandela's inauguration to the present, arguing for the continued salience of Surialanga's dance, even in the face of particularism and violence.

As South Africa's first democratically elected president, Nelson Mandela championed a vision of the nation that resolved the painful contradictions of apartheid into a metaphor for multicultural unity – the 'rainbow nation'. In the years since, however, this ideal has faded from national memory as narrow ethnic and racial identities continue to structure everyday life. Sabelo Ndlovu-Gatsheni argues that despite the efforts of African nationalists, the categories of race and ethnicity set up by colonial and apartheid regimes persist in particularistic identities that have overshadowed calls for multicultural unity, a legacy he calls the 'colonial matrix of power' that has remained in South Africa (2013, 176). This article explores how decolonising artistic projects in post-apartheid South Africa have worked to destabilise and counter this colonial matrix of power. It focuses on personal stories, drawing on the postcolonial theorist Walter Mignolo's notion of the decolonial artistic project, which is situated in specific individual experiences and does not seek to universalise (Gaztambide-Fernández 2014). Drawing from firsthand experience and interviews with members of the Surialanga Dance Company of Durban, I show that their decolonial and decolonising artistic projects, inspired by Mandela's vision, have also gone beyond it, centring Indian-Zulu cultural exchange as emblematic of the 'new' South

An invitation to make South African art

In the months leading up to the historic inauguration of Nelson Mandela as South Africa's first democratically elected president in 1994, Professor Suria Govender of the University of Durban-Westville received an irresistible invitation: to present a 'gift of art' from the Indian people to the nation's first black president. The programme would be part of the inaugural programme, 'Many Cultures, One Nation'. Govender, a Bharatanatyam dancer and teacher of Indian heritage and a lifelong Durban resident, went looking for the right piece of music.[1] Having grown up in a multiethnic cultural environment and participated actively in the anti-apartheid movement, Govender felt strongly about having her dance set to Zulu music. She went to her campus's radio station and asked them to suggest a beautiful piece. The moment she heard 'Asimbonanga', Johnny Clegg's 1987 hit protest Zulu and English song that had topped charts in France and the U.K., her mind was made up. The song reflected her own African and Western cultural influences while celebrating Mandela and paying tribute to the many leaders who had died in the anti-apartheid cause. 'Asimbonanga' was a perfect bridge between South Africa's past and its future.

In that moment perhaps, the vision for her company of Indian classical dancers started to take a decidedly nationalist direction. Govender recalled:

> I really wanted the dancers to focus on the message. In a way, I was forcing them to be nationalistic. That was a requirement. But I found people wanted to do it ... There was a lot of work, but off we went from the University of Durban-Westville [to the inauguration]. We danced all the way to Pretoria on the bus, rehearsing! It was a wonderfully buoyant thing. We were part of the inauguration of the first democratically elected president of our country. (personal interview, 14 August 2008)

On 10 May 1994, sixteen South African Indian women, clad in Bharatanatyam costume, performed what might have been South Africa's first public intercultural dance: a Zulu song, sung by a white man, danced by Indian women in silk saris on a national and global stage (Desai 1996, 112; Govender 1994). Using Bharatanatyam's language of hand gesture and stylized facial expression, the dancers expressed the Zulu lyrics of the song, which plaintively ask where "our Mandela" is being kept, unseen by his people. Their percussive steps kept beat with the Zulu maskandi rhythms as they celebrated the birth of the new South Africa, dubbed 'the rainbow nation'.

This auspicious beginning launched a project of culture-making that has persisted to the current day, involving Zulu men and Indian women dancing together in a fragile, yet powerful enunciation[2] of South Africa's post-apartheid nationalist project, which sought to reconcile a long history of racial and ethnic division. Since the exuberant years of Mandela's presidency, however, the intercultural vision of harmony that Govender's dancers projected at that most buoyant moment receded from public consciousness. 'Our rainbow is bleeding', Govender agonised, reflecting upon the rise of xenophobia and violence in post-apartheid South Africa (personal interview, 14 August 2008). Although these dynamics have intensified further in recent years, Surialanga's work continues, enduring the symbolic threats to the company's work and physical violence and death experienced by company members and their families.

My emphasis is on analysing the select cultural registers in which Surialanga's work has been operating since that 1994 inauguration: pedagogic, choreographic and embodied, all the while recognising the interconnections between them. I find that Surialanga engages in a subversive shift in dance praxis by reworking Bharatanatyam to reflect the South African context and to focus on Zulu-Indian relationships, while decentering white culture. Govender's intercultural dance threatens the notions of 'pure' Indian identity constructed by colonial rule and reinforced by apartheid, while also challenging the 'colonial matrix of power' that persists in the particularistic identities and unresolved economic contradictions of the post-apartheid period (Ndlovu-Gatsheni 2013). On one hand, its dances may shore up the problematic legitimacy of Bharatanatyam as a metonym for Indian identity[3] but on the other hand, it nudges to the margins those modes of engagement and bodily work required for validation in the persistently Eurocentric dance culture of South Africa (Friedman 2012). While dance in most postcolonial nations constitutes a powerful mode through which authentic pasts can be constructed and performed,[4] Surialanga's dances imagine a future that departs from South Africa's past of colonial exploitation of black and brown bodies. In pedagogical, choreographic and embodied arenas of interaction, Surialanga's decades of work have pushed for a transformative dance reliant upon an emergent, processual understanding of culture, rather than a static one (Kumar 2011). In the new rainbow nation, Surialanga's work suggests that racial identity, music and dance need not align in segregated black and brown bodies. Perhaps the 'colours' – cultural and racial – could blur into one another and whiteness need not be at the centre. Perhaps this 'bleeding' could be constructive. Through sustained, courageous experimentation, the Surialanga Dance Company of Durban has created a project that thus both draws from Mandela's vision and goes beyond it, interweaving the performing arts traditions of the people of colour who find themselves in post-apartheid KwaZulu-Natal.

'Indianness' and coloniality in post-apartheid Durban

The persistence of the term 'Indian' in present-day South Africa speaks to how colonial, apartheid and post-apartheid regimes of racial identification and classification have reinforced the perpetual foreigner status of those who trace their ancestry to the subcontinent (Reddy 2016, 122). Indian migrants came to South Africa mainly in two streams – first as indentured labourers following the formal ban of slavery in Britain and its colonies (1860–1911) and next as 'passenger' Indians who travelled to South Africa in search of economic opportunity in the early twentieth century. Today, most South Africans who identify as 'Indian', then, have had families living in South Africa for four to seven generations. While the colonial government greatly curtailed the freedom of Indian migrants regardless of their status, as famously experienced by Mohandas Gandhi upon his arrival to South Africa in 1893, apartheid rule created Indianness anew in the 1950s, razing multiracial neighbourhoods and forcibly relocating those bodies designated as 'Indian' into new racially segregated townships through the notorious Group Areas Act

(Freund 1995, Maharaj 1995, Reddy 2016, 122–151). This extreme act of apartheid social engineering set up a social landscape in which Indians were, symbolically and spatially, a buffer group between indigenous Africans and whites. Spatial segregation was reinforced by occupational segregation, such that certain types of low-level clerical work and skilled manual work were reserved for Indians, excluding black Africans (Freund 1995, 64–91). As a result of this brutal regime of separation, by the time apartheid ended in 1994, most South African Indians had internalised colonial and apartheid logics of racial purity, separation and white supremacy. For this reason, even though many South African Indians were passionately involved in the anti-apartheid movement and adopted the self-identification 'Black' for the purposes of engaging the Black cause, 'Indians' in South Africa voted overwhelmingly for the white National Party, rather than for Mandela's African National Congress party in 1994 (Desai 1996). In this context, Govender's dance, both at the inauguration and in the post-apartheid landscape, radically challenged internalised legacies of colonial and apartheid racial projects.

Mignolo emphasizes that decolonial artists specifically can destabilise their own sensibility as colonial subjects, who come into being in the gaze of the White Other. In doing so, decolonial artists can replace colonial aesthetics with what he terms decolonial *aesthesis* (drawing on Gaztambide-Fernàndez 2014, 201, emphasis in the original). While he acknowledges that we are all in a 'Western epistemic trap', projects that place local vocabularies at the centre highlight the practice of 'making' and nudge decolonial projects forward. To this end, Mignolo emphasizes the need to push against 'representation' and rather to highlight 'enunciation', by which he means to speak from a situated perspective that aims not to universalise, but to build upon previous articulations of that perspective (ibid). Mignolo finds great promise in the 'thousands and thousands of decolonial projects' underway worldwide, referring to a wide range of literary examples with diverse aesthetic strategies, unified by their situated, non-universalist perspectives (2014, 198).

When viewed as one of many decolonial projects worldwide, Surialanga's ongoing work advances the specific South African post-apartheid project of reconciliation while also extending beyond South Africa. Govender's choreography begins from her own situated perspective as a South African of Indian heritage, who grew up in a multiracial neighbourhood of Durban and enjoyed a deep familiarity with Zulu language and culture. Years of training in Bharatanatyam and later, performance, study and activism at apartheid South Africa's premier 'Indian' university unfolded in parallel with her commitment to the anti-apartheid movement and the black cause. Govender explained in an interview,

> I did this [intercultural dance] because this is an expression of what I want everybody to feel now. Also, I wanted to experiment to see how far it could go, all these things that I used to see and idealize about [as a student activist]. (personal interview, 14 August 2008)

Thus, Surialanga's particular intercultural dance project grew out of both a post-apartheid pan-nationalist project and Govender's biography. From her lived experiences of apartheid and the movement against it, cultural life in KwaZulu-Natal, the exclusionary attitudes of many South African Indian family and friends, as well as her embodied experience of learning, performing and teaching Bharatanatyam, a specific enunciation of interculturalism emerged – one focused on enhancing and harmonising Zulu-Indian relationships. These relationships were particularly fraught in Durban precisely because colonial rule and apartheid had worked so vigorously to pit these two groups against each other.[5]

But Govender's commitment to a Zulu-Indian model of intercultural harmony developed in a political context in which, perhaps ironically, Indians were renewing their commitments to their minority identities, often through increased emphasis on connection to the subcontinent. When I first arrived in South Africa in 2001, I found a vibrant Indian cultural scene in Durban that was only becoming more enthusiastic. Even though arts and culture from the subcontinent had long been at the centre of South African Indian communities, with the end of apartheid, many South African Indian families had renewed their interest in their Indian cultural heritage, often to highlight their distinctiveness from black Africans and to assert a minority identity (Desai 1996). In my research with South African Indian women, I found that many of them noticed that their children were more invested in an Indian identity than they were themselves, and they were then searching for avenues through which the next generation's sense of identity could be explored and realised (Radhakrishnan 2005). As a result of this widespread interest, there were dozens of Bharatanatyam dance teachers with large dance schools in and around Durban. The students who enrolled in these schools were learning Bharatanatyam because their families and communities understood the dance as an authentic expression of their cultural heritage. As in contemporary India, in colonial, apartheid and post-apartheid South Africa, Bharatanatyam was viewed as especially important for women to perform. Bharatanatyam performance allowed women in India – and even more often in the diaspora – to serve as boundary markers and cultural symbols (Chakravorty 1998). As a result of these dynamics, cultural gatekeepers in the Indian community often opposed Govender's work. In a televised debate after the inauguration, for example, pro-Indian activist T. P. Naidoo expressed outrage that Govender had chosen a song with Zulu and English lyrics to represent the Indian people. But this resistance only deepened Govender's resolve to further develop her particular artistic and cultural vision.

The growth of Surialanga's decolonial project

When the company returned from the inaugural performance in Pretoria, Govender started taking steps to expand its membership. She activated her existing connections with a community organisation in Clermont and started travelling there on Saturdays to teach dance to the children there who were already learning Zulu and gumboot dances as a part of a cultural dance programme. There, she met S'bu, Sandile, Stembiso, and Siya, among other children who were between the ages of 8 and 12 at the time. Once these children joined Govender's company, the direction of what previously had been her company of classical Indian dancers, all of Indian origin, shifted irrevocably. Surialanga, a fusion of the words in Sanskrit and Zulu for 'sun' ('suria' and 'elanga' respectively) came into being, an enunciation of Govender's own intercultural vision that nonetheless contributed to the pan-African imaginary of the new South Africa. Thus began a process that would unfold over several years for four Zulu boys who grew into young men, and several young Indian women who were part of the company.

The young women who became part of Surialanga auditioned for the company after many years of training and the completion of an *arangetram,* a strenuous debut performance requiring an intense dedication of time and resources. They all came from Hindu families for whom Bharatanatyam was also a form of religious expression, and many of them came from the same dance school, thus sharing similar ideas and training regarding Bharatanatyam. But the young men of Surialanga learned Bharatnatyam in a radically different context that Govender customised for their experiences and talents. Building upon their existing connection to Zulu and gumboot dances that were already familiar to them, as well as a celebration of their identities as Christians, Govender crafted dances for them with adapted footwork and expressions (as discussed below) that nonetheless fit in with a Bharatanatyam idiom. Through the processes of engaging the young Zulu men and the Indian women, a reworked, distinctly South African Bharatanatyam emerged, undermining the stability of Indianness as an authentic identity in the post-apartheid context.

The newly formed Surialanga Company began by commissioning an eponymous piece of music that reflected Zulu-Indian cultural sensibilities. Composed by the late Siva Devar, the piece featured Zulu njembe drums, drum set, tabla, xylophone, electric sitar, violin and piano – all recorded on an electric synthesiser. In this first dance, S'bu, Sandile, Siya and Stembiso adopted only the *attami,* or signature neck movements of Bharatanatyam, incorporating them into sequences of Zulu traditional dance that they choreographed themselves. In the choreography, Zulu boys and Indian girls smile at each other, and exchange touches and dance movements, sharing their mutual rehearsal and performance spaces. The Zulu boys deepened their engagement with Bharatanatyam and in the next dance they learned, a Tamil language song in praise of Jesus called 'Yesuvin Padangalai' (see Figure 1). They danced elementary Bharatanatyam steps and learned to act out the stories of Jesus's life to the refrain: Yesuvin padangalai/ naan dinum dinum/ yesuvin padangalai [To Jesus's feet I pray/every day/to Jesus's feet I pray]. By worshipping Jesus in the dance through mimed flower offerings, fire ceremonies and the enactment of two miracles from Jesus's life, the young men of Surialanga were able to forge a personally relevant path to learning Bharatanatyam. This path was not based on the prevailing colonial script that prefigured cultural authenticity according to outward appearance, gender and address, which were all scripts that readily provided the young women with a sense of direct identification with the form.

'Raghupathy Raghava', a Gandhian song in Hindi about the universality of all religions for all people, incorporated new modes of experimentation for both the Indian and Zulu members of the company. While the song is most often sung in a semi-classical style, the Surialanga dancers performed a version with a rock and roll interlude, taken from the popular Bollywood film, *Kuch Kuch Hota Hai* (1998). The repetitive percussive beats in this version were amenable to Bharatanatyam steps that mirrored the steps of gumboot dance. Govender created movements for the young men that incorporated cymbals in lieu of the traditional clapping that is a part of gumboot dance. The men executed gumboot-esque movements with cymbals in hand, while the women performed Bharatanatyam footwork with clapping, instead of the elaborate alphabet of gesture usually paired with such rhythmic footwork. In an interview, S'bu shared that it was easy for him and the other Zulu boys to pick up this dance because they could understand the steps right away, and they could enjoy it. Govender's choreography of 'Ragupathy' also departed from the

Figure 1. Yesuvin padangalai, Durban waterfront, 2002. Photograph by Alyssa Wilson.

conventions of Bharatanatyam as the women stomped in a standing position that mirrored gumboot, rather than in the traditional *araimandi*, or deep plié position. In these ways, Govender's choreography drew the two groups together to exchange their movements for a compelling piece of dance, but in so doing it also created an inclusive, interfaith representation of Indianness in South Africa. 'Ragupathy' thus succeeded in creating a deep connection and familiarity with Bharatanatyam for the young Zulu men of the company. S'bu and Sandile told me that they learned 'Asimbonanga' only after their studies of 'Surialanga', 'Yesuvin' and 'Ragupathy'.

S'bu and Sandile conceived of their commitment to Bharatanatyam in terms that may have departed from Govender's own vision, although their commitment could nonetheless work in concert with hers. Speaking with me over a decade after they joined the company, S'bu and Sandile explained:

S'bu   We are doing a cultural dance which you can't see anywhere. You can see township dancing, clap dancing, and if you go, you can see it each and every time. But when it comes to cultural dance? [It is rare] … So I think that's the best thing I can do. It's very special. Something different. People say, 'this man is doing a wonderful thing.' It's the same like what someone like Johnny Clegg is doing. He is doing

DANCE, MUSIC AND CULTURES OF DECOLONISATION

something different from his culture. Because everyone was doing ballet, singing English songs. You know? So he said, 'let me do something different. You know? And you see him, you can see he is feeling it. You know? Like really feeling it.

Smitha And you feel it.

Sandile [Smiling and nodding] Yeah, yeah. We are. We are. We are. And it's nice. We feel it (personal interview, 15 August 2008).

Because of the structural limitations of my position as a researcher as well as my inability to speak isiZulu, I was unable to adequately capture in an interview what was evident from years of work in the company: that the principal dancers in the Surialanga company were committed both to their identities as black Zulu men and their identities as Bharatanatyam dancers. But in rehearsal, this dual commitment became evident.

I had arrived after a span of three years at the historic Asoka Theatre for dance rehearsal with Surialanga on 10 August 2008. Soon, S'bu and Sandile arrive and greet me warmly. I'm delighted to see them and they find the door that has been left unlocked for us. The familiarity of the space washes over me as we file into the dusty theatre and put our bags down on the seats surrounding the stage. As we start to stretch and warm up, we chat. 'I heard from Suria that you've been studying some contemporary dance', I say. 'What are some of the new warm-ups you've learned? I'd love to see them and learn!' The two men look at each other and then at me. Sandile, the quieter of the two, smiling his broadest smile, begins the Bharatanatyam warm-ups I introduced to them years ago, and pipes, 'we haven't learned anything contemporary. We are Bharatanatyam dancers'. I was stunned and delighted by the casual confidence with which Sandile claimed ownership of Bharatanatyam, that quintessential symbol of Indianness in South Africa and around the world, even to the point of rejecting any association with (Western) contemporary dance styles. That year, Govender and I discussed what it might take to have an *arangetram* for S'bu and Sandile – how they would train, where it would be, and what might be included in the programme. Govender was considering a composition on a Zulu icon rendered in a Bharatanatyam idiom, which might extend the boundaries of the *arangetram*. S'bu and Sandile asked me what it was like to learn dance in India, and if I knew anyone who would teach them. After years of training and experience, these young men had become fully invested in the practice and performance of Bharatnatyam. They had committed to the form in a way not a single Indian woman in the company had done. Here, the contradictory dynamics of race, class and gender meant that even though young Indian women have symbolised Indianness, other economic opportunities turned them away from pursuing dance professionally. For S'bu and Sandile, however, limited economic opportunity outside of dance made full-time dance a viable profession, a set of circumstances that opened up the possible meanings of Indianness available in the realm of South African cultural production.

By fusing Indian classical dance and Zulu dances and creating a South African articulation of Bharatanatyam, Surialanga dancers challenged taken-for-granted, internalised understandings of essential difference between Indian and Zulu groups, differences naturalised through colonial logics and policies. While the usage of Bharatanatyam retained the colonial and apartheid category of 'Indian' in important respects, the lengthy process of teaching and working with Indian and Zulu dancers transformed it irrevocably. This process invited Zulu dancers to explore the form, thus expanding and legitimising it for them over ballet and other Eurocentric modes of dance expression, and destabilising Bharatanatyam for the experienced Indian women who participated in the project. These sustained pedagogic and choreographic interactions enabled the emergence of a radical decolonial project resonant with Mandela's vision, but also separate from it, centring on the experiences of those living in Kwa-Zulu-Natal to express the aspirations of the nation (see Figure 2).

However intensely those involved with the Surialanga experienced this project, the shifts in the country as a whole were evident. In the lead-up to Thabo Mbeki's second inauguration in 2009, Govender found herself in discussion with musician Mbogeni Ngema, who had been embroiled in controversy for the 2002 song, 'AmAndiya', considered by many to be anti-Indian.[6] Ngema was in charge of the celebration and officially requested Govender to bring Indian dancers to represent Indian culture: 'So, what if the guardians of Indian culture are now becoming African?' Govender asked Ngema. The real question, Govender insisted, is 'who are the custodians' of the art, not who are the race group. Ngema was not interested in this line of reasoning. Although Govender and a few Surialanga dancers did perform at Mbeki's second inauguration, the Zulu Bharatanatyam dancers were not among them. These dynamics hint at the

Figure 2. S'bu and Sandile portray Zulu-Indian interculturalism, 2008. Photograh by Ganesh Ramachandran.

persistence of particularistic racial and ethnic identities more than a decade after a project of national unity should have ideally rendered such distinctions untenable.

Dancing Mandela's vision then and now

Inspired by Mandela's vision, Surialanga has experienced both its magic and its limits. During the year I was an active member of Surialanga, in 2001–2002, Asimbonanga was the most requested and most performed song of the company's repertoire. During one of our many performances at the International Conference Centre in Durban in 2002, for example, I observed audience members moved to tears by that piece. The harmonious intercultural possibility portrayed on stage, set to a song that for many invoked the success of the anti-apartheid struggle and the legacy of Nelson Mandela, offered perhaps Surialanga's most important message for its audiences. In the dance, all the dancers, Zulu and Indian, wear Bharatanatyam costume and interpret the words of the song though Bharatanatyam gestures and expressions. They portray Mandela as a sage in meditation and as a prince. The gestures go with the English words of the song as well: 'Oh the sea is cold and the sky is grey/ Look across the island into the bay/ We are all islands, where comes the day/ We cross the burning waters?' Bharatanatyam gestures describe his literal captivity on Robben Island, while evoking the possibility of a shared future ahead. As Govender described, and as I witnessed during my many performances of the piece, Mandela is portrayed as 'the fighter, the yogi or one who meditates, as the prisoner, the man of letters or the advocate, and finally as the one who has evolved to the stage where his third eye has been opened'. Each of these aspects of Mandela's persona is explored through different Bharatanatyam gestures that vary each time the refrain of the song recurs (Govender 1994). Over the course of the dance, three other anti-apartheid activists – Stephen Biko, Victoria Mxenge, and Niel Aggett – are honoured with mimed offerings of flowers, incense and fire. These actions on stage forge a connection between Hindu worship and Zulu ancestor worship that audiences and dancers alike recognise.

Asimbonanga has also become a potent teaching tool. In the dance company's community activism, which involves teaching Bharatanatyam, Zulu and gumboot dance in schools all over the Durban area, a simple version of Asimbonanga is often the first piece Govender and company members teach young, predominantly Zulu students. From my own participation in these teaching programmes, I saw that students were most excited to learn this dance and perform it. Govender has long been acutely aware of this:

> For people from the outside and from this inside, it ['Asimbonanga'] unpacks the history of this country, and allows you to look at the history, of Zulu culture and Zulu language, and to unpack the symbolism of the Mandela legacy. And the Mandela personality and persona.

Even many years after Mandela left political office, Govender felt that teaching and performing the piece communed with Mandela at a time when the country seemed to be taking a turn for the worse. Despite Mandela's tremendous sacrifices, Govender felt that as a country, 'We have reneged on our promise to him'. By teaching 'Asimbonanga', that vision might be revived and the painful present and past might be reconciled. Govender reflected, 'We try, I think, in the dance company, to do those kinds of things that sort of deal with all the painful issues that we have to deal with in our country at this time' (personal interview, 14 August 2008). For Govender, Mandela's vision and work endowed her with a great sense of personal and artistic responsibility to deliver on his promise of a truly intercultural society. Despite this continuous struggle, however, she finds that her efforts have been stymied by factors outside her control.

Perhaps the boldest dance in Surialanga's repertoire, and the one that pushes its intercultural vision the furthest, is Vicky Sampson's acclaimed 'African Dream', which she performed at the opening and closing ceremonies of the African Cup of Nations Football Competition in South Africa in 1995. While still situated in the hopeful glow of apartheid's end, the song's rendition as a 'dream' speaks once again to possible and hoped for futures, which Surialanga interpreted in a distinctly South African intercultural mode. In this piece, women in Bharatanatyam costumes enter first with movements that jump forward for the first three drumbeats with the gesture of an opening flower, *alapadma*, and then turn away for the next three, changing the hand gesture to flattened palms, *pataaka*. These introductory movements form the prelude of the song, set only to drums. When the instrumentation swells and Sampson's voice begins to sing, the men then join them on stage in Zulu costume, smiling and running with raised knees. Standing in a row behind the women, they appear as a line of couples, as the women leave behind the ambivalence of jumping towards and turning away, and assume the *katakamukham* hand gesture with one hand at the chest, with the *dhola* gesture with the other hand at their side, a stance that denotes womanhood in Bharatanatyam. During a musical interlude later in the song, all the dancers depart the stage except for one woman and one man. The woman gathers flowers and makes a garland, which she then places over her partner's neck, suggesting marriage in an Indian context. The couple then dances together happily, exchanging movements; she borrows a passage of Zulu dance, he performs an abstract *adavu*, or foundational step; they both dance an abstract Bharatanatyam sequence in synchrony. The other dancers join them onstage for an exuberant conclusion of rhythmic movements.

While Asimbonanga's choreography was fairly literal, staying close to the Bharatanatyam conventions of mirroring word with gesture, in African Dream, these conventions are transformed. A flattened palm becomes a sign of confusion, and a garland becomes a sign of union, not just an interpretation of the words in the song. Where Asimbonanga articulates its homage to South Africa's freedom fighters and Mandela's legacy through identifiably Indian gestures and traditions, African Dream imagines something perhaps even more radical: an optional present and future in which cultural sharing and intercultural love is celebrated, even as the women remain marked and dressed as 'Indian' subjects and the men remain marked and dressed not only as 'Zulu', but also as 'African'.

Zulu-Indian intercultural dance has continued to have power for audiences in Durban, although its import has changed over time. In 2008, Govender reflected,

> I think people are still chasing after this, this thing, this dream. Partly it's because the dream is not being fulfilled in real life. You have to have a dream. And when you see it, you do cry or you, you're sometimes saddened by it, but you're sometimes inspired and heightened by it. And they say, like 'Ah, it is just so beautiful.' And just like, everybody's in tears. (personal interview, 14 August 2008)

By 2018, a decade of Jacob Zuma's regime had heightened xenophopia and particularism across South Africa, and Surialanga received invitations to perform less frequently. But

Surialanga's performances no longer signal a present dream, shared by all, but rather an exuberant dream deferred in the face of political, economic and social instability that highlights racial identity, rather than working across and against it. The kind of intercultural exchange that their dances portray ironically appears to be either an ideal of the past or perhaps an unattainable future.

By 2018, Govender's work with Surialanga, and particularly performances of 'Asimbonanga' and other pieces, served not just to promote Mandela's vision, but also to defend her own positioning in the country as a South African of Indian heritage. She explained,

> People are trying to keep the Mandela vision in their mind somewhere. Because there's a lot of exclusionary measures in the legal framework and in public and private life … so people are not valuing the contribution a person can make … I am very much more vocal about who I am and that I have to have a space to develop certain things. (personal interview, 15 August 2018)

Performing Surialanga's pieces have become a way to remember the buoyant founding moment of South Africa's democracy at a time when interracial divisions and anti-Indian sentiments have become commonplace.

Transforming selves

Mignolo's suggestion that decolonial artistic projects offer up the possibility of a new set of cultural sensibilities particularly relates to dance because of its embodied form. So, do these processes reconfigure deeply internalised understandings of racial and cultural divisions for the dancers themselves? In a 2003 reflection piece about Surialanga, I considered the distance between the imaginaries of interculturalism presented in their performances, and the reality of the dancers' divided everyday lives, where class, gender and race structured their interactions in rehearsal and beyond. I observed then that the men of the company congregated with one another in rehearsal downtime, usually speaking to each other in isiZulu, while the Indian women congregated in another part of the theatre, speaking to each other in English. Occasionally, a member of one or the other group would wander to the other end of the room to chat, but these exchanges were relatively rare, even though there was no overt animosity between them that I observed. I also observed that outside of rehearsal and performance, there was no interaction between the men and women, who lived segregated, class-stratified lives that by apartheid design excluded one another (Radhakrishnan 2003). Apart from these broad structural divisions, both groups had existing familiarity among themselves before joining the company. The young women were often drawn from the same Bharatanatyam school in Durban, the highly regarded Manormani Dance Academy. Some of the most senior dancers of that school had performed at Mandela's inauguration. Similarly, the young men had been training together for years, lived in the same township and were comfortable around one another outside the context of the company. Yet, over the years in the company the distance I observed in those early days shifted, proving to be yet another arena of transformation in Surialanga's ambitious decolonial project.

From the perspective of the young women, their initial hesitation in interacting with 'the guys' came from unfamiliarity. As a long-time company member Kobashnee explained, dancing with Surialanga was the first time the young women had danced alongside men or boys before, so just having young men in rehearsal felt uneasy. They had also never experienced making physical contact with fellow dancers during a dance, so that felt 'a bit uncomfortable at first' (personal interview, 16 August 2018). Kobashnee recalled being particularly conscious of her sweaty palms; she constantly apologised to the guys before and after she held their hands in rehearsal, but especially on stage, when the excitement and pressure made her perspire even more. Apart from the uneasiness of physical proximity and contact, Kobashnee explained that in the beginning, she was not sure what to talk to them about: 'culturally, you don't know what you're allowed to ask and not ask. So you're afraid of asking'. Surialanga's choreography required the women to do movements that were 'different' as well: gumboot, Zulu traditional, Western contemporary and others. The entire context was thus challenging because it prompted both the men and women of the company to transform their embodied understandings of themselves and those of the other dancers, even as it required them to learn new dances that challenged their previous intense training.

Govender was acutely aware of the distance between the two groups in the company, and always considered this distance to be the greatest challenge she hoped to address. She attempted many strategies. She hosted luncheons for the whole company whenever possible and she encouraged them to celebrate each other's birthdays. When she interacted with the young women, she prompted them to think about what the guys would like, just as she would ask the guys to think about what they would like to do for her and the girls. In the early days especially, she frequently destabilised roles within the company, and she made sure the expertise of the young men in Zulu and gumboot dance was recognised. Despite being extremely young at the time, she encouraged the young men to teach the young women traditional Zulu dance. Govender would design sessions where the four Zulu men would be in charge of creating and teaching a particular sequence, such as those that appear in 'Raghupathy' or 'African Dream'. This was extremely challenging. Govender explained,

> I think they [the women] found it very hard to actually go out of a role of a middle class Indian woman. Their only interaction with a person of colour, and definitely a black man, would be as a guard or gardener or something. So that whole power relation, the disparity, is seriously there. And it's difficult to undo that kind of thing and in a way, you've got to just let it be and grow.

There were many everyday instances in which this disparity stepped to the fore. In the early 2000s, for example, Govender recalled, 'the girls used to say to the guys, "can you bring the bag, please?" Like, their own suitcases! And we had to change that to, "No, you must carry your own bag"' (personal interview, 14 August 2008). Recalling the same time period, S'bu reflected,

> That time, we thought maybe because these things were still there – racist things and all those things. Blacks have to be with blacks, Indians have to be with Indians, whites have to be with whites. What they knew about blacks was that blacks were criminals. You see, that's the thing. So, if you don't want to talk to me, I'm not going to force you. I'll just chat with my friends. That's what usually we do. (personal interview, 15 August 2008)

Over time together in the company, however, the distance between the men and women of Surialanga diminished to a large extent, a result of retooled sensibilities and increased familiarity and openness from everyone involved. By 2008, S'bu and Sandile felt that their relationships with the young women of the company had changed for the better. Many of the women had ended their time in the company to begin full-time jobs or move to another city for work or because of a partner. The women who joined more recently seemed more willing to be friends, S'bu and Sandile felt. In parallel, the experience of international travel transformed the relationships of all company members. While visiting Washington D.C., Amsterdam, Singapore and South Korea, the dancers lived together full-time, staying at the same hotel, eating the same food, rehearsing together and exploring the city together, all representing South Africa. Recalling the company's first trip abroad together to France, S'bu noted,

> Right away, we started chatting in airports, in the plane. And we started to become friends. 'Okay, how's your life? And how's this and that?' We started to know each other. You know what made us start talking? Because everyone was so excited about going overseas. Because no one had been overseas [before]. Maybe if we had been in South Africa, it would have taken a long time. (personal interview, 15 August 2008)

For Kobashnee, travel was just one part of a bigger experience of performing together.

> It became more and more that the dancing kind of united us … You were sharing the stage … it was never like a solo performance, so you always felt you were part of something bigger. And of course, wherever we would perform – the reaction from people! People would be so enthralled and excited. It made you realize you're part of something different, something new. And then, when we were dancing together, we got to enjoy it more, you know? So you know, actually dancing made you more comfortable. And also getting the message out to people that dance knows no boundaries, that dance can unite us. To get that message out, we had to look it and show it. (personal interview, 16 August 2018)

Kobashnee felt that over time, the guys became more like colleagues with whom they could joke and laugh offstage, and engage with real smiles and caring onstage.

The ongoing project of bringing the 'girls' and the 'guys' together was always fragile and tense, and for Govender, always at the forefront of her consciousness. And although there were successes, she also realised her experiment could not reconfigure subjectivities entirely:

> I started realizing – and it was quite an awakening – that you can't actually, when you put the forms together, it doesn't necessarily, even if you make the relationship, even if you do the contact improv[isation] at certain points, there are issues … But I think to be a part of the company they had to buy into that. They knew that was my stance, whatever they thought of it, and however crazy they thought I was. That's okay. But that's the code. I won't accept any other kind of disrespect, you see … the treatment of people was not something you could compromise. (personal interview, 14 August 2008)

The experiment that was forged in Surialanga was thus radical and yet partial, lived in the flesh and yet not completely internalised within the minute muscles of the company members.

S'bu and Sandile agreed that they were much more comfortable with the women now, that they felt comfortable and could talk to each other. But the ease and familiarity came with caution. S'bu still had poignant questions lingering when we discussed their relationships with the young women. 'Why should we talk now, when we are going overseas? Why didn't you know me better while we're still at home? You know?' (Personal interview, 15 August 2008).

The disparities that structured their lives outside the company never completely left their lives inside the company. When I asked if they had ever visited each others' homes, S'bu and Sandile laughed, and they responded in unison, 'No, never. Never, never'. They said it would never come up, and they were afraid to invite anyone to their homes because they might not want to come, or might feel it to be dangerous (personal interview, 15 August 2008). Their laughter indicated the absurdity of the suggestion of visiting one another, as their emphatic answer gestured towards the violent inequities that continue to separate them.

Thus, in the years since I wrote my initial reflections on the dynamics within the intercultural artistic space of Surialanga, the relationships within the company grew and transformed, at once constrained by structural disparities and at times, free from them. What was clear especially from the recollections of S'bu, Kobashnee and Govender, however, was that for those directly involved, the decolonial project presented on stage was always experienced at the level of the senses. And the fragile project had to be practiced, as in a dance, to reconfigure ways of thinking, interacting, experiencing and feeling. Having experienced physical proximity and close familiarity with one another, they were able to convey a message that continues to move audiences to tears. And still, these transformations have played themselves out within limits prescribed by the persistent coloniality of the post-apartheid social landscape.

Post-Mandela: life, death, and the ongoing dance

The life trajectories of those involved in the company speak to the contradictions of post-apartheid social and cultural life over two decades after a joyous gang of sixteen Indian dancers boarded the bus to Pretoria for Mandela's inauguration. Most of the women who have been involved with the company moved onto professional careers. Many of them married, had children, purchased homes and have enjoyed upward mobility. Govender continued working at the University of Kwa-Zulu Natal, in the English department, but has more recently moved on to be Adjunct Professor at University of Stellenbosch, while consulting at other universities, including Duke University in the U.S. Govender set up long-term work opportunities for S'bu and Sandile at Hillview Primary School, just down the road from the Asoka Theatre where we rehearsed so often. For years, the pair lived there, teaching Zulu children Bharatanatyam, gumboot and Zulu dances as a regular part of the curriculum. They continued to travel abroad with the company for performances, and in 2017, S'bu travelled to Scotland with Hillview teaching staff for a training programme. When local performances came, S'bu and Sandile managed the music and the costumes for the company, and Govender did her best to make sure they were treated well and paid fairly at times she when was unable to be physically present. Despite these improvements, however, S'bu and Sandile's livelihoods remained tenuous and dependent on the opportunities provided by and through Surialanga, and Govender in particular, a situation that created interpersonal strife at times. Their family connections in Clermont Township meant they remained embedded in an economy of personal obligations that prevented them from saving money. In recent years, their teaching at Hillview has been more sporadic. Eventually, the programme they led came to an end, and they moved out.

The everyday violence of post-apartheid life has touched many company members, underscoring the fragility of Surialanga's particular decolonial project. In the spring of

2018, I was shocked to see a post on social media that Sandile had passed away at the age of 36. He had been ill for some time, but Govender had little idea of the nature of his illness. She only knew that he had dropped out of some recent performances, and had stopped coming to rehearsals. Unable to visit him or learn what was wrong, Govender only learned of his death after the fact. It was then that I noticed the patterns of violence that have plagued the company, sparing no group, but affecting Zulu company members most directly. In 2008, when I reconnected with Surialanga and found both S'bu and Sandile firm in their commitment to Bharatanatyam, I could not ignore that a visible scar had transformed S'bu's face. He had been stabbed near the eye during a robbery, and I learned that he had been unable to receive adequate medical care in time to prevent extensive and permanent scarring. From my recent interview with Kobashnee, I learned that violence had touched another member of the company, a young Indian woman with whom I had also danced. Her mother had been violently murdered in her own home. She had been making tea for the men who proceeded to kill her. Govender also shared with me in her interview that a new member of the company, a Zulu woman who was a contemporary dancer, passed away due to illness last year.

And still, the company performs. Many of the iconic pieces of their repertoire continue to be performed, and Govender continues to work with Zulu artists to produce new works as well. As the country continues to grapple with its identity as a nation, a company as old as the democratic state continues to promote a vision of intercultural harmony that moves from body to body through dance and touch, moving hearts and minds with a fragile sense of progress. Govender's work has never been simply a reflection of Mandela's national vision; rather it emerged from her own life experience and perspective as an artist embedded in diverse identity-making projects: Zulu, Indian and South African. As such, Surialanga's dance never sought to represent a universal vision of South African identity, but rather to 'enunciate' an expression of interculturalism particular to Durban – one that honours the culture, language and music of those particular groups who migrated to Kwa-Zulu Natal. While white culture is never completely erased – English lyrics, Western instrumentation and even Western contemporary dance pervade the company's repertoire – those elements are decentred. Learning and performing Surialanga's dances, the members of the company retool to some extent their taken-for-granted ways of knowing and classifying, thus challenging the colonial matrix of power. The persistent violence of post-apartheid life heightens the stakes of decolonial art such as Surialanga's, making South African Bharatanatyam an improbable – but evermore essential – articulation of post-apartheid belonging.

Notes

1. Bharatanatyam is a classical dance form of India that has come to represent Indianness around the world and was a key form of artistic production in the Indian nationalist movement.
2. I borrow this usage of the term 'enunciation' from Gaztambide-Fernandez's interview with Walter Mignolo, to be explored in greater depth in the next section (Gaztambide-Fernández 2014, 201).
3. Bharatanatyam itself has a contested history, embedded as it is in both colonial rule and in anti-colonial nationalist projects. A thorough explanation of these dynamics lies outside the

34 DANCE, MUSIC AND CULTURES OF DECOLONISATION

scope of this paper, but my consideration of Surialanga's work is deeply informed by this understanding (Chakravorty 1998, Thobani 2017).
4. For a discussion of other contexts where this has been true, as well as how this orientation shapes dance and the study of dance cultures, see Reed 1998.
5. This orientation also emerges from a contradictory history of Zulu-Indian relationships in the province of Natal and later, Kwa-Zulu-Natal (Xaba 2001).
6. See Itano 2002. Govender did later convince Ngema to include Zulu men in Bharatanatyam silks at an official event.

Disclosure statement

No potential conflict of interest was reported by the author.

ORCID

Smitha Radhakrishnan ⓘ http://orcid.org/0000-0002-1456-1293

References

Chakravorty, P. 1998. "Hegemony, Dance and Nation: The Construction of the Classical Dance in India." *South Asia: Journal of South Asian Studies* 21 (2): 107–120.

Desai, A. G. 1996. *Arise ye Coolies: Apartheid and the Indian 1960-1995.* Johannesburg: Impact Africa Pub.

Freund, B. 1995. *Insiders and Outsiders: The Indian Working Class of Durban 1910-1990.* Pietermaritzburg: University of Natal Press.

Friedman, S. 2012. *Post-Apartheid Dance: Many Bodies Many Voices Many Stories.* Newcastle upon Tyne: Cambridge Scholars Publishing.

Gaztambide-Fernández, R. 2014. "Decolonial Options and Artistic/AestheSic Entanglements: An Interview with Walter Mignolo." *Decolonization: Indigeneity, Education, and Society* 3 (1): 196–212.

Govender, S. 1994. "Interculturalism and South African Indian Fusion Dance." *Indic Theatre Monograph Series,* no. 3. Accessed October 24, 2018. Available at http://scnc.ukzn.ac.za/doc/ARTS/dance/SURIA.htm.

Itano, N. 2002. "Blacks and Indians Clash Over Divisive Zulu Song." *The Christian Science Monitor,* July 16. Accessed October 24, 2018. https://www.csmonitor.com/2002/0716/p07s01-woaf.html.

Kumar, A. 2011. "Bharatanatyam and Identity Making in the South Asian Diaspora: Culture through the Lens of Occupation." *Journal of Occupational Science* 18 (1): 36–47.

Maharaj, B. 1995. "The Local State and Residential Segregation: Durban and the Prelude the Group Areas Act." *South African Geographical Journal* 77 (1): 33–41.

Ndlovu-Gatsheni, S. J. 2013. *Coloniality of Power in Postcolonial Africa: Myths of Decolonization.* Dakar, Senegal: CODESRIA.

Radhakrishnan, S. 2003. "'African Dream': The Imaginary of Nation, Race, and Gender in South African Intercultural Dance." *Feminist Studies* 29 (3): 529–537.

Radhakrishnan, S. 2005. "'Time to Show Our True Colors': The Gendered Politics of Indianness in Post-Apartheid South Africa." *Gender & Society* 19 (2): 262–281.

Reddy, M. 2016. *Social Movements and the Indian Diaspora.* Abingdon: Routledge.

Reed, S. A. 1998. "The Politics and Poetics of Dance." *Annual Review of Anthropology* 27: 503–532.

Thobani, S. 2017. *Indian Classical Dance and the Making of Postcolonial National Identities: Dancing on Empire's Stage.* Abingdon: Routledge.

Xaba, T. 2001. "From Symbolic to Participatory Reconciliation: Race Relations in South Africa – The African-Indian Case." *Transformation: Critical Perspectives on South Africa* 45: 37–57.

Music competitions, public pedagogy and decolonisation in Trinidad and Tobago

Christopher L. Ballengee

ABSTRACT

This article examines music's role in decolonising processes in Trinidad and Tobago, focusing on postcolonial national identity politics with reference to the country's two largest ethnic groups: those descended from enslaved Africans and those from indentured labourers from India. First, the article traces the nationalisation of Creole culture – defined in terms of African-European syncretism – from the 1950s onwards, and it describes the state's use of music competitions and educational programmes to institutionalise Carnival, calypso, and steel pan, all associated largely with African Trinidadian culture. This impacted on Indian Trinidadians by excluding them from inscriptions of national identity. The article concludes with a discussion of Indian Trinidadian cultural resurgence, tassa competitions, and the growth of public pedagogy from the 1970s that established tassa as an icon of Indianness; and all illustrating how music was used in a complex decolonisation process (relating to colonial rule and the Creole mainstream).

Trinidad and Tobago is a twin-island nation state in the southern Caribbean that features a profound mix of ethnicities resulting from the entangled legacies of colonialism, African slavery, and Indian indentureship.[1] As independence approached in 1962, Trinidadian political leaders set upon a programme of cultural development to nationalise 'Creole' culture, narrowly defined in terms of African-European syncretism. This included subsidy and promotion of Carnival and its primary musical components calypso and steel pan as symbols of the burgeoning nation. Calypso and steel pan were (and continue to be) the subjects of a state-supported developmental programme including national competitions that shaped performance practice according to nationalist ideals and educational initiatives meant to affirm Carnival as key to Trinidadian identity. Such a nationalist project necessarily excluded non-African Trinidadian cultural practices, in effect barring minority groups from participating in the inscription of national identity. This most significantly impacted Indian Trinidadians, numbering about 40% of the country's population from the time of independence until now. In a period of increasing political assertiveness and cultural efflorescence in the 1970s and 1980s, Indian Trinidadian performing arts underwent a similar process of development with the emergence of major competitions, public pedagogy projects and accompanying political rhetoric that advocated for equal representation of Indian Trinidadian culture on the national stage. This article describes the role music competitions and corollary educational programmes play in establishing, maintaining and disrupting postcolonial national identity. It begins with an overview of the state's nationalisation of calypso and steel pan as part of a decolonisation programme initiated at the moment of independence. Then it focuses on Indian Trinidadian tassa drumming as a case study for what might be considered a second wave in the process of decolonisation that continues to push back against African Trinidadian cultural hegemony.

Nationalising Creole culture

At the end of slavery in the British Empire in the 1830s, planters turned to a system of indentured labour to maintain production on plantations. After efforts to recruit labour locally and abroad, they eventually found a steady supply of workers in India. Between 1838 and 1917, hundreds of thousands of agricultural labourers mostly from the Bhojpuri region of northeast India became enmeshed in a global labour scheme that fed workers into British, French, and Dutch territories in the Caribbean, Africa, the Indian Ocean, southeast Asia, Australia, and Oceania. Today, their descendants form distinct communities, some more integrated than others, within the postcolonial societies where they live. The contemporary twin-island nation-state of Trinidad and Tobago at the southern-most tip of the Lesser Antilles hosts a total population of about 1.2 million comprising a multiethnic, multicultural, and multi-religious society reflective of the intertwined legacies of slavery and indenture. Trinidad received nearly 150,000 Indian labourers throughout the indenture period, the majority working on sugarcane plantations. While some returned to India, many decided by choice or circumstance to remain.

Though contract requirements were modified at different points throughout the indenture period, Indian labourers generally agreed to a five-year contract, with the completion of another five-year contract required for free passage back to India. Trinidadian society largely regarded Indians as temporary visitors to the colony, this despite the fact that most decided to remain rather than return. Even as a sizable Indian population settled permanently, Indians continued to be regarded as outsiders, arriving as it were in an already-established racially stratified social hierarchy (Brereton 1979, 176–77). By 1900, Indians made up one third of the total population of Trinidad (Ramesar 1994, 131) with most residing in rural areas and working their own plots of land adjacent to their former estates, where many continued to engage in seasonal wage labour. In this way, Indian Trinidadians remained a largely rural people attached to the land for subsistence, far from urban centres of educational, economic and political power until the 1950s. Such geographic isolation coupled with a persistent outsider status resulted in Indian Trinidadians' relative marginalisation in matters of national representation.

As British colonisers gradually gave up power in preparation for independence in 1962, it was a mostly urban African Trinidadian middle class that claimed leadership by way of the People's National Movement (PNM), the dominant political party from the late 1950s to the early 1990s. The PNM was led by Eric Williams, an Oxford-educated historian, a leading figure on the history of slavery, the country's first prime minister, and the most important politician in Trinidad and Tobago until his death in 1981. As something of an independence gift to the nation, Williams laid out the first major historical account of Trinidad and Tobago written from the perspective of the country's formerly colonised people in his book *History of the People of Trinidad and Tobago* (1962). In it, Williams railed against European colonialism while explicating what Bridget Brereton calls an 'Afro-Creole nationalist narrative' in which 'people of African or part-African descent – Creoles in local terminology – were the most important constituent group in the nation, the core Trinidadians ... who had the historical "right" to succeed the British in the governance of the new nation' (2010, 221). Williams' *History* was of central importance as the PNM set upon a nation-building project that sought to establish Creole culture as national culture. From such a perspective, the PNM promoted 'interracial solidarity' and urged all ethnic and religious groups to prepare for 'complete integration in our cosmopolitan society' (Mohammed 1960, 2). For many Indian Trinidadians, 'solidarity' and 'integration' on these terms were tantamount to cultural suicide, and leaders quickly took up contrary positions in an effort to counter African Trinidadian cultural hegemony (Singh 1962). Therefore, at the moment of independence, Indian Trinidadians were 'relegated to the status of political oppositionists and cultural aliens' (Manuel 2000, 58), which allowed them to participate in the nationalist project in only a token way.

Carnival, calypso and steel pan as patriotic imperatives

As part of their nationalist agenda, the PNM focused on Carnival as a unique and appropriately celebratory symbol of the nation. Exerting control over Carnival with the advent of the Carnival Development Committee (CDC) in the 1950s, the PNM assumed oversight of a range of Carnival activities. Among other promotional programmes, the CDC established or took leadership of several regional and national calypso and steel pan competitions. Among these were Calypso Monarch (the national calypso competition) and Panorama (the national steel orchestra competition), still highly anticipated events in the Carnival season. Such contests, then and now, spurred interest and development in these genres while simultaneously affirming them as national musics (Guilbault 2011, 11).

Carnival-time music contests have a long history in Trinidad and Tobago. By the 1910s, informal calypso contests were common among working class African Trinidadians and they became a highlight of the Carnival season over the next decade with the proliferation of 'calypso tents' in which informal contests were staged as part of an evening's entertainment for paying audiences. Often critical of those in power, calypsos were simultaneously entertaining and potentially threatening to colonial order. Until the 1940s, various 'improvement committees' comprised of prominent businessmen, police and city officials made efforts to control and coordinate the activities of calypso tents (Guilbault 2007, 68–70). One strategy in this regard was to formalise the calypso competition such that the champion of each tent would compete with one another in a 'Calypso King' contest; (the name was changed to Calypso Monarch in 1978 to accommodate female competitors). Those who conformed to the expectations of the improvement committee were awarded top prizes. As the state assumed control over Calypso King through the auspices of the CDC from 1956 onward, it employed a similar approach in rewarding top prizes to calypsonians whose music emphasized national unity and avoided critiques of the ruling elite (Guilbault 2007, 71).

The steel pan was invented by working class African Trinidadians in the 1930s and it has been associated with Carnival as a performance context from the start. Early steel pans were noisy and colonial elites disparaged them, prompting authorities on several occasions to curtail steel pan performance and development. Undaunted, bands continued to cultivate the instrument and its repertoire (comprising calypso as well as foreign popular and classical music) to become essential elements of the Carnival season. By the 1950s, steel pan builders had sufficiently refined the instrument such that an all-star band billed as the Trinidad All Steel Percussion Orchestra represented the colony at the Festival of Britain in 1951. The PNM understood the potential of steel pan as a symbol of Creole creativity and worked to subsidise its development, in part through the creation of Panorama, the national steel orchestra competition held annually during the Carnival season since 1963. Panorama quickly became the centre of steel orchestral activities, shaping performance practices through contest rules that reward innovation and creativity within the bounds of 'tradition', in part defined by complex musical arrangements of calypso (as opposed to non-local genres) or using relatively standardised musical form and orchestration (Ziegler 2015). Those that deviate from this careful balance between tradition and innovation are typically unsuccessful in competition. After Birdsong Steel Orchestra finished in last place in the 2014 Panorama competition, the group's arranger, New York-based pannist and jazz musician Andy Narell, lamented the judges' unwillingness to accept something different (When Steel Talks 2014b). Discussion among Panorama aficionados, however, suggested Birdsong's poor finish was most importantly due to Narell being an American, a foreigner who dared to compete since 'Panorama is [our] thing' (When Steel Talks 2014a; Ziegler 2015, 89–90).

Calypso Monarch and Panorama come into view as political technologies that draw on and shape nationalist sentiment by rewarding exemplars and penalising nonconformists (Dudley 2003; Guilbault 2007). The prestige of these competitions, which has been established and perpetuated through government subsidy, continues to be underpinned by a multifaceted academic and public discourse by local and foreign observers that centres on calypso and steel pan as quintessential expressions of the nation. Histories of calypso sought roots in Europe and West Africa, thereby situating modern calypso as a hybrid musical practice with identifiable and ancient origins (Elder 1964; Hill 1967; Quevedo 1983; Warner 1983; Liverpool 1990). Steel pan was likewise historicised (Elder 1964; Johnson 2011), though many also focused on its technical and musical novelty (Seeger and Seeger 1956; Seeger 1958). Studies by foreign scholars have tended to focus on the economic, political, and cultural impact of the nationalisation of steel pan (Stuempfle 1995; Dudley 2008). Trinidadian expats living abroad, in the United States especially, established steel orchestral education and performance programmes that transformed steel pan into a cosmopolitan instrument, in turn increasing its cachet at home (Martin 2011; Gormandy 2017). Such performance projects and scholarly work have collectively positioned calypso and steel pan as patriotic imperatives worthy of preservation, development and critique within state supported national competitions and educational programmes. The latter includes the study of Carnival arts in primary and secondary school curricula, organisation of in-school calypso competitions, an exhibit on steel pan technology at the National Science Museum, and a range of opportunities at the St. Augustine campus of the University of the West Indies including a degree in Carnival Studies and a dedicated Steelpan Development Centre 'created to explore, support, and develop all aspects of the technology of the steelpan' and to provide 'technical, business, and administrative support' to pan builders (Copeland, Imbert, and Gay 2001). In part, thanks to this large body of work, the steel pan was officially made the national instrument of Trinidad and Tobago by prime ministerial decree in 1992.

Grassroots educational programmes have emerged also, most soliciting state subsidy or commercial sponsorship and many organised as offshoots of steel orchestras. For example, Birdsong Steel Orchestra started the Birdsong Academy in 2004 to offer tuition-free music literacy training including lessons in music theory and applied music instruction on a range of instruments. Since its inception, the programme has trained more than 1000 children, specifically targeting at-risk youth. According to stakeholders, the programme has been a great success, and not only in fulfilling their mission of music education. A majority of participants reported improved overall academic performance in school through 'increased focus and problem-solving capacity' learned at the Academy. Stakeholders also tout the Academy as a safe place for young people to avoid becoming criminals (Burke 2014, 90–91). In 2013, the Ministry of Community Development, Arts, and Culture (formerly The Ministry of Arts and Multiculturalism under the previous government) took notice of the Birdsong Academy model and lent its support to establishing similar programmes at six other panyards around the country ('Music Schools in the Community' 2015).

A general feature of twentieth-century Caribbean and Latin American nationalist movements was a middle class desire to define a national culture that in turn legitimised political autonomy. In the Caribbean, this process relied heavily on recovered or reinvented African Caribbean idioms, especially music and dance, in the absence of other easily identifiable indigenous practices (Austerlitz 1997; Averill 1997; Moore 1997; Turino 2003). This was indeed the case for Trinidad and Tobago. The reification of Carnival and Carnival-time musics is but one example where the state chose to selectively nationalise elements of African Trinidadian culture as part of a decolonisation programme that included subsidy of competitions and educational initiatives meant to institutionalise Creole culture. Other musics representing a range of constituent ethnicities and traditions were largely excluded from inscriptions of national identity at the moment of independence and beyond, an audible absence that continues to resonate within Trinidad and Tobago's cultural politics today (Munasinghe 2002, 663–64; Guilbault 2011, 16). In the following section, Indian Trinidadian tassa drumming provides one such case study in which tassa competitions and educational programmes demonstrate how Indian Trinidadians remain invested in celebrating their contributions to national history and culture. Such efforts collectively seek to counter the outdated yet still-potent perception of Indian Trinidadians as outsiders, in the process decolonising the conventional postcolonial concept of citizenship by advocating for equal recognition and inclusion.

The Indian Trinidadian cultural renaissance

The 1970s was a revolutionary period in Trinidad and Tobago. The first ripples of the Black Power Movement reached Trinidad in the late 1960s and came to a head in 1970 when students and activists staged a series of demonstrations that rocked Port of Spain. The government was hard pressed to contain building tensions, and protests became increasingly intense when police killed a protester, Basil Davis, on 6 April 1970. In response, some members of the military staged a mutiny, and at nearly the same moment, the sugar workers union, comprised primarily of Indian Trinidadians, halted work sparking rumours of a nationwide general strike. Eric Williams responded by declaring a state of emergency, in the process arresting many of the movement's frontline leaders. From the start, the Black Power Movement had looked to integrate Indian Trinidadians into its struggle by virtue of a shared history of colonial exploitation, though unity was never truly achieved despite some fleeting moments of solidarity. Indian Trinidadians were reluctant to identify with the movement, largely out of fear their Indian identity might vanish under the rubric of 'blackness' (Brereton 2010, 223). Indeed, throughout the 1970s and into the next decade, something of an Indian Trinidadian cultural renaissance arose inspired by and in counterpoint to the Black Power Movement.

One result was the greater visibility of Indian Trinidadian expressive arts, which became a vehicle for expressing cultural pride, though not necessarily in an overtly political fashion, in opposition to both the Black Power Movement and the dominant nationalist narrative. This cultural resurgence gave rise to

> all manner of music competitions, public and private performances and song sessions, religious events, mass media projects, academic conferences, scholarly publications and journals, classes in everything from Hindustani art music to wedding songs, and a general sense of healthy cultural assertiveness and pride. (Manuel 2015, 29)

The televised Indian talent programme *Mastana Bahar* ('Joyful Season'), created by brothers Sham and Moean Mohammed and premiered in 1970, profited from and played a key role in this renaissance. While much of the programme's content focused on renditions of Bollywood hits, local genres of Indian Trinidadian folk and popular music were also audience favourites. The Mohammed brothers additionally produced *The Indian Cultural Pageant*, an annual televised concert with a competitive element featuring Indian Trinidadian performers that ran from 1975 until 2000. These programmes exposed audiences to the diversity of Indian and Indian Trinidadian performing arts in an accessible and apolitical manner, providing even non-Indian audiences an easy portal for appreciating Indian Trinidadian music and dance (Niranjana 2006, 178). The influence of these programmes is evidenced by the reinvigoration of all manner of Indian Trinidadian performing arts, importantly including the emergence of new competitions for tassa drumming, chowtal singing, Ramayan singing, and other genres; and the invention of new musical styles like chutney-soca, a popular genre fusing African and Indian musical elements reflective of Trinidadian cultural mixing (Manuel 2000, 199; Ramnarine 2001). The following sections discuss one of these styles: tassa drumming, situating it in its historical and cultural context and then describing ways in which competitions and public pedagogy projects work in decolonising processes that challenge Carnival's centrality in the national narrative of expressive culture.

Contextualising tassa

Trinidadian tassa is derived from an amalgam of North Indian folk drumming styles. However, it maintains the most direct continuity with *dhol-tasha*, an Indian percussion ensemble comprising one or more semi-spherical *tasha* drums and a number of cylindrical double-headed *dhol* bass drums. To this is often added time-keeping instruments such as metal shakers, bells, gongs, or small hand cymbals called *jhanjh* or *jhal*. The ensemble remains popular in many parts of India and Pakistan where it provides music for processional and celebratory events in Hindu, Muslim, and secular contexts (Manuel 2014; Wolf 2017). *Dhol-tasha* has particularly enduring links with the Shi'a Muslim Muharram observance in North India where drumming facilitates the procession and imaginatively evokes the sounds of the Battle of Karbala (680 A.D.) in which the Prophet Muhammad's grandson Hussein ibn Ali, his family, and followers were martyred. This performance context was the most important vehicle for the global dissemination of *dhol-tasha* as the British exported Indian labour throughout the world. In Sumatra, for example, locals trace their *dol-tasa* tradition to the arrival of Indian soldiers recruited by the British East India Company in the late 1700s to man its fort in Bengkulu (Kartomi 2012, 78–81). Here *dol-tasa* is exclusively played for Muharram (locally termed *tabut*) where a single *tasa* leads a much larger number of *dol* players through a series of rhythms, each musically representing sections of the Muharram narrative (Kartomi 2012, 91–93). From the 1830s, indentured labourers were responsible for establishing virtually all other *dhol-tasha* variants outside the subcontinent. In Mauritius, the first place to experiment with importing indentured Indians in 1834, *dhol-tasha* is closely linked with Muharram, locally termed *Ghoon*. In this context, ensembles include a number of large double-headed *marfa* drums (instead of the cylindrical *dhol*) and a lesser number of *tassa* drums. The repertoire is repetitive and martial in character, with a lead *tassa* beating out musical cues and more skilled drummers engaging in limited improvisation. Drummers and spectators also sing prayers and exclamations along with the drumming.

In the Caribbean, the most pronounced *dhol-tasha* traditions are in territories that received large numbers of indentured labourers, namely Suriname, Guyana, and Trinidad. Of these, Trinidadian tassa is one of the world's most vibrant *dhol-tasha* variants with drummers having developed expectations of virtuosity and a high level of technical skill. Like *dhol-tasha*, the Trinidadian tassa ensemble consists of three instrument types: the bowl-shaped tassa, the doubled-headed bass drum (or *dhol*), and brass hand cymbals *jhal*. Tassa's enduring popularity is perhaps thanks to tassa's absorption of elements of other Indian musical styles that have since faded in Trinidad and Tobago. In this way, tassa has become something of a default Indian percussion ensemble called upon for a range of sacred and secular events. Tassa is indeed a vital component of the Muharram observance, locally termed *Hosay*, and it is essential for portions of the three-day set of Hindu wedding rituals. In these two cases, tassa's inescapable loudness reverberates into surrounding neighbourhoods sonically marking the boundaries of Indian Trinidadian cultural space in rural villages and urban centres alike.

In Indian Trinidadian drumming terminology, the word 'hand' refers to a distinct composite rhythm played by the ensemble. Tassa hands may differ from one another in a number of ways: a different bass line, a different supporting rhythm, the use a particular formal structure, etc. Most everyday tassa hands are adapted from other musical sources. The hand called *nagara*, for example, features rhythms typical of those played on the North Indian nagara drum pair, which is obsolete in Trinidad and Tobago today. In another example, the hand *chaubola* is patterned in name and structure from a common poetic form used in Local Classical Singing, a nostalgic and well-loved Indian Caribbean genre built from a fusion of North Indian folk, classical, and devotional music (Manuel 2000). Where a typical Local Classical song features a theka (the main body of the song) and a barti (a section featuring contrasting metre and/or rhythmic structure), so too does *chaubola* hand for tassa, rearticulating this theka/barti structure while marginally preserving the song form in the absence of singing. Hands are also derived from non-Indian sources. A good example is *calypso* hand whose rhythms are distilled from those typically played by the steel orchestra, an important accompaniment for calypso singing beginning in the 1930s (Ballengee 2018). Despite such eclectic source material, in all cases tassa repertoire proceeds according to a distinct Indian Trinidadian musical aesthetic encompassing notions of timbre, rhythm, and form that closely align with other Indian Caribbean genres.

Tassa competitions and public pedagogy projects

In 1984 Republic Bank of Trinidad and Tobago (RBTT) organised Tassa Taal, the country's first formal tassa competition. RBTT sponsored the competition as part of a series of developmental projects around the country with staff and wealthy customers at the Penal branch (located in an area comprising a predominantly Indian Trinidadian demographic) deciding on creating a competition to 'elevate' the public's perception of tassa (Ballengee 2013, 196–97). Tassa Taal quickly became a popular annual event drawing bands and audiences from across the country. Nearly two decades later, the Tassa Association of Trinidad and Tobago (TATT) established its own national contest in 2000. First billed as the Tassa Monarch Competition (evoking Carnival-time competitions like Calypso Monarch, Soca Monarch, etc.), it has since been renamed the National Tassarama Competition of Trinidad and Tobago (evoking Panorama). Tassa Taal and Tassarama both emerged as independent commercially sponsored events outside of the Carnival season (and most often held outside the capital city Port of Spain), each with the objective of approaching the prestige of Carnival-time competitions while providing a national stage for Indian Trinidadian expressive culture.

All tassa competitions generally require bands to condense their most impressive talents into a skilful, short, and entertaining staged presentation. Judges award points in categories that focus on accuracy of performance and stage presence; the latter often accounting for costumes and other extra-musical elements. Unlike Panorama and Calypso Monarch, in which competitors are expected to perform new material from year to year, tassa competitions have until recently emphasized mastery of a very small set of common repertoire deemed both traditional and accessible for a range of skill levels, with all bands in a given competition playing essentially the same four or five hands as prescribed by contest rules. Since competition performances rarely require bands to perform more esoteric hands, bands work to create memorable, well-rehearsed, and often ostentatious arrangements of common repertoire. Much like the development of steel pan and calypso was incentivized in their respective competitions, many drummers I talked to agreed that the potential prestige and cash prizes that come with placing well in competitions have catalysed refinements in tassa performance practice that bolster new standards for precision, virtuosity, and professionalisation despite the relatively static repertoire restrictions. In the early 2000s, a new generation of drummers began to lobby for changes in contest rules to allow for more individualisation. In response, both national tassa competitions today require one original composition, a significant change for a musical tradition that has conventionally minimised such innovation.

Bands are typically required to play a suite of five hands, four chosen by the contest organisers and one original hand (or sometimes a 'hand of choice' that need not be an original composition) that may be performed in any order. Within these constraints, bands frequently 'act the music' (a technique involving actors, dancers, and props to enhance the meaning of a musical performance) to create a coherent narrative that holds the audience's attention and makes an impression on the judges. Such a narrative usually centres on Indian Trinidadian culture, especially historical themes of Indian arrival, indentured agricultural labour, and emergence of diasporic culture in the post-indenture period. Mimed wedding scenes are commonplace as are vignettes of plantation labour and Indian arrival, the latter frequently evoked via maritime imagery including fanciful models of the *Fath-al-razak*, the ship that brought the first indentured Indians to Trinidad. Also common are scenes that involve reference to Trinidad and Tobago's multiculturalism. A memorable competition performance in 2014, for example, featured a tassa drumming arrangement of music used for African Trinidadian Shango religious ceremonies together with actors miming a Shango ritual on stage. While some bands eschew extra-musical elements all together, relying instead on musical performance alone to impress the judges, most bands will have at least a few dancers if not a more elaborate production. A good example of the latter is illustrated by a performance at the Tassarama finals in 2009 by Trinidad & Tobago Sweet Tassa, a band founded and directed by Lenny Kumar.[2] Below, I give a general account of this performance.

The band began with their original piece called *Punjabi*, a hand Kumar adapted from Indian bhangra rhythms. In an opening flourish, three dancers entered the stage with a brief choreography evocative of Bollywood-style dancing. Bollywood is an easily recognisable marker of Indianness for Trinidadian audiences. Therefore, this introduction set up the performance's narrative by referencing India as a starting point, a place of origin. The next hand was *nagara*, serving to advance the narrative from Indian origins to the re-articulation of Indian cultural practices in diaspora. This association was made clear by enacting a scene from *matikor*, a fertility ritual performed exclusively for and by women on the first night of the three-day set of Hindu wedding rituals (Ramnarine 2001, 100–118). The word *matikor* roughly means 'digging dirt' (from Bhojpuri *matti*, 'earth', and *khora*, 'dig'), referring to the primary action of *matikor* puja that involves digging up and collecting a bit of earth to be used as part of the marriage altar. Prior to the puja, women process toward the puja site accompanied by tassa drumming. Once the puja is completed, tassa provides music for dancing that often involves overtly sexual movements. For Trinidad & Tobago Sweet Tassa's competition performance, actors dressed as old women crossed the stage in a relatively reverent manner evocative of a *matikor* procession then began to mime digging the earth with a long-handled hoe. Almost immediately after establishing the scene, however, all five abruptly dropped the pretext of the puja and began dancing in the traditional suggestive manner, much to the approval of the gathered crowd. The band next played a hand called *chutney*, which adapts rhythms typically played on the double-headed hand drum dholak within the folk music style of the same name. Where *nagara* represents an older tradition originating in India and transformed in the Caribbean, *chutney* represents a style invented in Trinidad (though proceeding from a general Indian aesthetic). Therefore, *chutney* advances the narrative to suggest integration of Indian culture into the fabric of Trinidad and Tobago.

The fourth and fifth hands in the sequence were *dingolay* and *calypso*, each meant to convey a sense of cultural fusion. Structural elements of *dingolay* are akin to the high-energy dholak drumming patterns common in North Indian-derived folk and devotional music in Trinidad (Ballengee 2013, 140–41). However, by virtue of its Creole name (which means 'to dance wildly') and its relative similarity to certain West African drumming patterns, *dingolay* is often assumed to be an example of African and Indian musical fusion.[3] This idea was reinforced in the competition performance by a pair of dancers wearing patriotic colours (red, white, and black) dancing to *dingolay* with choreography featuring a hybrid of African- and Indian-identified movements. Next, a female African Trinidadian *bèlè* dancer emerged at the start of *calypso* to emphasize this hand's adaptation from an African Trinidadian musical style.[4] After a short while, the tempo increased at which point the actors and dancers from previous scenes began forming the final vignette downstage right. Driven by 'acting the music', the final moments of the performance transitioned from a celebration of cultural fusion to that of multiculturalism. The *bèlè* dancer continued her choreography as the *dingolay* dancers came out to flank her. A female actor in Chinese costume (representing the country's significant Chinese minority) began moving from upstage to downstage right behind them. Then, a male dancer in white trousers, a red sequined top, and a black sash draped across his shoulder to embody the national flag danced Carnival-style into the centre of the group. As the music increased in tempo and intensity, fireworks shot up from behind the stage and the male dancer thrust aloft a large red, white, and black umbrella to symbolise, as Kumar described it to me later, that 'we're all under the umbrella of T&T'. With a final flourish, the music ended, the group took a bow, and the crowd roared with enthusiasm.

With generous portions of formality, pageantry, and spectacle, tassa competitions create a heightened sense of occasion framed within a clearly defined Indian Trinidadian cultural space. In this way, such contests comprise an 'invented tradition' (Hobsbawm 1983) wherein orchestrated retellings of Indian arrival and past struggles sit comfortably alongside seemingly contradictory notions of cultural fusion and individuality. Indian Trinidadian orientations to national belonging are expressed both aurally and visually. Tassa's timbres, textures, and performance practice signal clear affinity with India as a place of origin, yet equally locate Trinidad and Tobago as home given the music's rootedness in diaspora. The expectations of tassa competitions, as with many folkloric music competitions (Stillman 1996; Bakan 1998; Dudley 2003), reward refinement and presentation of traditional music while also encouraging transformations in repertoire and performance practice as arrangements cultivated for the stage feed back into bands' everyday performances. Many veteran drummers lament these changes, often deriding contemporary tassa as mere noise. Despite such criticism, competitions continue to provide an important space where tassa receives the kind of critical attention afforded other performing arts of national importance.

The efflorescence of Indian Trinidadian performing arts and corollary educational initiatives from the 1970s onward have been accompanied by an evolving discourse centred on the promotion of performing arts as a cultural imperative to keep Indian Trinidadian culture 'alive' and to push back against African Trinidadian socio-political hegemony. Just as an intellectual body of work helped establish and continues to nurture Carnival-time musics as key to Trinidadian national identity, so too has a similar discourse emerged, though much smaller in scope, that positions tassa as a quintessential expression of Indian Trinidadian culture (Ballengee 2013; Manuel 2015). Such is tassa's iconicity that some cultural activists have led a campaign since 2005 to pressure the state to recognise tassa as the country's co-national instrument alongside steel pan, a demand that has yet to be considered by three successive governments (Ballengee 2017).

Teaching and learning tassa has long been an informal process, with knowledge of technique and repertoire passed down orally through patrilineal family lines. Drummers tell me that most tassa bands of past generations were indeed made up of family members or close family friends. With the advent of formal competitions and with increasing professionalisation, however, bands today are typically comprised of talented musicians who seek out each other as opposed to the family bands of the past. This transformation has therefore modified traditional lines of teaching and learning. While most drummers get their first lessons from family members, the most dedicated will typically enter a kind of informal apprenticeship with a more experienced drummer, over time building a mutually beneficial professional relationship. The past decade has also seen cracks in the patrimony of tassa as a number of women have made serious inroads into the tassa scene. Based in San Juan, Trinidad, the band D'Evergreen Tassa Group is well known for their excellent jhal player Donna Ramsumair, and Lenny Kumar's two daughters Lennita and Lenora formed the country's first all-female tassa group in 2009 with neighbourhood friends (see Figure 1). The Caribbean community in Florida is home to a handful of tassa bands including the Florida Tassa Girls. While female drummers are still regarded as a novelty in Trinidad and Tobago and in diaspora, these women are indeed serious musicians who are regularly hired to play for weddings and other functions and have placed well in local and international music competitions (Goslin 2016).

Figure 1. The Trinidad & Tobago Sweet Tassa Girls Band performs at the opening of the Sweet Tassa Academy, March 2017. Photo courtesy of lime.tt.

Meanwhile, some entrepreneurial drummers and community organisations have offered more formalised tassa training. For example, Lenny Kumar conducts after-school tassa workshops at a number primary and secondary schools throughout the year and has provided a tassa drumming course as part of the Siparia Deltones Steel Orchestra youth music programme (Figure 2). Kumar's most important achievement, however, is the recent establishment of the Trinidad & Tobago Sweet Tassa Academy. Opened in early 2017 with financial and logistical support from the band's sponsor, the National Gas Company of Trinidad and Tobago, the Academy currently offers tuition-free weekly sessions for students of all age groups who learn four common hands alongside lessons on the history and development of tassa. At the close of each session, students participate in a graduation ceremony and are granted certificates of completion. 'I always had a vision to extend my knowledge … into an academy,' Kumar said in a press release, 'a place for persons to come and learn about the tassa drumming art form … to occupy their time and keep them out of trouble. Now, I have decided to create my legacy by opening this academy' (National Gas Company of Trinidad and Tobago 2017).

Tassa is ever-present in the Indian Trinidadian soundscape and as such has become an icon of Indianness in Trinidadian public discourse. The impact of tassa's iconicity is reflected, for example, in grassroots performance projects that position tassa as the Indian Trinidadian counterpart of the steel orchestra. Examples include a number of steel pan and tassa collaborations for Panorama as early as 1972 (Johnson 2006, 55), most notably Leon Edwards's arrangement of the Mighty Trini's Indian-flavored

Figure 2. Lenny Kumar teaches tassa to young students at the Siparia Deltones Steel Orchestra panyard. August 2012.

calypso 'Curry Tabanca' for the Trinidad All Stars Steel Orchestra in 1987 which featured tassa drummers on stage and tassa rhythms integrated into the steel orchestra. As musical director of the Lydian Singers, a choir comprised of amateur singers, the late Pat Bishop also staged a number of performances that intentionally sought to fuse musical styles of Trinidad and Tobago's constituent ethnicities. Memorable among these was a 2009 performance of Handel's *Messiah* featuring a pit orchestra in part comprised of steel pans and tassa drums. That Bishop chose to arrange this iconic work for both steel pan and tassa speaks to the widespread perception of these instruments as representative of African and Indian identity, respectively. But perhaps more importantly, these examples of musical fusion look to the potential of racial harmony while acknowledging the distinctiveness of each constituent culture, thus calling into question the validity of creolisation, at least in its conventional sense, as the basis of national belonging.

Conclusions

At the moment of independence, the state moved quickly to decolonise Trinidad and Tobago's cultural policy by reifying creole cultural practices regarded as reflective of the nation. Indian Trinidadian traditions were therefore largely excluded from the nationalist project, in this way transforming a racial divide into a political one in which Indian Trinidadian leaders continue to seek the symbolic and material benefits of state support for their distinctive cultural practices (Wilson 2012, 151). Opposition comes especially from those who see Indian Trinidadians' petitions for equal representation as a prelude to an Indian takeover of the country.[5] In early 2013, for example, a Tobagonian politician warned a group of supporters that voting for the People's Partnership (the coalition headed by then Prime Minister Kamla Persad-Bissessar) would result in a 'Calcutta ship' invading Tobago: 'That ship is waiting to sail to Tobago; they are waiting to get the results of this election, if you bring the wrong results, Calcutta ship is coming down for you! You must stop that ship!' (*Trinidad Express* 2013). Such inflammatory rhetoric draws on a symbolically important image of Indian presence in Trinidad and Tobago, that of the voyage across the *kala pani* (black water) from India to the Caribbean. While Indian Trinidadians evoke this idea as a touchstone of their heritage, here the image of the ship is appropriated as an ominous emblem of invasion that reflects enduring characterisation of Indian Trinidadians as social outsiders.

It is in such a light that perceptions of inequities in state support of the country's constituent cultural practices take on greater significance. While the state has increasingly subsidised Indian Trinidadian culture since the 1980s, Carnival arts, including calypso and steel pan, have continued to receive the lion's share of state cultural funding (Diethrich 2004, 284 and 288). This share of state subsidy, fuelled by a long-standing academic and popular discourse, and in cooperation with political efforts, has worked to affirm Carnival, calypso, and steel pan as constituting national art forms. It then became a matter of national pride to establish school curricula, independent academies, university courses, and other programmes to perpetuate these art forms. Competitions were an important element in this process of nation building, shaping performance practice while stimulating investment in calypso and steel pan. Indian Trinidadians for their part have worked to maintain and develop their own cultural forms without the expectation of significant state support (Manuel 2000, 58). In this regard, Tassa Taal and Tassarama, largely independent commercially-sponsored competitions, are important examples that not only showcase Indian Trinidadian creative expression, but also aim for its promotion and preservation just as Carnival-time competitions similarly generate interest in calypso and steel pan. And while educational initiatives worked to affirm and perpetuate the national importance of calypso and steel pan, so too has the Indian Trinidadian community established programmes that aim to contextualise tassa as a powerful symbol of Indian arrival, transformation and integration.

This article has outlined the role of music in complex decolonisation processes firstly, against colonial rule and, secondly, in which Indian Trinidadians have struggled against a narrow definition of national belonging. The former sought political autonomy, not by erasing the legacy of European colonialism, but by embracing the achievements of the colonised – however highly selective this process may have been – as a means of establishing an independent national identity. Similarly, the latter has not sought the erasure of African Trinidadian culture, but instead advocated for multiculturalism, not for creolisation per se, as the central component of a redefinition of national identity in more inclusive ways.

Notes

1. For simplicity, throughout this article I refer to the country as Trinidad and Tobago and citizens of the country as Trinidadians.
2. Video of this performance can be accessed on YouTube at the following address: https://www.youtube.com/watch?v=DdQbbsx5jEw.
3. Frank Korom illustrates such assumptions about African Trinidadian influence when he observes that *dingolay* is 'a hybrid hand influenced by indigenous soca rhythms' (2003, 167). This is unlikely since recordings of tassa by Emory Cook in the 1950s captured *dingolay* in its present form well before the advent of soca in the 1970s. Both Peter Manuel (2015) and I (2013) argue that *dingolay* corresponds to an Indian Trinidadian source rather than having any significant African Trinidadian influence.
4. *Bèlè* refers to a range of African Caribbean contradance styles common in the francophone Caribbean and areas, like Trinidad and Tobago, that featured significant francophone influence prior to British colonisation. In Trinidad and Tobago, *bèlè* is usually danced by women only (though men participate on occasion), either solo or in synchronised groups, using an easily identifiable folkloric style featuring sweeping choreographic gestures and colonial-era dress.
5. Trinidad and Tobago has elected two Indian Trinidadian prime ministers, Basdeo Panday (1995–2001) and Kamla Persad-Bissessar (2010–2015). In each case, anxieties about Indian infiltration into the highest ranks of government were expressed in various public forums.

Disclosure statement

No potential conflict of interest was reported by the author.

References

Austerlitz, Paul. 1997. *Merengue: Dominican Music and Dominican Identity*. Philadelphia: Temple University Press.

Averill, Gage. 1997. *A Day for the Hunter, a Day for the Prey: Popular Music and Power in Haiti*. Chicago: University of Chicago Press.

Bakan, Michael B. 1998. "Walking Warriors: Battles of Culture and Ideology in the Balinese Gamelan Beleganjur World." *Ethnomusicology* 42 (3): 441–484.

Ballengee, Christopher L. 2013. "From Indian to Indo-Creole: Tassa Drumming, Creolization, and Indo-Caribbean Nationalism in Trinidad and Tobago." PhD diss., Gainesville, FL: University of Florida.

Ballengee, Christopher L. 2017. "Steel Orchestras and Tassa Bands: Multiculturalism, Collective Creativity, and Debating Co-National Instruments in Trinidad and Tobago." In *Global Perspectives on Orchestras: Collective Creativity and Social Agency*, edited by Tina K. Ramnarine, 81–99. Oxford and New York: Oxford University Press.

Ballengee, Christopher L. 2018. "Tassa Drumming as an Icon of Indianness in Trinidad and Tobago." *Centre for Integrated Caribbean Research*, January 22. https://cicr.blogs.sas.ac.uk/2018/01/22/tassa-drumming-as-an-icon-of-indianness-in-trinidad-and-tobago/.

Brereton, Bridget. 1979. *Race Relations in Colonial Trinidad 1870–1900*. Cambridge: Cambridge University Press.

Brereton, Bridget. 2010. "'All ah we is Not One': Historical and Ethnic Narratives in Pluralist Trinidad." *The Global South* 4 (1): 218–238.

Burke, Suzanne. 2014. "Creative Clustering in Small Island States: The Case of Trinidad and Tobago's Carnival Industries." *Caribbean Quarterly* 60 (1): 74–95.

Copeland, Brian, Clément Imbert, and Derek Gay. 2001. "The Steelpan Development Centre at the University of the West Indies." *The Journal of the Acoustical Society of America* 110 (5): 2673.

Diethrich, Gregory Michael. 2004. "'Living in Both Sides of the World': Music, Diaspora, and Nation in Trinidad." PhD diss., Urbana, IL: University of Illinois at Urbana-Champaign.

Dudley, Shannon. 2003. "Creativity and Control in Trinidad Carnival Competitions." *The World of Music* 45 (1): 11–33.

Dudley, Shannon. 2008. *Music from Behind the Bridge: Steelband Spirit and Politics in Trinidad and Tobago*. New York: Oxford University Press.

Elder, J. D. 1964. "Color, Music, Conflict: A Study of Aggression in Trinidad with Reference to Role of Traditional Music." *Ethnomusicology* 8 (2): 128–136.

Gormandy, Mia K. 2017. "Pan in Japan: Cultural Adoption and Adaption of Trinidad and Tobago's National Instrument." PhD diss., Tallahassee, FL: Florida State University.

Goslin, Ted. 2016. "First All-Female Tassa Group Wins Awards at World Championship of Performing Arts." *Pan Magazine*, July 27.

Guilbault, Jocelyne. 2007. *Governing Sound: The Cultural Politics of Trinidad's Carnival Musics*. Chicago: University of Chicago Press.

Guilbault, Jocelyne. 2011. "The Question of Multiculturalism in the Arts in the Postcolonial Nation-State of Trinidad and Tobago." *Music & Politics* 5 (1): 1–21.

Hill, Errol. 1967. "On the Origin of the Term Calypso." *Ethnomusicology* 11 (3): 359–367.

Hobsbawm, Eric. 1983. "Introduction: Inventing Tradition." In *The Invention of Tradition*, edited by Eric Hobsbawm, and Terence Ranger, 1–14. Cambridge: Cambridge University Press.

Johnson, Kim. 2006. *If Yuh Iron Good you is King: Pan Pioneers of Trinidad and Tobago*. Port of Spain, Trinidad: Pan Trinbago.

Johnson, Kim. 2011. *From Tin Pan to TASPO: Steelband in Trinidad, 1939–1951*. Kingston, Jamaica: University of the West Indies Press.

Kartomi, Margaret J. 2012. *Musical Journeys in Sumatra*. Champaign, IL: University of Illinois Press.

Korom, Frank J. 2003. *Hosay Trinidad: Muharram Performances in an Indo-Caribbean Diaspora*. Philadelphia: University of Pennsylvania Press.

Liverpool, Hollis Urban. 1990. *Kaiso and Society*. Deigo Martin, Trinidad: Juba Publications.

Manuel, Peter. 2000. *East Indian Music in the West Indies: Tān-Singing, Chutney, and the Making of Indo-Caribbean Culture*. Philadelphia: Temple University Press.

Manuel, Peter. 2014. *Drumming for Ganesh: Music at Pune's Ganapati Festival*. Streaming video: https://vimeo.com/100255733.

Manuel, Peter. 2015. *Tales, Tunes, and Tassa Drums: Retention and Invention in Indo-Caribbean Music*. Champaign, IL: University of Illinois Press.

Martin, Andrew Richard. 2011. "Pan-America: Calypso, Exotica, and the Development of Steel Pan in the United States." PhD diss., Minneapolis and St. Paul: University of Minnesota.

Mohammed, Kamaluddin. 1960. *Unifying Our Cosmopolitan Community: A Speech on Interracial Solidarity*. Port-of-Spain, Trinidad: P.N.M. Pub. Co.

Moore, Robin D. 1997. *Nationalizing Blackness: Afrocubanismo and Artistic Revolution in Havana, 1920–1940*. Pittsburgh, PA: University of Pittsburgh Press.

Munasinghe, Viranjini. 2002. "Nationalism in Hybrid Spaces: The Production of Impurity out of Purity." *American Ethnologist* 29 (3): 663–692.

'Music Schools in the Community'. 2015. Culture Division -Ministry of Community Development, Culture, and the Arts. January 30,. Accessed September 3, 2018. http://www.culture.gov.tt/training/music-schools-in-the-community/.

National Gas Company of Trinidad and Tobago. 2017. "The NGC-Sponsored Trinidad & Tobago Sweet Tassa Band Launches Tassa Academy".

Niranjana, T. 2006. *Mobilizing India: Women, Music, and Migration between India and Trinidad*. Durham, NC: Duke University Press.

Quevedo, Raymond. 1983. *Atilla's Kaiso: A Short History of Trinidad Calypso*. St. Augustine, Trinidad: University of the West Indies, Department of Extra Mural Studies.

Ramesar, Marianne. 1994. *Survivors of Another Crossing: A History of East Indians in Trinidad, 1880–1946*. St. Augustine, Trinidad: School of Continuing Studies, University of the West Indies.

Ramnarine, Tina K. 2001. *Creating their Own Space: The Development of an Indian-Caribbean Musical Tradition*. Kingston: University of West Indies Press.

Seeger, Peter. 1958. "The Steel Drum: A New Folk Instrument." *The Journal of American Folklore* 71 (279): 52–57.

Seeger, Peter, and Toshi Seeger. 1956. *Music from Oil Drums*. New York: CCM Films/Folkways Records.

Singh, H. P. 1962. *Hour of Decision*. San Juan, Trinidad: Vedic Enterprises.

Stillman, Amy Ku'Uleialoha. 1996. "Hawaiian Hula Competitions: Event, Repertoire, Performance, Tradition." *The Journal of American Folklore* 109 (434): 357–380.

Stuempfle, Stephen. 1995. *The Steelband Movement: The Forging of a National Art in Trinidad and Tobago*. Philadelphia: University of Pennsylvania Press.

Trinidad Express. 2013. "TOP Accuses Opponents of Waging Race War." January 6.

Turino, Thomas. 2003. "Nationalism and Latin American Music: Selected Case Studies and Theoretical Considerations." *Latin American Music Review* 24 (2): 169–209.

Warner, Keith Q. 1983. *Kaiso! the Trinidad Calypso: A Study of the Calypso as Oral Literature*. London: Heinemann.

When Steel Talks. 2014a. "Can a Foreign Arranger or Steelband win a Parorama in Trinidad & Tobago?" April 1. http://whensteeltalks.ning.com/forum/topics/can-a-foreign-arranger-or-steelband-win-a-panorama-in-trinidad.

When Steel Talks. 2014b. "Pulling No Punches: Andy Narell, Arranger for Birdsong Steel Orchestra, Speaks on the 2014 Panorama Season." April 3. http://www.panonthenet.com/tnt/2014/invue/andy-narell-3-14-2014.htm.

Williams, Eric Eustace. 1962. *History of the People of Trinidad and Tobago*. Port-of-Spain, Trinidad: PNM Pub. Co. Ltd.

Wilson, Stacy-Ann. 2012. *Politics of Identity in Small Plural Societies: Guyana, the Fiji Islands, and Trinidad and Tobago*. New York: Palgrave Macmillan.

Wolf, Richard K. 2017. *The Voice in the Drum: Music, Language, and Emotion in Islamicate South Asia*. Champaign, IL: University of Illinois Press.

Ziegler, Aaron Michael. 2015. "Challenging the Trinidad and Tobago Panorama Construct: An Analysis of Compositional Styles of Ray Holman, Liam Teague, and Andy Narell." DMA diss., Iowa City, IA: University of Iowa.

The *BBC Young Dancer* and the decolonising imagination

Magdalen Gorringe ⓘ *

ABSTRACT
The process of decolonisation requires a radical re-imagination of how we construct our identities – one that steps away from fictions of independence and essentialism to acknowledge the complex webs of dialogue and interdependence. It requires a self-conscious abandonment of identities that privilege nostalgia for an idealised past, whether this is perceived as lost through geographical dislocation or through the changes of history. This is a nostalgia that tends to underplay cultural interweaving in favour of cultural essentialism. This article discusses the televised competition, the BBC *Young Dancer*, which offers a model, albeit imperfect, for navigating between essentialism and assimilationism, thereby contributing to a decolonised imagination of our future. It includes a South Asian dance category that is situated as equally representative of 'British' dance. In this way it helps us to imagine a decolonised future, which acknowledges the past to allow us to shape new identities.

On 23 January 2017, in a studio theatre within the glass walled post-modernist building of The Lowry arts centre in Manchester, the young bharatanatyam practitioner, Akshay Prakash, performed a short section of an *abhinaya*[1] based dance on the Hindu god Anjaneya – or Hanuman, and his relationship with Lord Rama. Cheeks and chest puffed out, and alternating impressive crouches and leaps with the depiction of a sedate and dignified gait, Prakash swapped between the roles of the strong ruler of the monkey army (Hanuman), and, with his left hand raised in *shikara* to show a bow, and right hand by his side in *kapitha*[2] to represent an arrow, the Lord Rama.[3] While there can hardly have been more than 100 audience members in the theatre in Manchester, Prakash's piece and those following it, were filmed, edited and (interspersed with footage of the competitors in training and going about their everyday life) broadcast to an audience of approximately 189,000 people on prime-time Friday night UK television,[4] with many more watching it on catch-up.[5] This was the final for the South Asian dance category of the British Broadcasting Corporation's (BBC) initiative, the *Young Dancer 2017* – only the second round of a competition launched by the BBC in 2015.[6]

The presentation of art forms originating from a former colony (India) by the mainstream media of a formerly colonising power (Britain) is bound to be a sensitive area. No less a figure than Stuart Hall observed in 1999 that it is 'really very complex to

---

*This article is dedicated to the memory of Professor Andrée Grau.

understand how appropriately minority communities should now be represented in mainstream British cultural and artistic institutions' (1999, 19). The approach taken to this competition and its component dance categories by an institution previously branded by its then director-general, Greg Dyke, as 'hideously white'[7] provides an illuminating case study through which to consider the perception and representation of South Asian dance forms in Britain[8] and through this, the challenges facing the wider project of decolonisation, particularly within the UK.

As the post-colonial studies scholar Anibal Quijano observes:

> despite the fact that political colonialism has been eliminated, the relationship between the European, also called 'Western' culture, and the others, continues to be one of colonial domination ... This relationship consists, in the first place, of a colonization of the imagination of the dominated. (2007, 169)

It is not just the imagination of the dominated, but of all of us, dominators and dominated, formerly colonised and former colonisers, that is restricted, limited and truncated by a universal cosmology whereby one worldview dominates, rather than being extended, challenged and invigorated by what the biologist and philosopher Humberto Maturana calls a 'multiversal' understanding of the world – whereby we avoid the 'temptation of certainty' ([1987] 1992, 18), in cultivating an approach of holding 'objectivity-in-parenthesis' (1988, 29). Such 'parenthetical objectivity' challenges the dogma and paternalism of colonialism in the same way that it challenges any dogmatism – by proposing 'many different, equally legitimate ... explanatory realities, [where] ... disagreement is an invitation to a responsible reflection of coexistence, and not an irresponsible negation of the other' (1988, 32).

For the semiotician and literary theorist Walter Mignolo, such 'multiversality' is key to any attempt at 'decoloniality', which he believes 'means working towards a vision of human life that is not dependent upon or structured by the forced imposition of one ideal of society over those that differ' (2007, 459). My contention is that the *BBC Young Dancer* offers a valiant if flawed attempt at such multiversality while, in the challenges it faces to do this, it also reminds us of the size of the decolonisation project and the length of journey there is yet to travel. The discussion is based on participant – observation methods. I have conducted over 40 semi-structured interviews with artists and administrators working within or supporting the development of classical Indian dance forms in Britain, and have attended over 30 performances and events, as part of a broader project on the professionalisation of classical Indian dance forms in Britain. Interviewees covered a wide age-range of dancers, who practice a cross section of styles, focusing on bharatanatyam and kathak. Of particular relevance for this article, I attended the live performances of the BBC Young Dancer South Asian Category finals 2017 (described above), as well as the Grand Finals performed at Sadler's Wells theatre in London on 22 April 2017. In addition, I watched broadcasts of the finals for each category, as well as the Grand Finals, for both 2015 and 2017. I gathered further material from reviews together with observations made on blogs and social media for both rounds of the competition. My research is grounded in over 25 years spent training and working as a bharatanatyam dancer, teacher, administrator and researcher based in different parts of the UK. This experience has given me a proximity and investment in the field which has been both an advantage and disadvantage in undertaking participant-observation. I attempt to be alert to my own interests and investments, echoing the social anthropologist Kate Fox, who wryly concludes in *Watching the English* that 'while participant observation has its limitations, this rather uneasy combination of involvement and detachment is the best method we have for exploring cultures, so it will have to do' (2004, 4).

The BBC *young dancer*

The BBC *Young Dancer* is a biannual British dance competition established in 2015 for young dancers aged between 16 and 21. It is based loosely on the model of the competition the BBC *Young Musician* established in 1978. Perhaps unsurprisingly given the time at which it was established, the focus of the competition is classical music, and as Bruce Marriott, the editor of the dance website Dance Tabs put it, it really ought to be called '*BBC Young Classical Musician*'[9] (though I would argue for the yet more specific '*BBC Young Musician of Western Classical Music*'). The competition is highly influential in the world of British classical music, and several of the winners and finalists in the competition have gone on to stellar classical music careers.[10]

With the *BBC Young Dancer*, as Jane Hackett, former Director of Creative Learning at Sadler's Wells and dance consultant on *BBC Young Dancer* explains, the BBC had been thinking about a dance equivalent to the *Young Musician* for some time. Rather than attempt to cover every possible form, Hackett suggested a focus on four categories of dance – ballet, contemporary, hip hop and South Asian. Within the South Asian category, the forms are limited to bharatanatyam and kathak. The limit of four categories, she felt, would allow both the BBC and the viewing public to gain a deeper understanding of each form presented (Hackett, personal interview via Skype, 3 September 2017). The choice of forms was clearly difficult, and inevitably, the BBC received 'a lot of letters from musical theatre and other groups contesting the category selection' (ibid). However, the decision was not arbitrary, and was based on a combination of factors including the popularity of the forms in terms of the numbers of people engaged in them, the fact that 'each style has a very rigorous and detailed technique' and the presence of a 'highly skilled set of dancers taking the form in a different direction' (ibid).

Dancers compete within their categories, culminating in 4 category finals broadcast on BBC 4. The winners of each of the category finals together with one 'Wildcard' then compete against each other in a Grand Final, which takes place on the main stage at Sadler's Wells in London and is broadcast live on BBC 2.

The inclusion of a South Asian dance category – initial responses

The inclusion of the South Asian dance category in the competition has been widely welcomed by both organisations and individual artists working within the sector. Mira Kaushik, for example, Director of the London based Akademi South Asian Dance in the U.K,[11] an organisation committed to the promotion of South Asian dance in Britain, felt that its inclusion was 'the best news for South Asian dance in Britain' (Kaushik, personal interview, 22 February 2017). An online Tamil journal covering the *Young Dancer 2017* drew attention to the participation of dancers of Tamil heritage, Anjelli Wignakumar and Piriyanga Kesavan, remarking with some satisfaction, 'Congratulations to the talented young Tamils for representing our art on the world stage'.[12] Mira Balchandran-Gokul, bharatanatyam dancer and teacher based in Southport, who is a founder member of the *Sankalpam* dance company, said, 'I think it's brilliant' (Balchandran-Gokul, personal interview, 6 February 2017).

There are voices, however, that are more cautious. Bharatanatyam dancer, teacher and choreographer Nina Rajarani feels that 'although the inclusion of the category is a welcome move, it does not entirely "work"' (Rajarani, personal interview, 24 April 2018). As artistic director of *Sristhi Dance Creations*, she is concerned that,

> while the eye that is watching it [the competition] is not necessarily one that can fully appreciate the nuances of classical Indian dance … I don't think we will ever get a winner, and I think that sends out a negative message that we don't need.

A further informant, while recognising the value of the competition in several ways, at the same time asked with some frustration, Why do we need the BBC to recognise an Indian dance award? (Anonymous, personal interview, 23 August 2017). In the following section, I will explore each of these responses, looking in greater detail at both the opportunities and the challenges the competition presents to the sector before considering more widely what this case study suggests for the decolonising imagination.

The inclusion of a South Asian dance category: benefits for the sector

> This is the biggest outreach project that could ever happen
>
> (Hackett, interview 2017)

Education

An obvious benefit of the *Young Dancer* for South Asian dance is the impact it has had on the visibility of the sector. Appearing on primetime evening television, and then available on catch-up, within the context of a framework designed to have a broad appeal, the programme has brought South Asian dance forms to more people in Britain than ever before. British dance artist and former Chief Executive of the London based dance centre (and home to London Contemporary Dance School), The Place, Kenneth Tharp, celebrated this achievement when he blogged:

> I witnessed many comments [by people] on social media … and what their comments had in common was that watching a full hour of classical Indian dance on T.V had clearly been a huge eye opener. Many were thrilled and surprised at the combined beauty of the music, dance, performances and costumes … What the BBC Young Dance did alongside showcasing and inspiring young talent was to allow huge numbers of people to enjoy a whole range of dance they might not otherwise have seen.[13]

Hackett agrees: 'There is actually very little known about South Asian dance forms outside the immediate dance world – and we have had a lot of feedback from people on Facebook for example saying, "*I had no idea that South Asian dance had that much in it*"' (interview 2017, my emphasis).

It is noteworthy that the Facebook commentator Hackett refers to above is left with a greater appreciation of the complexity of South Asian dance forms. This in part reflects the BBC's framing of the performances in a manner which, true to the mission statement of BBC founder John Reith, strives not only to entertain but also to 'inform' and 'educate'. The 2015 South Asian category final included short introductions to the forms from contemporary and kathak dancer and choreographer Akram Khan and bharatanatyam dancer and choreographer Seeta Patel, and the website features links to more information about all the categories featured, including South Asian dance. This information provides a basic sketch of the 'narrative' of the different dance styles, in the sense used by aesthetician Noel Carroll, meaning 'placed in an evolving tradition of art' (2001, 63). This allows the viewing public an appreciation of the dance forms with at least a sense of their historic and artistic context. As the editors of the South Asian arts website *Finding Lila* noted, 'When else would you hear *abhinaya* being discussed on Friday night TV?'[14]

From this perspective, Hackett's insistence on restricting the categories selected to four to allow the viewing public scope to acquire a greater depth of knowledge about the selected styles seems justified, and doubtless contributes to the sense of the programme possessing a greater weight and a greater commitment to artistic integrity than is commonly found in other televised dance competitions. Hanna Weibye, writing for the specialist arts website, *the arts desk*, for example, commended the competition as being 'remarkably gimmick free' and 'light years away from the razzmatazz, sparkling scoreboards and celebrity judge in-fighting of the BBC 1 show [*Strictly Come Dancing*]'.[15] Kenneth Tharp, agreed, noting,

> I remember watching the very first contemporary solo and what struck me immediately from the first 30 s was that the quality of the performance and that of the choreography was not the kind of wham-bam razzmatazz showpiece you might expect from a competition piece.[16]

The BBC *Young Dancer* then, raises the profile of the sector, and moreover it does so in a way that aims to highlight the skill and complexity of each of the represented forms, inviting the audience to engage with different aesthetic values. This is important because it marks an attempt, in Mignolo's terms (2007, 497), to expand the 'space of experience' and the 'horizon of expectations' of viewers, reminding them of the world's 'pluriversality', and of the existence of multiple aesthetic codes and multiple dance canons.

The manner of assessing or judging the competitors has again been approached with some care. For each competitive round leading up to the Grand Finals, the panels of judges comprise figures with an established experience, expertise and standing in the dance fields represented by the categories.[17] Here again, the limit imposed on the categories represented enables judgement by specialists (dancers, choreographers, researchers) from each category chosen, each one conversant with the 'narrative' framing an individual performance. Hackett explains,

> We didn't want the competition to be a repeat of *Britain's Got Talent*, so we needed forms that would have clear criteria upon which to make a judgement – so that the decision wouldn't just be a question of personal preference. (interview, 2017)

The knowledge of the 'narrative' of an art form, allows for an informed assessment and guards against mistaken judgements made about the dance forms 'because inappropriate assumptions about the art are imported' [from other narratives] (McFee 2005, 369). It also means, in response to Rajarani's concern voiced above, that at least some of the 'eyes' watching the competition can indeed appreciate the 'nuances of Indian classical dance'.

This portrayal of South Asian dance, evaluated by experts from within the field assessing the category on its own terms, (meaning for South Asian dance, through reference to *abhinaya, rasa, nrtta, talam* and so on), has then been broadcast to phenomenal numbers, with viewing figures for the South Asian Category Final 2017 being 189,000, as noted above, and for the Grand Final 2017 being 636,000 by transmission.[18] Such exposure serves to educate people in two ways – it informs them about forms they may not have been aware of (hence Hackett – this is the largest outreach project that could ever happen) and it helps to expand, to follow Mignolo, the 'horizon of expectation'.

Equal representation?

In incorporating a diversity of dance styles, and in doing so in a manner that accords equal time and coverage to each dance category selected, the competition has taken a significant step away from the *Young Musician*, a competition that, as described above, has no space for music outside that of the Western classical music tradition. One might think that in twenty-first-century Britain such diversity should be taken for granted, so it is sobering yet necessary to be reminded that this is far from the case. As Hackett, explains,

> When I joined they were going to have to have three categories – ballet, contemporary dance and "Other". They seemed to think that everything else – from Irish dance to musical theatre, to South Asian dance forms, to hip hop would go into one category. (interview, 2017)

This view is far from anomalous, as several commentators clearly felt that this was the approach they should have taken. Marriott wrote for example 'ethnic dance came down to South Asian, but what of other ethnic dance? … I hope a wider view can be taken next time and perhaps a catch-all section introduced'.[19] Similarly Ismene Brown writing for the *Spectator* suggested as a possible improvement, 'Rethink the categories more broadly to admit jazz, tap and any ethnic dance – rather than only hip-hop and kathak'.[20]

The dance anthropologist Joann Keali'inohomoku pointed out the meaninglessness of the term 'ethnic dance' almost half a century ago: 'by definition, every dance form must be an ethnic form. Although claims have been made for universal dance forms … it is doubtful that any such dance form can exist except in theory' ([1969] 2001, 39). Despite this, the assumption that Western classical and contemporary dance forms inhabit a class of their own, somehow unmarked by cultural origins, or that at best, to follow the title of an article by dance ethnographer Theresa Buckland (1999, 3), 'all dances are ethnic, but some are more ethnic than others' remains a deep seated and widely prevalent belief. It is worth then pausing to welcome the fact that the *Young Dancer* has at least to some extent bucked this trend, and has refused to dump South Asian dance within an 'ethnic dance mixed bag' but has accorded each of the dance categories selected equal time and respect.

This is significant for members of the British South Asian dance community. Kaushik explains her enthusiasm in these terms:

> I think it's the best news for the position of South Asian dance in this country because all this time South Asian dance has been perceived to be a community activity. In this context, where it is put alongside ballet, contemporary dance and other forms … the inclusion of South Asian dance is big and good news (interview, 2017)

Again, for Mira Balchandran-Gokul, the programme reinforces the British presence of South Asian dance as art – '… you are seeing it not just as a cultural form, you are seeing it alongside all the different dance forms' (interview 2017). Somasundaram and

Basu noted that many of those who watched the programme felt that it was 'the first time that South Asian dance had been presented on an equal footing with ballet, hip hop and contemporary dance on mainstream T.V'.[21]

While it is debatable whether this is the first time the BBC has presented South Asian Dance 'on an equal footing', it is significant that this is how the competition has been perceived by parts of the South Asian dance community. Many in the sector (including Jeyasingh herself) do not align Jeyasingh's or Akram Khan's work as representative of 'South Asian' Dance forms, and it is difficult to think of another programme that has profiled classical bharatanatyam and kathak alongside other dance styles in this way.

Clearly, questions remain. How far the representation can be considered equal when ballet and contemporary are each assigned their own categories, while the dance styles kathak and bharatanatyam (which are at least as distinct from each other as ballet and contemporary dance) are judged under one heading is a moot point. The competition however faced an invidious task in its selection of dance categories, which necessarily needed also to reflect the numbers of practitioners engaged in each dance style. In this light, the incorporation of the two classical Indian dance styles most widely practiced in the UK under one heading, while not ideal, is a pragmatic decision that nonetheless positions classical Indian dance forms as an integral and important part of the British dance ecology. It serves as both a recognition and validation of the contribution of these dance styles, and as such it has largely been warmly welcomed, as discussed above.

Institutional endorsement

The idea of 'validation' leads to a third benefit to the South Asian dance sector brought by the competition – that of institutional endorsement. While the informant quoted above, is understandably frustrated by the sense of a need for 'outside validation', it remains the case that the positioning and choices of institutions – particularly of influential and symbolic institutions such as the BBC – play an important role in shaping the perceptions of ourselves and others as to our place and value within a wider cultural framework. To follow political theorist Bhikhu Parekh, 'Notions of cultural value, belonging and worth are defined and fixed by decisions we make about what is or is not culture and how we are represented (or not) by cultural institutions' (2000, 159). The dance anthropologist Andrée Grau makes a similar point: 'institutions have a claim to the right of legitimacy. They are established, recognised as such and in the example of the arts they have helped in the creation of aesthetic canons' (2001, 29).

The BBC, founded in 1925, has an indisputable historicity and an iconic status which, in partnership with the equally iconic Sadler's Wells, lends an undeniable status, visibility and credibility to the art forms it chooses to represent. Thus, despite understandable reservations about representation on mainstream media, when an institution such as the BBC presents four categories to represent dance in Britain, and South Asian dance is one of these categories, it is, hard to argue with Kaushik's view that is 'big and good news'. This is especially the case for classical Indian dance forms given the BBC's role in helping to shape narratives of 'Britishness' both at home and abroad (Higgins 2015; Seaton 2007). It is, as journalist Charlotte Higgins puts it, an institution at the heart Britain. The BBC defines and expresses Britishness – to those who live in the UK and to the rest of the world. The BBC ... as well as informing, educating and entertaining, permeates and reflects our existences and infiltrates our imaginations. (2015, 1)

Thus, the BBC's clear acknowledgement of the significance of classical Indian dance forms in Britain represents a step towards a re-imagination of British identity, as a nation in which Indian classical dance forms are integrally British – a further expansion of the British dance canon. In this way, it is a step towards the decolonisation of Britain's imagination of itself.

Dialogic representation

A further challenge in the endeavour to decolonise the imagination is the essentialist imaginary, encompassing both 'orientalism' and 'assimilationism'. The dangers of orientalism are now well-rehearsed, whereby artistic and cultural forms from outside the Western cultural establishment are presented as 'static, frozen, fixed eternally' (Said 1995 [1978], 208). On the other hand, lie the dangers of assimilation, whereby these art forms are valued most when 'sufficiently processed to meet the Western palate' (Sporton 2004, 88) – so processed that they can no longer be said to display the distinctive technical and aesthetic vocabularies characteristic of these dance styles (what Slavoj Žižek, 2010, describes as the 'Other deprived of Otherness' – or the 'decaffeinated other'[22]). How does one avoid the presentation of Asian classical dance forms in 'concert halls and festivals in the west' whereby, as dance scholar Anthony Shay puts it, 'over a century since the appearance of Asian dance in world exhibitions, [Western] audiences search for meaning and truth in "ancient" and "timeless" traditions of dance and music they feel lacking in their own lives' (Shay 2008, 167)? At the other extreme is the question voiced by an audience member at the Academy of Indian dance debate 'Traditions on the Move', back in 1993, and echoed repeatedly since then in a variety of contexts, which is that with innovation, is there a line where 'work stops being Indian dance?' (Tucker 1993, 2). Where is the line between innovation within a technique and the creation of a new technique? Clearly this question stands across dance forms, though the reality of dominant economic and cultural power structures makes more likely the assimilation of South Asian art forms in Britain into a dominant cultural framework. The problem is raised by Akram Khan, who has voiced the need to ensure that 'on the one hand ... South Asian dance [is] still protected in a sense of its form', while on the other allowing artists to 'find a way to experiment ... by taking aspects of South Asian dance to a more contemporary place' (Khan, interviewed for BBC Young Dancer 2015, South Asian Final, broadcast 1 May 2015, BBC 4).

The cultural anthropologist Dwight Conquergood, as a way out of the 'moral morass and ethical minefield of performative plunder, superficial silliness, curiosity seeking and nihilism' proposes a model of 'dialogical performance' meaning 'a kind of performance that resists conclusions ... more than a definite position, this dialogical stance is situated in *between* competing ideologies. It is more like a hyphen than a period' (2013, 75, emphasis in original). The BBC *Young Dancer* encourages such dialogic performance, allowing space for classical together with less conventional interpretations of South Asian dance that seek to challenge and extend classical boundaries. As an illustration, for the 2017 category finals, the kathak dancer Jaina Modasia presented first a compelling nrtta or abstract dance piece, *In Akbar's Palace*,[23] highlighting the rapid footwork and dramatic turns of classical kathak. Her duet, with the contemporary dancer Peter Camilleri, combined kathak with partner work, including lifts and weight exchange with her partner that took her work well beyond the parameters of the classical form, which is conventionally a solo art, and where even when performing together, there would not normally be any physical contact between performers.[24] This piece, and the competition rubric that suggested it, is I feel problematic in some ways (which I discuss below). Nevertheless, the encouragement of works that extend conventional classical boundaries helps to puncture the sense of classical Indian dance forms existing as a 'somehow timeless and ever available means of accessing Indianness' (Pillai 2002, 15).

The *Young Dancer* has facilitated such a dialogical representation, steering between, and thereby avoiding, both essentialist and assimilationist ideologies. There is a further discussion to be had about what should be defined as normative, transgressive, conventional or exploratory, and in what context – and I address this later. For the moment, it is important to acknowledge that the programme avoids over simplification, and embraces complexity by encouraging a breadth of representation of the dance forms. The *Young Dancer* poses a long overdue challenge to the established British canon by positioning South Asian dance and hip hop as equals next to ballet and contemporary, and moreover it does so in a nuanced manner that avoids an over emphasis on either 'Otherness' or 'Sameness'. Given all this one might ask, what's not to like?

The inclusion of a South Asian dance category – challenges and risks

South Asian dance in Britain – mind the gap!

Firstly, while not a result of the competition, and while equal representation is in many ways welcome as discussed above, a problem with this is that the competition presents as equal competitors dancers from sectors that are very unequally resourced. As Brown points out, 'There's a muddle here, as there is no level playing field for ballet, South Asian, contemporary and street dance'.[25] Looking at the steps of the career ladder for South Asian dance in Britain, there is no institution providing full-time vocational training; there are no apprentice schemes for newly trained dancers and there are hardly any dance companies to which a trained dancer can apply for a job. In 2018, there were only two classically rooted South Asian dance companies in the U.K operating with the relative stability of RFO (regularly funded organisation) status – Sonia Sabri Company and Aakash Odedra Company – and employment opportunities offered by both are limited as both artists frequently perform solo. Akram Khan made the point at the South Asian dance conference *Navadisha* 2016, 'there just isn't enough access to long-term serious classical training, and the many opportunities needed, to make a full-time career as a classical [South Asian] artist today' (Khan cited in Gibson 2017, 25–26). The only vocational training available for South Asian dancers in Britain is through a 'portfolio' training arranged through their teacher, or guru, and the best chance of employment is through forming their own company. With such gaps in progression routes it is only to be expected that, for the *Young Dancer* 2017, in marked contrast to ballet and contemporary contestants, all of whom were engaged in full time vocational training, only two of the South Asian dance category finalists were engaged in dance full time, and both must find a way to negotiate their training and practice themselves without institutional support.

With lack of resource comes the accompanying risk that placed alongside dancers institutionally enabled to train full time for at least 3 years, South Asian dance forms could end up appearing less technically rigorous than other dance forms – simply due to the lack of full time training available. For Graham Watts of Dance Tabs, the South Asian dancer in the 2017 Grand Finals evinced 'the least potential for diverse movement flexibility of the contestants'.[26] There is a possibility that this opinion could reflect more on Watts' own insight and 'diverse flexibility' as a critic, which might prevent him from acknowledging the full potential for diverse movement contained in more nuanced shades of hand, foot and eye movements. Equally, the lack of opportunity and resource available for this dancer could prevent him from doing justice to such nuances in a way to summon the attention of an untrained eye. The level of surrounding ignorance about the dance forms means that the competition can have a disproportionate influence on public perceptions of the styles – for good or ill. In this way, presenting such unequally resourced dance styles on an equal platform could result in the *Young Dancer* reinforcing the very assumptions about the greater mastery and skill inherent in Western dance forms that it seeks to question. I put this risk to Mira Kaushik, whose reply was characteristically feisty:

> That's not the risk – that's the reality. Ballet is supported by numerous institutes that enable intensive and dedicated training at all levels – we haven't anything parallel to this. However, it IS worth the risk to take part. Yes, it is not a level playing field, but South Asian dancers have been remarkable in competing on a par with ballet and contemporary dancers despite this. We should not undermine what we have achieved given our circumstances. We are daring to be on a par with these well nurtured sectors (Kaushik, personal phone interview, 3 March 2017).

Category confusion and 'contemporary' dance?

Despite efforts to escape it, the *Young Dancer* remains subject to the stranglehold of the Western aesthetic hegemony, which is such that, true to any hegemony, its full extent passes unnoticed. The impact of this on the competition is seen in at least two ways, one I label 'category confusion' and the other being the vexed question of 'contemporary' dance. By 'category confusion' I mean the kind of misperception identified by McFee (2005) whereby artwork is incorrectly understood because it is read with 'inappropriate assumptions' (2005, 369). This leads to the mistaken (and essentially unthinking) application of what works for Western contemporary dance on to classical Indian dance styles. Thus, the competition rubric suggests that the second South Asian dance solo might 'contain elements of vocabulary from another South Asian dance style' (BBC *Young Dancer* Competition Guidelines 2017). This misapplies what is appropriate for Western contemporary dance onto South Asian forms. The rubric for the contemporary dance solos also asks that they 'show the essence of differing techniques, e.g. Graham, Cunningham' (ibid). The crucial difference is that contemporary dancers expect to train in a variety of these techniques, while asking a bharatanatyam dancer to use vocabulary from kathak for example, is more like asking a ballet dancer to use vocabulary from Release technique. To apply the same rules for both is to start from the standpoint of Western contemporary dance and to assume that this will work for very different art forms.

The problems with referring to the term 'contemporary dance' arise because within the dance world in the U.K, 'contemporary dance' is widely assumed to mean 'Western contemporary dance' – which is indeed how the competition itself uses the term in certain contexts. There is therefore an almost inevitable ambivalence when the competition rules state that for the obligatory duet, for South Asian dance, 'your partner work should be a contemporary duet' (ibid). Questioned about this, Hackett explained 'The duet is not part of the traditional form ... So, in this sense any duet choreographed will necessarily be contemporary'. The word 'contemporary in this context, is "contemporary" with a small "c" – meaning "of this time"' (Hackett, interview 2017). Hackett's intention here aligns with that of Akram Khan when he selected artists for the 2017 *Darbar* festival at Sadler's Wells, based on their bringing 'a contemporary sensibility to the classical work' – which he explained as their asking a 'very present question' (Khan Interviewed by Alistair Spalding, Darbar festival, Sadler's Wells, November 9, 2017). That this distinction is not clear to competitors is, however, borne out by the experience of the competition producers themselves. Independent arts manager Anita Srivastava, Director of *New Dimensions*, was recruited by the BBC to help with 'reaching out and getting in touch with the SA dance sector' (Srivastava, personal interview 21 September 2017). She explains, 'In 2014, ... BBC advertised the young dancer competition ... But up to the first deadline, they did not receive a single one [application for the South Asian dance category] ... the word that they used [in specifying a contemporary duet] ... that was definitely one of the stumbling blocks for many of the teachers thinking "I don't teach contemporary, so how can I present this?"' (ibid).

Clear definition is the more important given the deeply entrenched 'rhetoric of modernity' (Mignolo 2007, 463) which has aligned, since the Enlightenment, the contemporary, the 'modern' the 'new' with the values and cosmology of Western Europe (and later the USA) as opposed to the perceived 'traditionalism' of alternative cosmologies. Returning to Modasia's duet discussed earlier, I wondered if this was why the choreographer, Sujata Banerjee, had prioritised a set of somewhat indifferent lifts rather than, for example, a complex battle of rhythms. Would any of the 'contemporary' or ballet dancers have attempted to make a battle of footwork central to their duets? Is Modasia's duet the result of playful creativity and a transgressive exploration of artistic boundaries? Or is it an attempt to align the aesthetic of her piece with that of (dominant) Western contemporary dance practice in an instance of what Quijano terms the 'colonization of the imagination of the dominated', whereby 'European culture became a universal cultural model'? (2007, 169), together with setting the standard for all that is 'new and now'. Kathak dancer and choreographer Sonia Sabri voices this concern: 'I do feel that there is a second-class syndrome around whereby people feel that "if I don't do contemporary ... I'm not good enough". But it should really be about making our own art form shine' (Sabri, personal interview via telephone, 31 August 2018).

This relates to the question of what should count as normative, transgressive, conventional, experimental, 'traditional' or 'new', and from whose perspective? As practitioner and academic Janet O'Shea points out, 'lack of familiarity with choreographic codes often leads non-South Asian viewers to assume that bharata natyam choreography, no matter how recent its composition, is "ancient" and "traditional"'(2007, 57). A South Asian dancer interpreting the term 'contemporary', is acutely aware of the fact that an audience that might, for example, see nothing new in Seeta Patel's inventive interpretation of a classical *margam, Something Now, Something Then* (which uses space, direction, combinations of *adavus*, lighting and staging in ways that mark a clear departure from more conventional interpretations),[27] and is also responding to funding guidelines that have been seen to privilege a specific interpretation of innovation. Against this context, a lack of confidence in what will be perceived or accepted as 'contemporary' may result in pushing boundaries in a manner more forced than organic. Beyond the fact of being performed 'in the now', what is meant by 'contemporary'? The competition falters with the deep-seated identification of the 'contemporary' with the 'Western'.

Conclusion

The *Young Dancer* is a considered, intelligent competition with a commitment to artistic integrity that treats with respect all the dance forms with which it engages, and which strives to avoid stereotypes through a dialogical performance that accepts and accommodates the 'permanence-change dialectic' (Freire [1970] 2017, 152). The deliberate engagement with and invocation of the artistic narratives of different cultural forms, through the judgement and commentary of dancers and choreographers from these forms at least in part fulfils Mignolo's plea for the 'pluriversality' (the demand that 'basically we cannot have it all our own way' (2007, 500)), and the vision of a world in which 'many worlds will co-exist' (2007, 499), that he believes is key to the on-going project of decolonisation. At the same time, the competition has been 'a huge profile raiser' that 'has created a lot of excitement and an environment of ambition within students and parents' (Piali Ray, Director, Sampad Arts, personal interview, 2 June 2017). It has also offered valuable institutional endorsement helping to reframe perceptions of what forms the canon of British dance, and thereby, of what it means to be British.

However, important as the *Young Dancer* is in these many ways – its goals and purposes remain to an extent thwarted and undone by the sheer weight of the cultural sphere that surrounds it. The disparity of the resources available to Western classical and contemporary dance forms as opposed to other dance styles means that the competition is skewed from the outset. Equally, despite a committed attempt at 'multiversality', shifting a perspective that continues by default to hold 'the elite values of European art ... as the pinnacle of human endeavour' (Buckland 1999, 8) will necessarily involve more than an attempt to accord equal respect and airtime to each different dance category considered, particularly while the full extent of this ingrained perspective remains unperceived and unacknowledged. In 2017, a contemporary dancer won the *Young Dancer* grand final for the second time, and once again, the space of the Wild Card was awarded to a contemporary dancer. Could this be because related to the fact that for the Grand Final 2017, three out of the six-member jury panel had a contemporary dance background? (As Watts observed, this seems 'a bit too contemporary-heavy'.[28]) Such blatant discrepancies however remain relatively easy to redress (once acknowledged) when compared to the more insidious dominance of the Western contemporary and classical dance aesthetics and values, which remain compelling even while an effort is made to resist such dominance. The *Young Dancer* works hard to broaden its horizons, yet it cannot extricate itself from setting its competition rules from the perspective of Western contemporary dance. The Arts Council strives for genuine 'diversity' and yet a senior dance officer within the Council still perceives Jeyasingh and Akram Khan's companies as offering viable employment routes to classically trained South Asian dancers (personal communication, Navadisha conference, Birmingham, 20 May 2016). A choreographer seeks to include classical Indian dance vocabulary within his work, and yet bemoans the lack of 'dual-trained [Western contemporary and classical Indian] dancers' (personal communication, post-show event, South Bank, 24 May 2017). A training in Western contemporary dance is a prerequisite for his work, even as he aspires to include elements of classical Indian dance vocabulary. In this context, Rajarani's reservations about the competition given the inscribed bias of the 'watching eye' are hard to dismiss.

This brings us up against more fundamental questions concerning competition and its undergirding philosophy of meritocracy. The problems with the *Young Dancer* are visible not only with respect to South Asian dance. Again, to quote Watts, 'It seems oddly counter-intuitive that 80% of the finalists in the first two iterations of this event have been young men, which is probably in inverse proportion to the gender balance amongst those seeking entry into the vocational schools'.[29] The problem with South Asian dancers appearing to possess 'the least potential for diverse movement flexibility than the other contestants' or with young men appearing 'generally stronger at the elite end of the young dancer spectrum'[30] is that such perceptions are self-reinforcing. For the *Young Dancer* to avoid damaging the very young talent it hopes to nurture, it may have to acknowledge the inequality of the context in which it exists, and consider the importance of positive discrimination. Furthermore, to genuinely engage with the project of decolonisation so as not to simply 'fall back in the same house while just changing the carpet' (Mignolo 2007, 500), it will need to accept the significance of the vocabulary it uses, recognising the context in which it is situated. It could start by considering within its framework what it means by the term 'contemporary' dance – to crack open the horizon for a truly pluriversal understanding of 'contemporariness' which can posit a welcome challenge to the Western monopoly on the 'now'. The competition as it stands works hard to accommodate South Asian dance. However, for both the competition and the wider project of decolonisation, the starting point for genuine change cannot be with good intentions, benevolence and generosity, but instead with wonder, diffidence and humility. The impetus must arrive not from the desire to teach, but to learn; not to include, but to be included. In other words, the starting point for the decolonised imagination is a healthy appreciation of one's own insignificance (if from a position of dominance), and a cultural perspective wide enough to allow that it forms just one, limited (though equally valuable) perspective amidst a plethora of differing cultural perspectives. The starting point for the decolonised imagination accepts the necessary discomfort of uncertainty (resisting, as Maturana advocates, the 'temptation of certainty' (1992 [1987], 18)), and admits that what it took for compass points are in fact no such thing, but only the four corners of a very small room.

With all this in mind, the *Young Dancer* nevertheless takes an important step in the right direction. If pursued, at least within the UK, the start of such self-reflection on the part of so iconic an institution as the BBC could in time develop to allow the recognition of a set of fundamentally alternative cosmologies that might, ultimately, extend our horizons such that a dance competition is not necessarily the chosen model to showcase and nurture young talent – though that of course, is another question.

Notes

1. A complex term *abhinaya* is a means of conveying and exploring narrative and emotion through the codified use of posture, gesture and facial expression.
2. *Shikara* and *kapitha* are two of the 28 'single hand gestures' used within classical Indian dance forms, as codified in Sanskrit texts such as the *Natyasastra* and the *Abhinayadarpana*.
3. [3] *Anjaneya*, chor. Prakash Yadagudde. Performed by Akshay Prakash, BBC Young Dancer South Asian Category Final, The Lowry Theatre, Manchester, January 23, 2017. Recordings of this piece and all the others from this final are available at https://www.bbc.co.uk/programmes/b07gbzxt/clips.
4. Figures provided by the BBC to Anita Srivastava, sent to me via personal communication, May 3, 2017
5. I assume. The BBC was unable to provide me a figure, but merely from the circumstantial evidence of talking to friends and colleagues, I believe this to be a safe assumption.
6. The subject of 'competition dance' is contentious, raising questions about the balance between accessibility, display and artistry. For discussion on this topic see Marion (2008), Morris (2008) and Weisbrod (2014).
7. Amelia Hill, 'Dyke: BBC is hideously white', *The Observer*, January 7, 2001. Accessed September 6, 2018. https://www.theguardian.com/media/2001/jan/07/uknews.theobserver1.
8. In this article, the dance forms discussed, when considered collectively, are variously referred to as 'Classical Indian dance' and 'South Asian dance'. The question as to which label is politically and aesthetically most apt has been debated by the sector for over twenty years, without conclusion. It has been the subject of articles and of a conference organized by Akademi (Pinto 2004; McFee 2005). This article follows the sector lead in using both terms.
9. Bruce Marriott, 'Young Dancer Award 2015 – Some Thoughts', *Dance Tabs,* May 18, 2015. Accessed September 6, 2018. http://dancetabs.com/2015/05/bbc-young-dancer-award-2015-some-thoughts/.
10. The winner of the 2016 Young Musician, for example, Sheku Kanneh Mason, topped the classical charts with his first CD and was the first artist to be invited to appear at the BAFTA awards ceremonies for 2 years running.
11. It is interesting (and somewhat ironic in the context of this article) that Kaushik and eight other members of the South Asian dance sector have been awarded Orders of the British Empire for their services to dance. Kaushik was awarded an MBE (Member of the British Empire). Of the other informants in this article, Nina Rajarani was also awarded an MBE, and Piali Ray an OBE (Officer of the British Empire).
12. Thamarai 'Tamil Dancer competes in BBC's Young Dancer 2017'. *Thamarai.* January 24, 2017. Accessed September 6, 2018. http://www.thamarai.com/dance/tamil-dancer-competes-bbcs-young-dancer-2017.
13. Kenneth Tharp 'What a difference a year makes' March 30, 2016, *The Place.* Accessed September 6, 2018. http://www.theplace.org.uk/blog/kenneth-tharps-blog/what-difference-year-makes.
14. Nisha Somasundaram and Urbi Basu, 'Editorial: What Does BBC Young Dancer 2015 Mean for South Asian Dance?', *Finding Lila, South Asian Arts UK,* June 5, 2015. Accessed March 17, 2017. http://www.findinglila.com/articles/editorial-bbc-young-dancer-south-asian-dance. This site has been closed since I last accessed it. However other articles from the same authors can be found at https://globalrasika.com
15. Hanna Weibye, 'BBC Young Dancer, BBC 4', *the arts desk,* April 18, 2015. Accessed September 6, 2018. http://www.theartsdesk.com/dance/bbc-young-dancer-2015-bbc-four.
16. Tharp, 'What a difference'
17. The South Asian category final judges for 2015 were Mira Balchandran Gokul and kathak dancer Pratap Pawar; and for 2017 they were bharatanatyam dancer Chitra Sundaram and kathak dancer Kajal Sharma.
18. Anita Srivastava, personal communication, May 3, 2017
19. Marriott, 'Young Dancer'

DANCE, MUSIC AND CULTURES OF DECOLONISATION

20. Ismene Brown, 'Why dance needs a Simon Cowell', *The Spectator*, May 15, 2015. Accessed September 6, 2018. https://blogs.spectator.co.uk/2015/05/why-dance-needs-a-simon-cowell/#.
21. Somasundaram and Basu, 'What Does BBC'
22. Slavoj Žižek, 'Liberal Multiculturalism masks an old barbarism with a human face', *The Guardian*, October 3, 2010. Accessed September 6, 2018. https://www.theguardian.com/commentisfree/2010/oct/03/immigration-policy-roma-rightwing-europe.
23. *In Akbar's Palace,* chor. Sujata Banerjee Performed by Jaina Modasia, BBC Young Dancer South Asian Category Final, The Lowry Theatre, Manchester, January 23, 2017.
24. *Seven Heaven,* choreography by Sujata Banerjee. Performed by Jaina Modasia and Peter Camilleri, BBC Young Dancer South Asian Category Final, the Lowry Theatre, Manchester, January 23, 2017.
25. Brown, 'Why dance needs'
26. Graham Watts, 'BBC Young Dancer Award 2017', *Dance Tabs*, April 23, 2017. Accessed September 6, 2018. http://dancetabs.com/2017/04/bbc-young-dancer-award-2017/.
27. *Something Now, Something Then,* Performed by Seeta Patel, the Arena Theatre, Wolverhampton
28. Watts, 'BBC Young Dancer'
29. Ibid.
30. Ibid.

Acknowledgements

I am in receipt of a Vice Chancellor's Scholarship from the University of Roehampton, gratefully acknowledged, to conduct a doctoral research study on 'The Professionalization of South Asian dance forms in Britain.' This article also owes a debt of thanks to the late Andrée Grau, Professor of the Anthropology of Dance at the University of Roehampton, whose idea it was in the first place. I thank Professor Ann R. David, Dr Hugo Gorringe and Professor Tim Gorringe for their very helpful comments. Finally I would like to acknowledge the generous contributions of all members from the South Asian dance sector who have given their time to this research.

Disclosure statement

No potential conflict of interest was reported by the author.

ORCID

Magdalen Gorringe ⓘ http://orcid.org/0000-0002-4206-7700

References

Buckland, Theresa. J. 1999. "All Dances Are Ethnic, but Some Are More Ethnic Than Others: Some Observations on Dance Studies and Anthropology." *Dance Research: The Journal of the Society for Dance Research* 17 (1): 3–21.

Carroll, Noel. 2001. *Beyond Aesthetics: Philosophical Essays.* Cambridge: Cambridge University Press.

Conquergood, Lorne Dwight. 2013. *Cultural Struggles: Performance, Ethnography, Praxis*, edited by E. Patrick Johnson. Ann Arbor: University of Michigan Press.

Fox, Kate. 2004. *Watching the English.* St Ives: Hodder and Stoughton.

Freire, Paulo. 2017. *Pedagogy of the Oppressed.* St Ives: Penguin Random House. [originally published in 1970].

Gibson, Rachel. 2017. *Navadisha 2016: Conference Report.* See http://navadisha2016.co.uk/wp-content/uploads/2017/01/Navadisha-Report-final-lr.pdf.

Grau, Andrée. 2001. *South Asian Dance in Britain – Negotiating cultural Identity through Dance.* See https://www.researchgate.net/publication/282019278_Report_South_Asian_Dance_in_Britain_SADiB.

Hall, Stuart. 1999. "Unsettling 'The Heritage': Re-Imagining the Post-Nation." In *Whose Heritage? The Impact of Cultural Diversity on Britain's Living Heritage*, 13–22. London: Arts Council England.

Higgins, Charlotte. 2015. *This New Noise: The Extraordinary Birth and Troubled Life of the BBC.* London: Guardian Faber Publishing.

Kealiinohomoku, Joann. 2001. "An Anthropologist Looks at Ballet as a Form of Ethnic Dance." In *Moving History/Dancing Cultures*, edited by A. Dils, and A. C. Albright, 33–43. Middleton Connecticut: Wesleyan University Press. [originally published 1969].

Marion, Jonathan S. 2008. *Ballroom: Culture and Costume in Competitive Dance.* New York: Berg.

Maturana, Humberto, R. 1988. "Reality: The Search for Objectivity or the Quest for a Compelling Argument." *The Irish Journal of Psychology* 9 (1): 25–82.

Maturana, Humberto, R., and Francisco Varela. 1992. *The Tree of Knowledge: The Biological Roots of Human Understanding.* Boston: Shambhala Publications Inc. [originally published 1987].

McFee, Graham. 2005. "The Artistic and the Aesthetic." *The British Journal of Aesthetics* 45 (4): 368–387.

Mignolo, Walter D. 2007. "Delinking – The Rhetoric of Modernity, the Logic of Coloniality and the Grammar of de-Coloniality." *Cultural Studies* 21 (2/3): 449–514.

Morris, Geraldine. 2008. "Artistry or Mere Technique? The Value of the Ballet Competition." *Research in Dance Education* 9 (1): 39–54.

O'Shea, Janet. 2007. *At Home in the World: Bharata Natyam on the Global Stage.* Middletown, Conn.: Wesleyan University Press.

Parekh, Bhikhu. C. 2000. *The Future of Multi-Ethnic Britain: Report of the Commission on the Future of Multi-Ethnic Britain.* Runnymede Trust: Commission on the Future of Multi-Ethnic Britain. London: Profile Books.

Pillai, Shanti. 2002. "Rethinking Global Indian Dance Through Local Eyes: The Contemporary Bharatanatyam Scene in Chennai." *Dance Research Journal* 34 (2): 14–29.

Pinto, Shiromi. 2004. "No Man's Land – Exploring South Asianness", Report on Akademi Symposium held 22 May 2004. See http://akademi.co.uk/wp-content/uploads/2014/02/No-Mans-Land-Report.pdf (Accessed 22.1.17)

Quijano, Anibal. 2007. "Coloniality and Modernity/Rationality." *Cultural Studies* 21 (2/3): 168–178.

Said, Edward. W. 1995 [1978]. *Orientalism.* Reprinted with a new afterword. London: Penguin.

Seaton, Jean. 2007. "The BBC and Metabolising Britishness: Critical Patriotism." *The Political Quarterly* 78: 72–85.

Shay, Anthony. 2008. *Dancing Across Borders: the American Fascination with Exotic Dance Forms.* London: McFarland and Co.

Sporton, Gregory. 2004. "Dance as Cultural Understanding: Ideas, Policy, and Practice." *Dance Research Journal* 36 (2): 80–90.

Tucker, Catherine. 1993. "Traditions on the Move". *Academy of Indian Dance, Traditions on the Move conference report. June 9, 1993, London.* Accessed September 6, 2018. https://vads.ac.uk/x-large.php?uid=47115&sos=1&pic3=ak31-4.

Weisbrod, Alexis A. 2014. "Defining Dance, Creating Commodity, the Rhetoric of So You Think You Can Dance." In *The Oxford Handbook of Dance and the Popular Screen*, edited by Blanco Borelli, 320–334. Oxford: Oxford University Press.

Decolonising Indian classical dance? Projects of reform, classical to contemporary

Sitara Thobani [ID]

ABSTRACT
Now contained under the rubric 'classical', several dance practices in India underwent significant 'reconstruction' in the heyday of twentieth-century anti-colonial politics reliant upon the nationalist claim of a cohesive cultural identity. Such restoration of prestige to a supposedly denigrated cultural practice offered a positive 'artistic' counterpoint to alleviate nationalist anxieties regarding the purity of the nation and the uniqueness of its identity. Within a few decades of this nationalist reconstruction, Indian classical dance forms were regarded as emblematic of Indian culture and tradition. This article builds on important critiques of the nationalist reconstruction of Indian classical dance in India to examine how this project is enacted in the transnational present. It argues that both diasporic and non-diasporic (British) dancers uphold the foundational assumptions of the reconstructive Indian nationalist movement even as they are located within, and identify with, a very different national and political context, namely multicultural Britain.

In the transnational present, Indian classical dance is doubly Othered – first in alignment with the mid-twentieth-century Indian nationalist politics that shaped its 'reconstruction', second in the multicultural politics of representation that frame its twenty-first century performance. These politics are not, of course, limited to the UK, the specific site of my research; they manifest in varied forms in the many multicultural contexts where diasporic South Asians, like members of other diasporas, continue to produce and perform their 'cultural' practices as well.[1] This duality complicates the analysis at hand, namely that of present day Indian classical dance performances[2] and their relationship to processes of decolonisation. For not only must such an analysis contend with the enduring legacy of colonial representation that continues to shape Indian classical dance performances, it demonstrates the role that contemporary multicultural politics now play in shaping such representations as well. In other words, the re-production of nationalist narratives linking Indian classical dance with notions of antiquity, cultural purity and tradition are revealed to work in tandem with multiculturalist discourses to further essentialise Indian classical dance practices in the present. As I demonstrate, although the nationalist imperatives that shape dance performances in India and the multicultural politics that currently frame performances of 'ethnic' art in the UK are indeed distinct, they nonetheless come together in the transnational field of contemporary Indian classical dance performance and shape this field in turn.

In this paper, I wish to build on this synergetic relationship between postcolonial and multicultural forms of representation and their relationship to Indian classical dance to focus on the pedagogical value of such performances given their ability to construct 'Indian' culture and disseminate this 'cultural' knowledge to diverse dancers, their audiences and communities. I interpret pedagogy broadly here, pointing to the ways in which performances such as Indian classical dance – as well as the related but distinct genre of Contemporary South Asian dance – serve to teach performers and audiences about notions of cultural difference. This is made evident, for example, by the claims of many of the dancers with whom I worked that their dance performances provided a way to 'educate' British society about the traditions and culture of India, and by extension the South Asian diaspora. Such interventions confirm Britain's status as multicultural beneficiary, while simultaneously delineating between British national identity and its multicultural Others upon whom the burden to provide such 'education' necessarily falls.

My interest in such pedagogy leads me to examine more closely the complex ways in which British-based dancers, diasporic or otherwise, activate particular imaginaries – colonial, diasporic and multicultural – to delineate cultural-national identities even as they seek to break with the essentializing limitations these very categories entail. The paradox that ensues as dancers reproduce the very assumptions they claim to want to challenge calls into question the possibility of decolonising dance practices that have yet to be fully understood in relation to their embeddedness in the post/colonial situation. This embeddedness, I suggest, results from the continued essentialization of Indian classical dance as well as its offshoot, Contemporary South Asian dance. While dancers often engage in critiques of the limiting narratives that frame dance performances and their reception in the present, they fall short of challenging the colonial logic laying the very ground for their performances. Thus they extend this logic into the present, which is now in alignment with contemporary practices of state-sanctioned multiculturalism.

The history of Indian classical dance development, as a number of scholars have already observed, is a relatively familiar postcolonial story of nationalist cultural production that cannot be understood outside the context of Indian nation formation. Now defined as 'classical', several dance practices in India underwent significant processes of reconstruction at a time when anti-colonial politics strove to instil cohesive claims of a stable pan-Indian cultural identity. Through this process, the architects of these reconstructive movements delinked the practice of dance from its hereditary performers – namely women associated with temples and courts, seen by the twentieth century to have fallen into disrepute – to sanitise these practices as 'Indian' cultural and artistic heritage (see Allen 1997; Soneji 2012; Srinivasan 1985).

It is not my intention to rehearse this history here. However, important to my project is the ongoing nature of this history, which is under continual construction through the work of dancers in a context far removed – temporally, politically and culturally – from that of the nascent Indian nation. Whereas many critiques of the nationalist production of Indian classical dance present 'reconstruction' as a chapter in Indian classical dance history that has since been closed, I maintain that this project is actively continued through the works of Indian classical (and Contemporary South Asian) dancers in the present. Thus my aim is to examine the ways in which this history shapes contemporary dance practices, even as it is in turn protracted and extended through them.

An addition to this ongoing history, especially in the UK, is the burgeoning category of Contemporary South Asian dance. Although Indian classical and Contemporary South Asian dance are expressed as distinct genres, they are nonetheless mutually constitutive categories; dancers of each style produce the other through their very struggles to define their own forms. Taken together, Indian classical and Contemporary South Asian dance can be seen to constitute the metacategory of British Asian dance, a kind of spectrum on which Indian classical and Contemporary South Asian dance both lie; although the two genres are not interchangeable, their demarcation is often left to be articulated by dancers themselves, with each drawing a slightly different line.[3] The complex and interdependent relationship between the two is neatly summed up in the words of one such dancer I interviewed: 'contemporary, yeah, very interesting isn't it. For me, contemporary is anything that's not classical'.

I have argued elsewhere that the relationship between the two genres, especially as articulated by Indian classical and Contemporary South Asian dancers in the UK, temporalizes the two to constitute an evolutionary schema – that unrelenting cornerstone of colonial logic (see Thobani 2017b). Contemporary South Asian dancers, I argued, are engaged in a new project of reform that parallels the classicizing project of the twentieth century in that both can be seen as attempts to claim historical agency and respectability in relation to hegemonic discourses (be they colonial or multicultural). In short, where Indian classical dance reformists sought to prove their civility by casting aside the supposedly degenerate history of *nautch*[4] to align classical dance with nationalist ideas of modernity (which still included space for 'tradition'), Contemporary South Asian dancers in the UK seek to prove their compatibility with British contemporaneity by rejecting the cultural stasis they associate with Indian classical dance.

Alongside this temporalization however is another, equally complex phenomena similarly rooted in the legacy of colonial logic. For, as I argue below, the relationship between Indian classical and Contemporary South Asian dance also corresponds with the co-production of 'Indian' and 'British' national-cultural identities. While the performance of Indian classical dance signals the success of Indian nationalist narratives glorifying constructs of uninterrupted cultural-artistic heritage beyond the bounds of the Indian nation, Contemporary South Asian dance enables celebratory projections of British national identity as cosmopolitan and multicultural while still relying upon the reification of 'Indian' culture. The bid to modernise South Asian dance in the UK – increasingly advocated for by those who aspire to a greater professionalisation of their art form – re-articulates the colonial politics of difference, constructing 'Indian' and 'British' as homogenised entities in the process to suture postcolonial relations between the two-nation states on the terrain of diasporic arts.

Building on this discussion, I focus in this paper on the ways in which the temporalizing narratives that frame Indian classical and Contemporary South Asian dance in the British context are simultaneously coterminous with processes of cultural essentialization. The result is to demonstrate the salience of categories of ethnic and cultural difference, in both contemporary dance practices as well as in the origins of these practices as we know them. In the next section, I explore the ways in which Indian classical dance is fixed through its association to an essential Indian identity by all dancers of this genre.

I then turn to the nascent category of Contemporary South Asian dance in the following section to examine the paradoxical ways in which dancers of this genre construct Indian classical dance in ethnic and cultural registers despite their stated desire to break free of the cultural stasis they perceive to be inherent in Indian classical dance. Together, the next two sections draw attention to the pedagogical and disciplinary value of both constructs – Indian classical and Contemporary South Asian dance – which while appearing to be in a state of conflict, nevertheless achieve similar aims of educating dancers and their wider audiences about the delineation of 'Indian' and 'British' identities, past and present. Moving beyond an analysis that simply attempts to define a genealogical relationship between the two genres, my aim in this paper is to interrogate the role these mutually constituted forms play in the politics of difference, embedded as they are in both the postcolonial and multicultural context.

Dance and identity in the transnational present

The privileged status accorded India as 'homeland' of Indian classical dance continues to enact, and therefore ensures the success of, the nationalist script that tied dance to nation. Importantly, this is a script that also ties nation to ethnicity, whether through discourses that posited national identity as determined by one's blood, or through the Orientalist fantasies that laid the foundations for many representations of 'exotic' Indian art and culture, including Indian classical dance (for more, see Thobani 2017a). This connection to ethnic-cultural identity is evident in the different ways one's proximity (and thus claim) to Indian classical dance is conceived and articulated. Not surprisingly, such proximity comes into question for non-Indian (diasporic and non-diasporic) dancers especially and is often discussed by them in turn.

In India, 'foreign' (diasporic and non-diasporic, Western) dancers often find themselves being 'Indianized' when celebrated for their abilities as dancers. For one example, successful American Odissi dancer Sharon Lowen has been described as

> an American Jew [who] possesses startlingly Indian looks. With dark hair, a pair of large eyes, and typical oriental features she has the looks of an Indian dancer. She has imbibed the spirit of Odissi and is a serious exponent of the form. (Kothari and Pasricha 1990, 130)

Written by one of the leading dance critics and scholars in India, this account was clearly intended as a compliment. Yet one cannot help but question the priorities for assessment that are raised in this account, not to mention the multiple and symbiotic levels of Orientalism that are activated as a result. Implicit in this statement is not only a description of Lowen the dancer, but more importantly, a delineation of what an Indian classical dancer (and thus what Indian classical dance) should be. What is more, the Indianization of Lowen necessarily entails the further racialization of the Indian dancer, with her dark hair, large eyes and 'Oriental' features. This identity of the dance, inextricably linked here with processes of racialization, is fixed even as room is made to include, and indeed celebrate, a diverse range of dancers.

Such compliments to 'foreign' dancers might be interpreted to suggest a correlation between 'looking Indian' and the acquisition of particular forms of body language, demonstrating the extent to which the physical body can be trained into behaving in certain culturally prescribed ways (see Bourdieu 1977; Connerton 1989; Csordas 1990; Mauss 1973).

That diasporic dancers are also praised in this way suggests at first glance that 'looking Indian' might rely upon more than one's physical appearance; for such compliments often correspond with references to the diasporic dancer's ability to capture the embodied nuances presumed to be specific to the original (local) context of the dance form they practice. Upon closer analysis however, it soon becomes clear that such notions of cultural competency in the form of trained body language are not far removed from a focus on a given dancer's ethnic identity. For even when dancers are celebrated for their technical skill, this celebration is overwhelmingly expressed through references to somatic traits as demonstrated in the description of Lowen above. Such traits, it appears, remain the primary mode through which 'cultural competency' is articulated.

In the UK, where 'race', 'ethnicity' and 'culture' are so routinely conflated, one's somatic appearance is often perceived to determine one's 'natural' abilities – and affinities – for Indian classical dance. The extent to which diasporic dancers are thought to be more naturally inclined to Indian classical dance in the UK stands in contrast to the ways in which they are more likely to be grouped (at least initially) with other 'foreign' (non-diasporic) dancers in India. Take for example this excerpt from an interview with a South Asian dancer based in London:

> I think when you are Indian, you're really lucky because ... if you are Indian you have the natural rhythm of India ... Because you know, as you're Indian, you're born in the Indian family, you have the Indian rigour, the Indian way of life, you have the praying, the language, you listen to music. If you're Western, and when you learn the dance and then you go back home, you're very Western again. Your parents don't have that kind of thing. But [the dance is] for everybody. Everybody can learn the dance. What I'm trying to say is, classical Indian dance – like [names a white dancer in London] for instance, she's a wonderful dancer but there's *no dance* [speaker's emphasis], there's no soul in it. It's just movement. Because she doesn't have that rhythm, that attunement [*sic*] with the classical Indian music. For example, when [addresses a diasporic dancer] dance[s], you can tell [she's] at one with the music because [she] can feel it ... You can see in [the white dancer] that's lacking. She's very English ... she does her *bhangi* [pose] quite nicely but you don't see the *bhangi* has an Indian thing any longer.

Race of course is a social construct produced through its articulation in the act of differentiation (Balibar 2004; Banks 1996; Fanon 2008; Gilroy 1992; Hall 1996, 1991a, 1991b). While this dancer begins by asserting a fundamental relationship between Indian classical dance and 'the Indian way of life' in line with the conventional perspectives on Indian classical dance, the speaker goes further to discuss the unequivocal contrast between the way of life it poses and what is perceived to be 'Western' – coded here as English, non-diasporic and therefore presumably white. So doing this speaker constructs ideas of what it means to be Indian and Western, leaving little room for the myriad of complex subjectivities that lie between. The Indian classical dance of the diasporic dancer is presented to be of a different quality or essence than that of the technically adequate non-Indian/white dancer by virtue of the 'natural rhythm' they are presumed to embody.

It must be noted that, on the whole, most diasporic South Asian dancers I encountered denied any tangible (technical) differences in ability between them and their white counterparts. Even the dancer cited above continued to say 'we should be open to everybody ... As teachers and givers, we have to give them [white students] 110% of it [the dance]'. However, even if not expressed in terms as blatant as those in the excerpt cited above, notions of difference persisted amongst the dancers I encountered, albeit in more subtle ways. Importantly, such notions existed for the non-Indian (white) dancers as well. For some for example, this difference was articulated in terms of good teaching, as it was for this white dancer in London describing her experiences:

> It [learning to dance] was definitely harder for me than say people born in India or in the Indian, the South Asian community. Because, when I came [*sic*] to India for the first time, to learn, I could very clearly see the difference. Because even if you are practicing for a long time, but if you are kind of not within this environment, if you don't really have Indian teachers, Indian performances, if you don't come to performances often, then you kind of – you're basically on your own …

Although this dancer makes reasonable observations about access (or lack thereof) to accomplished role models and the limited choice of teachers in the UK, she nonetheless conceives of the problem as unique to her and not shared by people 'born in India *or the Indian, the South Asian community*' (emphasis added). Glaring in this account is how the greater resources this dancer observed in India are presumed to be more easily accessible to dancers in the South Asian diaspora by virtue of nothing more than their circumstances as people born into this community; this in spite of the fact that those in the South Asian community (diaspora) would have access to the same teachers and performers as this dancer living in the UK. Diasporic dancers are here conflated with those in India, demonstrating the extent to which racialized identity is seen to determine one's proximity to Indian classical dance. Such conflation would not of course occur in India, where the diasporic dancer would be perceived of as similarly disadvantaged by the supposed lack of training opportunities and resources abroad.

In expressing as unique the challenges of training she encountered as a non-South Asian dancer, this speaker is not alone. Another difficulty identified by white dancers in the UK pertained to their self-awareness of their non-Indian identity and how this might be interpreted during, or impact upon, the particular context of their classical dance performance. As another dancer described in an interview:

> Sometimes I did feel a bit conscious that I was doing something outside of my own culture, but rather than [pauses] I was only uncomfortable with that sometimes when I was performing it to someone within the culture. So, I was just worried that I was understanding it and doing the right thing, and not stepping on somebody's toes or being an impostor or something like that. But where I was performing it to people who it was new to, no it was just a case of I think most people found it interesting. Some people found it odd, but then they would just not watch.

It is interesting to note how this dancer's self-awareness extends to their performance for South Asian audiences, and not those to whom the dance 'was new'. Implicit in this assertion is the idea that the dance would not be 'new' to 'someone within the culture', as well as that someone outside 'the culture' would not already have preconceived ideas of what an 'Indian' dance performance should look like. Both positions are of course untenable: Indian audiences – diasporic or otherwise – are not inherently familiar with Indian classical dance, especially given the caste, class, religious and cultural diversity of the country and its diaspora. Neither are non-Indians completely free of longstanding ideas about India, its culture and even its dancers, ideas that have circulated for centuries in the Western (colonial) imaginary. Crucially, both positions rely upon the fundamental essentialization of Indian classical dance, simultaneously associating it with the knowledge presumed to be inherent to the Indian community while disassociating it completely from its long encounter with the West.

As a result of these essentializing gestures, white dancers must contend with the very real consequences that result from notions of 'natural' advantages and disadvantages, even though these are based on perceptions of difference. Dancers, both South Asian and white, often spoke of the perception that it was more difficult for the latter to secure performances and teaching positions because of their presumed lack of authenticity compared to South Asian dancers. For example, according to one South Asian Bharatanatyam dancer:

If I was teaching a workshop and I couldn't do it, I would sub-out to someone who was not Indian [white] because those are the people that I know do it best. And I don't see that [amongst other dancers]. But they [the white dancers] will still have problems, both here and [in] India, because they're not Indian and this idea of authenticity comes up. So I feel, and I get some flack about authenticity because I'm not from India, but not as much as those people [white dancers].

The overall focus of this account is on the limitations faced by 'non-Indian'/white dancers, even as they are identified as the ones who 'do it best'. It is telling that South Asian dancers did not speak of their 'authenticity' being questioned in the UK in the same way as non-South Asian (white) dancers, despite the fact that their families often came from regions different from those with which their dance is associated, did not necessarily speak any Indian languages, or were second or third generation diasporic members. The relative lack of concern with authenticity for diasporic dancers suggests that ethnic identity overrides the acquisition of cultural knowledge and bodily training in the UK, for it is on the basis of this identity that dancers are or are not offered opportunities to perform and have their dance practice taken seriously. Training the body to move in culturally prescribed ways – that is, to 'look Indian' – still requires navigating constructions of ethnicity in order to be coherent, reconfirming these very constructions once again.

Whiteness was not always perceived as a disadvantage relative to the advantages equated with the cultural identities of diasporic dancers. Indeed, these tables could and did turn as some white dancers identified their whiteness/Westerness as inoculating them against the 'cultural baggage' they equated with South Asian dancers. This advantage also extended from the greater association of whiteness with professionalism; recall the assertion made by the diasporic dancer cited above who described white dancers as 'the people that I know do it best'. Take for another example the following:

It's strange that as a [white European] dancer I've been able to make a living out of Indian classical dance. I think it's partly to do with the fact that dancers with an Indian background see it as a mediated dance. They see it as something to link their background, cultural heritage and they don't see it as an art form, they don't take it as seriously. Whereas dancers from other backgrounds, they see it as an art form and they take it seriously. And also they have to do more research, you can't assume that it's in my blood or I just know it because I grew up with it. You have to look for the answers, you have to do much more research.

Aside from this dancer's striking reference to blood and the innate proclivity to Indian classical dance this is meant to signify, the suggestion that dancers of Indian background see the form as 'mediated' by its allegedly resilient cultural moorings reflects fairly popular assumptions. Implicit in this assertion is the notion that diasporic dancers may not have to work as hard as their white/Western counterparts for the greater cultural gap the latter are thought to have to bridge. And yet, the relative ease diasporic dance students are presumed to enjoy is countered by the belief that for them, dance is a purely personal and community-oriented affair, not a viable or desirable profession. Ultimately the category of Western (exclusive now of diasporic Indians) is here presented to suggest a greater penchant towards professionalism, the category through which the racialization of Indian classical dance is perhaps most subtly furthered in the British context.

Performing ethnic dance par excellence

I have been arguing until now that the suturing of Indian classical dance to the nation-culture of India operationalises constructions of ethnic and cultural difference for South Asian and white dancers and audiences alike. These processes are furthered in the multicultural context, where the practices and performances of 'Other' cultures are routinely overdetermined such that they are made to represent the entire culture, history, traditions and practices with which they are associated, no matter how diverse or conflicted these may actually be. While the approach of most classical dancers continues to tether their dance forms to formations of ethnic and cultural (and thus national) identity, also striking are the ways in which similar ends are achieved by those who wish to break with this very essentialization. I turn now to discuss this second group of dancers, the new reformists who aim to transcend the cultural stasis they equate with classical dance to pursue more 'relevant' artistic agendas.

Those dancers wishing to escape the cultural asphyxiation often equated with Indian classical dance take recourse to creating works signalled as innovative under the Contemporary South Asian dance banner. As suggested in the previous section, the classical/contemporary binary translates into an amateur/professional distinction whereby those who seek to develop Contemporary South Asian dance instead of Indian classical dance are able to call upon greater access to resources, funding and institutional support. Moreover, Contemporary South Asian dancers are more likely to perform at professional venues in the city centre, furthering the association between Contemporary South Asian dance and professionalism. For dancers who wish to pursue professional careers in the arts, the genre of Contemporary South Asian dance appears to be the clearest, if not only, option.

Notably, almost all of the dancers pursuing this line of choreography are of South Asian background. That almost no white dancers take up Contemporary South Asian dance, despite the growing interest of white dancers in Indian classical dance, indicates the complex and intimate relationship imagined to exist between Indian classical dance and Indian 'culture' writ large. This association is further underscored by the fact that Contemporary South Asian dancers almost exclusively collaborate with the genre of Western Contemporary dance (see Erdman 2000). The exclusive preference for such collaborations indicates the extent to which Contemporary dance (Western) enjoys a hegemonic position free from any 'cultural' markings; as such, practices associated with Western Contemporary dance provide the most immediate route to professionalism for South Asian dancers. In short, while its association to culture makes Indian classical dance increasingly attractive to non-Indian dancers (to varying degrees), this very association leads many diasporic

DANCE, MUSIC AND CULTURES OF DECOLONISATION

dancers to pursue contemporising genres in an attempt to claim both individual and artistic agency.

Of course, in order for Contemporary South Asian dance to be appreciated, it must first be *recognized* as contemporary. This challenge is aptly captured in the following excerpt from an interview with a presenter working for a major South Asian dance organisation based in the UK. Explaining the unfolding relationship between a leading Contemporary dance venue in London and South Asian dance, the presenter continued:

The director of [the venue] in London decided to do an Indian Summer Festival. So first year was Indian Summer and he had brought in a whole host of theatre groups and dance groups, visiting groups and local groups [and put them] together in the Indian summer festival. That year he came back to me and said, well actually we are a dance venue. We should be doing a dance event only. So theatre was out. So that year we had dancers, local dancers and visiting dancers. Classical, traditional, all sorts of dancers ... were programmed in. It was [after] the end of that festival that he came in and said well, that's rubbish, we are actually a Contemporary dance venue, we should be programming a contemporary dance festival. Fine. So he asked all the dancers to make bids and tell him what was going to be contemporary about their work. So one dancer ... applied and said I want to work on Ashta Nayika, which is a new [interpretation] and I would do a show with 8 heroines. She was in. A Bharatanatyam dancer applied and said I want to work with Hindustani music – an experimentation. Well, she was in. And so on ... It was the end when this man came and said to me, 'well what is experimental about it?' This was a white man who didn't understand the language, he didn't understand the context. What he was watching was people, these beautiful girls dressed up in all of this costume and jewellery, a lot of it, doing the same kind of technical routine. He didn't understand the context of Ashta Nayika or Hindustani music. It was the same. Now juxtaposed against that was another contemporary dancer, a classical dancer who was starting to create her contemporary shows ... She was someone who understood the trends within the contemporary dance. Who understood that contemporary dance audiences cannot have an informed journey into Hindustani or Karnatik music. Understanding that you cannot bring in stories with which we have grown up in South Asia ... But these audiences had no insight into Indian philosophy. Understanding Shaivism or Vaishnavism, understanding those two philosophies and identifying with the emotional baggage, which these very specific philosophies bring into the art form, was something very foreign for these audiences. So she created the whole piece, which didn't have stories, she used local Western musicians, and she was a hit.

I have quoted this excerpt at length for it resonates with issues that continue to impact dancers in the present despite pertaining to interactions that occurred over twenty years ago. The bids to reinterpret the *Ashta Nayika* – eight types of heroines in love outlined in the *Natyashastra* – or to combine Bharatanatyam (based on South Indian music systems) and North Indian Hindustani music are undeniably inventive; on paper, they were innovative enough to be successful in the application process for the Contemporary dance festival being organised. Ultimately however, these projects remained confined within their presumed sense of tradition for it was the dancer who conceptually, visually and aurally discarded her classical dance to adapt her performance to the requirements of the festival, venue and audience that was singled out as successful. The point is not to deny her artistic creativity or aptitude in knowing and anticipating her audience, but to indicate the role that audience reception (and mainstream recognition) plays in determining which performances are deemed contemporary and which are not.

It is no surprise then that dancers overwhelmingly choose to draw on what they know, or perceive to be, Western Contemporary techniques in their performances. When I first began my fieldwork in London, I was struck by the extent to which Contemporary South Asian dance dominated the British Asian dance scene, arguably the largest such site in the global South Asian diaspora. One of the first performances I attended was by an 'Asian-inspired dance company ... showcasing their new innovative and collaborative work ... featuring a triple bill of 5 female dancers, fus[ing] the ancient South Indian classical dance Bharata Natyam with contemporary techniques' (from programme notes). The performance consisted of three pieces, the last of which demonstrated more explicit choreographic references to Bharatanatyam than the first two. Perhaps the most successful – based on audience response – was the first piece, which featured four of the five company dancers. The piece began with the dancers physically struggling with one another for the microphone so that they might be able to share their personal biographies with the audience; as soon as one could grab hold of the mic, the others quickly stole it away so that each of their stories was left to be told in fragments. The audience was thus introduced to the dancers who appeared to be playing themselves: a Chinese Canadian woman, a white American woman who introduced herself as Hindu (although her family had 'left the temple'), a French-English woman and an 'Anglo-Indian' woman who (nonetheless) identified herself as English. The white Hindu woman spoke of how she felt lost when her family moved away from the Hare Krishna community when she was a child and how people would react oddly to her Hindu name; the Anglo-Indian woman responded that she did not know what it meant to be 'part Indian' and wondered if that was why she was 'so hairy'. Comedy, bordering on satire, was used throughout the piece to explore the complexities and absurdities of cultural essentialism, often eliciting laughter from the audience in response.

Later in the piece, the white Hindu woman began to perform classical Bharatanatyam; she was the only dancer trained in any style of Indian classical dance, although all four were very clearly trained in Western Contemporary dance to professional standards as was evident from their biographic information. The Anglo-Indian woman quickly grabbed the microphone to act as interlocutor for her partner's movements, calling out possible interpretations of the choreography as if playing a game of charades: 'she's picking flowers', 'she's happy', 'she's getting married', 'she's determined', 'she's on a boat', 'she's stomping because she is determined'. The last comment was in reference to the stylistic feature common to most forms of Indian classical dance (including Kathak, Bharatanatyam and Odissi) whereby dancers produce rhythmic patterns by slapping their bare feet on the ground.

This sequence brought attention to the potential for observers to misunderstand and outright mock Indian classical dance forms (many a dancer's fear) while at the same time making fun of the spectator's random if not outlandish speculations. The conjecture that 'she's getting married' in particular resonated strongly with the stereotyping of Asian culture and its assumed obsession with matrimony and grandiose weddings. Interestingly, a similar sequence was to occur later with the Chinese-Canadian dancer with 'she's getting married' offered once again as a possible explanation; the same did not occur while the French and English women performed their 'Western' solos respectively.

The piece concluded with the use of specific props through which the dancers could express their cultural identities; somewhat predictably (and perhaps once again drawing attention to and finding amusement in the cliché), food became a major cultural signifier. At one point, all four dancers were on stage, improvising movement individually so as to be dancing around themselves, yet, still in group formation. Each would again grab the microphone, this time to announce their favourite cultural foods. Chicken tikka masala and balti were those of the Anglo-Indian-as-English woman. The relationship of cultural identity to food was then demonstrated literally as the dancers proceeded to each bring forward a basket, emptying its contents to display before the audience. Along with food, the women presented clothing and other material objects that held personal or cultural significance. The French woman revealed a bottle of wine, a baguette, a beret and some sausage, while the English woman pulled out a box of PG Tips tea bags and a picture of the Queen. As the piece concluded the lights dimmed, shifting the focus of the audience to a pre-recorded conversation between the dancers regarding their experiences of immigrating to the UK and how this affected their understandings of home. Such were the cosmopolitan identities in the making.

Despite its very literal performance, the piece was nonetheless able to demonstrate the frivolity and humour of clichés without necessarily becoming one itself; it therefore was an important exploration of the composite identities that come together in the context of state-sanctioned multiculturalism in the transnational present. However, notwithstanding the diversity of the dancers involved and their abilities to perform multiple dance styles (the Chinese Canadian woman performed a ribbon dance in her solo while the French English woman performed ballet in hers), the performance was still marketed as – and ultimately reduced to – Contemporary *South Asian* dance. This is not to say that Contemporary South Asian dance is not capable of complex investigations on its own, but it is worth asking why it was selected – or at least articulated – as the medium from which to explore the multiplicity of cultural forms and identities that were presented on that London stage.[5] Why is the signifier South Asian highlighted in this exploration of racial-cultural diversity and anxiety, and how is it fixed through this production in turn?

The performance pivoted around the very sense of cultural dynamism that it effectively foreclosed for the Indian classical dance forms that were identified as its inspiration. What is even more striking then is how this performance, in its very attempt to define Contemporary South Asian dance (with all the limitations of this category), relied on the specific construction of *Indian classical dance* to ground this definition. Take for example the closing lines of the promotional material for the production, which suggested the audience:

> Expect to see precise and well articulated movement which challenges ideas of form, identity and artistic freedom, all executed with the utmost grace. By reducing the cultural specificity and religious associations of Bharata Natyam, [the Company] revives the language of South Indian dance and makes this unique art form more accessible.

In a complex manoeuvre, the generic metacategory of British Asian here becomes the ethnic dance *par excellence* as a result as Indian classical dance – strongly associated with Indian 'cultural specificity and religious associations' – becomes the grounds from which Contemporary South Asian dance can emerge to explore perceptions of cultural difference. 'Reducing the cultural complexity' and 'reviving the language of South Indian dance', this performance signals a new project of reform shaped by transnational politics of cultural difference, just as the older project of reform that produced Indian classical dance was informed through the colonial politics of civilizational difference. Indian classical dance is marked as the abject yet indispensable category that anchors the very (Indian) culture Contemporary South Asian dancers find so confining. As this

Conclusion

The project to classicize those dance forms that underwent processes of 'reconstruction' in India was premised upon nationalist attempts to ground their claims to cultural heritage and civility in the distant past. This temporalizing project tied Indian classical dance to glorified notions of antiquity and cultural essence in order to prove the durability of this culture and its traditions in spite of the experience of British colonisation. In the present multicultural context, however, this very association with antiquity serves to deny (diasporic) dancers entry into the fold of (British) contemporaneity. Dancers thus find themselves in search of ways to prove their contemporary credentials, a need that can only be met by the visible appearance of breaking with the 'cultural' limitations perceived to be inherent in their Indian classical dance forms.

Analysis of both (Indian) classicizing and (diasporic) contemporising projects reveals that such temporalizing moves simultaneously operate on, and contribute to, constructions of ethnic identity. For the temporal conundrum that diasporic dancers experience in the present is expressed through, and furthered by, constructions of ethnic identity as inherited from colonial logic and extended through multicultural discourse. This relationship between temporality and ethnicity is made clear by examining the genre of Contemporary South Asian dance; in order to transcend the limitations of their Indian classical forms, diasporic dancers must demonstrate their compatibility with the referents of Western contemporaneity (artistic or otherwise). The irony lies in the role the resulting genre of Contemporary South Asian dance plays as the ethnic dance *par excellence* in the British multicultural context. Here is a genre that is marked by its Otherness even as it continues to Another Indian classical dance once more. The mutually constitutive relationship between temporalizing narratives and constructions of ethnic identity remain firmly rooted in place.

Notes

1. In maintaining this point, it is not my intention to treat these various multicultural locations – from the UK to North America, elsewhere in Europe and Australia – as synonymous, for the multicultural policies and practices of each of these states are historically, socially and politically distinctive. Instead, tracing the similarities between different multicultural contexts draws attention to the transnational network in which Indian classical dance is presently practiced, and the extent to which it is impacted upon by various multicultural (racializing) narratives. In other words, the British context is shown to be part of the larger global circulation of Indian classical dance in the transnational present.
2. There are currently eight styles of Indian classical dance. While my research is focused on the three most common styles in the diaspora – Bharatanatyam, Kathak and Odissi – I am interested in how these distinct forms are together categorised under the umbrella term Indian classical dance. In treating as synonymous different forms of Indian classical dance, this term contributes to the construction of a uniform and coherent national-cultural identity.
3. Of course, as I will soon discuss, an individual dancer's articulation of what is 'Contemporary' must also be recognised as such by mainstream programmers, funders and audiences. Herein lies the crux.

4. The Anglicized form of the Hindustani word *naach* (dance), *nautch* operated as a catch-all category for those dance performances (and performers) that came to be viewed as debased by the late nineteenth and early twentieth centuries. These perspectives culminated in the anti-*nautch* movement, which targeted female performers associated with both 'religious' and 'secular' institutions.
5. A similar production toured a year later when a Kathak Company presented a feature length performance that sought to explore the complexity of cultural identity as essentialized through the phenomenon of 'ticking boxes', referring to having to select one's ethnic identity on state census forms. In this production too, the only practitioner of Indian classical dance was the founder of the Company, who performed with three other dancers (two of whom were trained in Western Contemporary dance and one in b-boy/break dancing). Both performances, although powerful and engaging, were much more than performances of South Asian dance. Yet, by presenting them as South Asian-inspired (even if they were indeed South Asian-inspired), naturalised the connection between South Asian dance and anxieties of cultural identity.

Disclosure statement

No potential conflict of interest was reported by the author.

ORCID

Sitara Thobani ⓘ http://orcid.org/0000-0002-8697-2753

References

Allen, Michael Harp. 1997. "Rewriting the Script for South Indian Dance." *The Dance Review* 41 (3): 63–100.

Balibar, Etienne. 2004. *We, the People of Europe?: Reflections on Transnational Citizenship*. Princeton, NJ: Princeton University Press.

Banks, Marcus. 1996. *Ethnicity: Anthropological Constructions*. London: Routledge.

Bourdieu, Pierre. 1977. *Outline of a Theory of Practice*. Cambridge: Cambridge University Press.

Connerton, Paul. 1989. *How Societies Remember*. Cambridge: Cambridge University Press.

Csordas, Thomas. 1990. *Embodiment as a Paradigm for Anthropology*. Cambridge: Cambridge University Press.

Erdman, Joan. 2000. "South Asian Dance: The British Experience, Choreography and Dance." *The Dance Review* 44 (3): 180–113.

Fanon, Franz. 2008 [1952]. *Black Skin, White Masks*. Translated by C. L. Markmann. London: Pluto.

Gilroy, Paul. 1992. *'There Ain't No Black in the Union Jack': The Cultural Politics of Race and Nation*. London: Routledge.

Hall, Stuart. 1991a. "The Local and the Global: Globalization and Ethnicity." In *Culture, Globalization and the World-System*, edited by A. D. King, 19–40. Basingstoke: Macmillan.

Hall, Stuart. 1991b. "Old and New Identities, Old and New Ethnicities." In *Culture, Globalization and the World-System*, edited by A. D. King, 41–68. Basingstoke: Macmillan.

Hall, Stuart. 1996. "Who Needs 'Identity'?" In *Questions of Cultural Identity*, edited by P. Du Gay, and S. Hall, 1–17. London: Sage.

Kothari, Sunil, and A. Pasricha. 1990. *Odissi: Indian Classical Dance Art*. Bombay: Marg Publications.

Mauss, Marcel. 1973 [1934]. "Techniques of the Body." *Economy and Society* 2 (1): 70–88.

Soneji, Davesh. 2012. *Unfinished Gestures: Devadāsīs, Memory, and Modernity in South India*. Chicago: University of Chicago Press.

Srinivasan, Amrit. 1985. "Reform and Revival: The Devadasi and Her Dance." *Economic and Political Weekly* 20 (44): 1869–1876.

Thobani, Sitara. 2017a. *Indian Classical Dance and the Making of Postcolonial National Identities: Dancing on Empire's Stage*. New York: Routledge.

Thobani, Sitara. 2017b. "Projects of Reform: Frictions of Generation and Genre." *MUSICultures* 44 (1): 163–186.

Gender, new creativity and Carnatic music in London

Jasmine Hornabrook ⓘ

ABSTRACT
This article examines creative projects amongst second-generation, British Tamil diasporic female musicians (focused on Sri Lankan examples) located within London's Carnatic music scene. Several scholars have suggested that the twentieth-century Indian nationalist project constructed ideals of femininity that positioned women as bearers of tradition during colonial rule to uphold the inner core of Indian culture [Bakrania 2013; Chatterjee 1989], and which were also reflected in the restricted performance and creativity of Carnatic music for female musicians [Subramanian 2006; Weidman 2003]. This article focuses on second-generation musicians, who combine their Carnatic background and 'South Indian' sound with other everyday sounds in Britain. Their creative projects shift from an aesthetic that was responsive to colonialism in India to highlight female creativity and hybridity in decolonising processes. This article presents examples of how cultural expectations of women as bearers of tradition are decentred, repositioning them as creative agents in a transnational diaspora.

In her review for the Carnatic music-inspired performance, 'Subduction Zone', Seetal Kaur wrote:

> There are some stories that get swept under the rug. Perhaps there aren't enough opportunities to express them, or there is an assumption no-one is listening ... The unique and complex identity of British Tamils is one of the stories that are often hidden ... but now the next generation is unfolding the richness of their refined cultural traditions and combining them with their equally strong urban influences (2016, 22).

'Subduction Zone' is the story of a British Tamil woman growing up in East London, expressed through Carnatic South Indian classical music, along with North Indian Hindustani and British pop music, South Indian classical dance and street dance. The performance explored experiences of growing up in diasporic settings, facing competing cultural interests and tackling discrimination and sexism. Through the sounds of the *veena* (lute), Carnatic songs, guitar and live electronics, the unique and shared stories unfolded. The performance was curated by a second-generation, Carnatic musician, who learned the South Indian *veena* as part of her Tamil upbringing. Her creativity, expression and experimentation through the performance were in sharp contrast to the cultural expectations and ideals of South Asian femininity, such as that of restrained female musicianship that emerged in the context of British colonialism in India.

This article looks at emerging creative projects among second-generation female musicians within Tamil, focusing on Sri Lankan, diasporic communities. First, it introduces the Carnatic music scene in London, discussing musical practices among the diasporic second generation. Carnatic music is an integral feature of a constructed Sri Lankan Tamil cultural identity that emerged in the face of ethnic persecution, and connects with Tamil Nadu in India in an act of Tamil cultural and ethnic solidarity. Despite being geographically associated with the whole of the South of India, the Carnatic music scene in London was largely the result of the displacement of thousands of Tamil people from Sri Lanka from the late 1970s. A brief discussion follows on the Indian nationalist project and the position of women as 'bearers of tradition', and on how ideas of 'ideal femininity' developed in Carnatic music, which are being challenged in the Tamil diaspora. Finally, the article argues, through looking at two artists in London, that female artists in diasporic settings are emerging as creative agents amid a music scene that retains ideals instated during the British colonial era. While the mention of female second-generation Sri Lankan Tamil musicians brings to mind artists such as the rapper M.I.A, the discussion here is on artists who have significant involvement with Carnatic music in the U.K. and in India. The first artist is Mithila Sarma, the *veena* player behind 'Subduction Zone' and various other projects using the *veena* in recontextualized settings. The second is Abi Sampa, who juxtaposes her South Indian and Euro-American vocal styles and recontextualizes Carnatic compositions on the electric *veena*. Their musical projects contribute to the visibility of women's roles in Carnatic music in a postcolonial diasporic context in the decolonising era.

In her book of interviews with female Indian musicians, dancers and painters, C. S. Lakshmi suggests that looking exclusively at female artists could be an essentialisation of their gender or their art, but can be portrayed also as a kind of counter-culture of matriarchal aesthetics (2000, viii). Looking at creative projects among female musicians, who learn Carnatic music as part of their Sri Lankan Tamil heritage is necessary, not only because second-generation female musicians are pro-active in the field, but also because the majority of literature on British South Asian music focuses on the male-dominated styles of Bhangra and Asian Underground (Bakrania 2013; Murthy 2009; Shukla 2003). Complex identity politics, and intergenerational, class, caste and gender gaps are key themes in this literature. Falu Bakrania states that, within Bhangra, male DJs dominate with women only appearing as vocalists on various tracks and as Bhangra references folk styles, it is associated with the working class (2013, 6). Asian Underground, on the other hand, is more gender neutral and is associated with the middle classes because of its use of classical South Asian music (2013, 6). Bakrania's fieldwork was carried out in the late 1990s and 20 years later the 2018 British South Asian Alchemy festival – held in London's Southbank Centre – included a day of curated events by Shaanti, a British South Asian production company focusing on issues of inequality. The events showcased British South Asian female musicians, DJs and writers to promote gender equality and opportunities for women working in music. Such a focus on new creative projects by female musicians is timely.

Creativity is deeply intrinsic to Carnatic music. *Manodharma sangeetham*, or 'creative music' in Sanskrit, refers to the rule-bound improvisation in Carnatic music. Carnatic music is highly standardised – with musicians strictly following conventions of performance, instrumentation, the use of *raga* melodic frameworks, and standardised repertoire, and the style is surrounded by discourses of musical purity. Within Carnatic music scenes, 'fusion' often describes both a creative process and an emerging popular genre expanding beyond the rigid rules of *manodharma sangeetham,* as well as Carnatic music more broadly, which incorporates individual creative ideas, popular music and explicit non-South Asian or 'global' musical influences. 'Fusion' is contested, however; hence the term 'new creativity' is used in this article to refer to individual, non-Carnatic creative processes, i.e. creative processes informed by the music that is heard on an everyday basis – through Carnatic music lessons, on the radio, in the temple – and appropriated in various, 'non-rule based' ways by the musicians. 'New creativity' is thereby distinguished from the established creative concept of *manodharma sangeetam* and opens up to broader ideas of creative transformations.

Carnatic music in London

Seetal Kaur's observation that the story of British Tamils is often hidden is reflected in my extensive fieldwork in London with the Tamil diaspora. Tamil cultural events, such as concerts by world-class Carnatic music artists, take place in temples, school halls and suburban theatres, and they are often promoted only within Tamil diasporic networks and in the Tamil language. As the island nation went through severe ethnic tensions throughout the twentieth century, Tamil cultural nationalism was consolidated and symbolised by the practice of the Tamil language, Carnatic music, *bharatanatyam* dance and Hindu religion. Many of Sri Lanka's Tamils looked to India for solidarity. India was referred to as 'Mother India' in Tamil Sri Lanka and as an ethno-linguistic, spiritual and cultural home (Russell 1982, 136). Chennai, the capital of Tamil Nadu, became a significant centre of Tamil politics, culture and music from the early twentieth century onwards (see Daniel 1996; Reed 2010; Wilson 2011), and many aspiring Sri Lankan Tamil musicians studied music there. Mass forced migration from Sri Lanka took place after the devastating anti-Tamil riots of July 1983, which resulted in civil war, and lasted until May 2009. The forced migration created a highly-dispersed diaspora, stretching from India, Southeast Asia, Australia and North America to the U.K. and other European nations, which has been active in establishing cultural and religious organisations. Forced migratory experiences resulted in a strong desire to upkeep Tamil community cohesion. Through music and other cultural practices, my research participants have explained that this is a way of 'becoming one again' after the 'scattering' of Tamil migration; diasporic gatherings are facilitated by common cultural practices performed concurrently in multiple locations around the world (see Hornabrook 2017).

While Carnatic music and *bharatanatyam* dance were significant cultural markers in twentieth-century Sri Lanka, many of the first generation in the U.K. were unable to learn or complete their training due to the troubles on the island. The second generation is encouraged to connect to their Tamil heritage through participation in Tamil supplementary schools, where many study Tamil language, Carnatic music, *bharatanatyam* dance and Saiva Hinduism. As a result, there is a significant generational gap between the first and second generation in terms of musical and dance education and experiences of learning and performance. Carnatic music pedagogy in the U.K. is based on the same

500-year-old learning system that is used in India, Sri Lanka and in other diasporic sites. Purandara Dāsa (1484–1564) composed graded musical exercises to teach Carnatic music and these exercises form the basis of musical tuition today. Young students are trained primarily through lessons from the 'blue book', a series of foundational exercises and basic songs designed to combine *tala* rhythmic cycles, *raga* and ornamentation, and lyrics (Panchapakesa Iyer 2008). The voice or instrumental style is trained to acquire the 'correct' sound through *varishais*, sequences for singing/playing in rhythm, cultivating ornamentation and extending vocal range, and *swaram,* composed syllabic passages, often in the seven-note Carnatic *raga* mayamalavakoulai. Over time, these exercises shape the voice and/or playing style so that there is a flow between each note, rather than accenting each individual step of the *raga*. Students progress to sing or play compositions, such as *Geethanams, Varnams* and *Kirthanams,* in various *raga* and *talam* and often in line with the graded syllabus of exam boards such as Oriental Examination Board London, Oriental Fine Arts Academy of London and Academy of Fine Arts (London). Musical skill is developed throughout the student's musical education, through such exercises, graded songs, and imitation of the *guru*'s singing or playing, with *gamakas,* or ornaments, integral in achieving the correct sound and aesthetic. Sarma observes that learning Carnatic music in the U.K. was not just about learning the musical system and style, it was a way that parents hoped would impart elements of Tamil culture:

> So that means I don't just learn sa ri ga ma pa dha ni sa. I learn what to wear, I learn how to respect my instrument, I learn how to act around my instrument, how I should act when I perform, what I should do, how I should perform my repertoire, what starts, what ends, my religious beliefs are based around my compositions or how I devote which song to which god at which time during the performance, so you learn it as a whole kind of package of culture, tradition, religion and everything else. I don't think there's anything wrong with it but it is kind of what we're fed and we're actually conditioned in a certain way we think 'Carnatic music' (Mithila Sarma, personal communication, November 2016).

As Sarma suggests, Carnatic music became an integral part of a constructed and essentialised Tamil diasporic culture passed onto the second generation, reflecting Sri Lankan Tamil cultural nationalism during the twentieth century. As a result, musical participation is fairly balanced between male and female students, although gender divisions do remain for certain practices and instruments. For instance, very few female students learn the *mridangam* double-headed barrel drum and few male students learn the *veena*. The violin, flute and vocal tuition is balanced in terms of gender participation, whilst *bharatnatyam* dance is predominantly learned by female students.

A significant, although voluntary, part of the learning process in the U.K. is the performance of an *arangetram* – a lavish debut performance ceremony consisting of the student's first full concert accompanied by professional musicians and symbolising the beginning of a young musician's career. *Arangetrams* are often regarded as graduation ceremonies in diasporic contexts, and it is quite rare that the student pursues their musical career, despite having performed a ceremony that costs their family tens of thousands of pounds. Unlike dance *arangetrams,* music *arangetrams* are relatively balanced in terms of male and female participation. The dancer and scholar, Priya Srinivasan refers to the dance *arangetram* in the United States as having a dual function: first, to teach 'young Indian American girls to become ideal Indian women cultural citizens' and, second, to demarcate difference in American multicultural discourse and society (2012,

142–43). The *arangetram* is a means of demarcating difference and asserting Tamil cultural identity in multicultural Britain, but the music *arangetram* does not emphasise the transition of British Sri Lankan girls into ideal South Asian women, as is the case of the dance ceremony in the U.S.A. Nevertheless, the high participation by London's Sri Lankan Tamil families in the *arangetram* symbolises a commitment to Tamil cultural continuity. A South-London-based music teacher told me that,

> In this country, this [the *arangetram*] is the one thing the Sri Lankans are doing [a lot] because of what we are missing. We are missing our part of the country, our culture … we are scared of losing our traditions, so we are unlimited in the way we are pushing our children. Our generation has lost a lot, education, wealth, independence, happiness, our aims; our life in a way. We had been living in our country, our land, we had to depart from that part of the country and make a new life, so we are scared of losing our culture (anon. personal communication)

The *arangetram* is also a significant marker in terms of the creative agency of young musicians. A prominent *veena* teacher in North London told me that the *arangetram* is the point at which the student gains the *guru*'s blessing to experiment musically. She said the *arangetram* symbolised the completion of her student's training with her; therefore, she gives her blessing to them to experiment with their performance style (personal communication, October 2012). The *arangetram* is widely performed by second-generation musicians, including the two musicians I refer to in the examples later, and is thus a significant part of the pedagogic process towards forging a new creativity.

The *arangetram* ceremony originates from the female temple artisans, or *devadasis,* who were custodians of music and dance and intrinsic to ritual worship in the temples of South India. Under colonial rule, *devadasis* were considered immoral and regarded as prostitutes as they were financially supported by wealthy patrons and therefore contrary to ideas of morality and female respectability in society and in music (Subramanian 2006, 120–21). The *devadasi* act of 1947 was brought in to abolish the artisan – patronage system. With this, the original custodians of the classical arts were eliminated under colonial rule. Music and dance were re-introduced as the recreations of urban middle-class Brahmin girls to enhance matrimonial potential and display ideals of South Asian femininity.

Carnatic music has a long history, from its origins in the Sanskrit Vedas and the Tamil *pannisai* music system to its current presence in South Asian diasporic culture, yet it was deeply impacted by British colonialism. Partha Chatterjee (1993) argues that there were two domains of Indian nationalism in the face of British colonialism: the inner, or spiritual sphere, and the outer, material, sphere. The spiritual sphere represents the inner self and the social space of the home, 'imagined to be India's uncolonized interior' (Weidman 2006, 146), while the material sphere reflects the world, the outer self and the direct influence from colonialism. Therefore, the material elements of 'modern Western civilization' were combined with the distinct 'spiritual essence of the national culture' (Chatterjee 1989, 623–24) to create a 'modern' India while retaining its spiritual core. These worlds placed women within the inner, spiritual domain and ideals of femininity positioned women to uphold the inner sphere of Indian culture as the 'bearers of tradition', and as Falu Bakrania states, their 'performance of femininity [w]as equivalent to national survival' (2013, 17). The practice of Carnatic music and *bharatanatyam* dance by middle-class Brahmin girls and women was a significant part of this performance of femininity and bearing of tradition. Lakshmi Subramanian argues that Carnatic music lay at the heart of Indian sovereignty that was not open to any negotiation or compromise in the twentieth century (2006, 17). Despite being placed within the inner, spiritual sphere of the Indian nation, contemporary Carnatic music reveals deep colonial influences. With colonial administration, Carnatic music underwent urbanisation moving from the temples and courts of Tanjore to the Brahmin-dominated music institutions of Madras, now Chennai. Subsequently, Carnatic music was consolidated as a classical genre, to stand as an Indian equivalent to the classical music of Europe. This consolidation project included the emphasis on written sargam notation, the concert hall performance format and refining and standardising repertoire (Subramanian 2006, 84), notably through the hailed institution of the Madras Music Academy. Carnatic music has retained the characteristics it acquired during the colonial era in South India's and Sri Lanka's postcolonial diasporas.

In her book *The Singer and the Song*, C. S. Lakshmi and her female Carnatic musician interviewees note how their gender has created limitations in their artistic careers (2000). A number of the interviewees remain active in the South Indian music scene in India and around the world and a number of high-profile female artists speak about continued gender inequality in Indian media. The next section looks at two lasting aspects of the Indian nationalist project on Carnatic music and gender, and how these are being challenged in the diasporic South Indian music scene, before moving onto two detailed examples of new creativity in Carnatic music by Mithila Sarma and Abi Sampa.

The voice, devotion and ideal femininity

The voice, in particular, was impacted by the Indian nationalist project. Symbolising 'authenticity' and 'Indianness', the voice is central in Carnatic music with melodic instruments, particularly the European violin, introduced during the colonial era, emanating a vocal quality in their performance. Amanda Weidman suggests the contemporary Carnatic vocal style is a 'distinctly modern and postcolonial desire' to create a 'natural and authentic' Indian sound, and that it is 'a metaphor for a tradition and a self that have survived colonialism' (2006, 57). She suggests that during the twentieth century it was not just a certain kind of voice that was valued, but the voice itself, 'identified with chaste womanly behaviour, [which] came to be privileged as karnatic music's locus of authenticity' (Weidman 2003, 195). This voice was encapsulated by M. S. Subbulakshmi, who was from a Devadasi family but showed the domesticity, 'sublime devotion' and Indian womanhood desired by Indian nationalism. The naturalness and beauty of the voice conveys the emotion of *bhakti* divine devotion and was gendered as female, reflecting gendered notions of sublimity and beauty from Euro-America (Weidman 2003, 208). Revered as the Nightingale of India, M. S. Subbulakshmi is known for her rendering of Carnatic and devotional repertoire, her focused performance as *bhakti* devotion, her traditional attire and her seamless, ornamented vocal performance. In her performance of 'Nagu-momu Kanaleni' by the eighteenth-century saint-composer, Thyagaraja, Subbulakshmi sings through the song in her highly-ornamented style in the piece's *raga* abheri, without deviation from the *raga* or the melodic character of the song (see M. S. Subbulakshmi 2008). Subbulakshmi's voice is accompanied by her female students, the violin, the *mridangam* drum and *ghatam* clay drum.

M. S. Subbulakshmi represented 'Indian womanhood' and domesticity: as a housewife who made flower garlands for the pooja room and knew nothing but music (Weidman 2003, 136). It is interesting to note, however, that M. S. Subbulakshmi came from the exact *devadasi* community of music and dance custodians that were so-called immoral and ostracised during colonial rule. There has been recent controversy within Carnatic music circles when the Carnatic vocalist and social activist, T. M. Krishna, publicly questioned whether M. S. Subbulakshmi's voice would have been regarded in the same way had she not behaved as a Brahmin woman, marrying a Brahmin man and fulfilling the constructed ideals of South Asian femininity (*Deccan Chronicle*, no author given, 2017). Krishna's questions were received with outrage on the most part, but some readers concurred and suggested that such questions are significant for the challenge of gender and caste inequality in Carnatic music. Priya Srinivasan has also brought M. S. Subbulakshmi's background to the fore in her piece 'Becoming Subbulakshmi', a 'talking dance' which positions archival recordings of Subbulakshmi's voice with the history of her background, problematising the discrimination of *devadasis* in direct relation to the celebration of Subbulakshmi's voice (Srinivasan 2016).

As part of the concepts of 'Indian womanhood' and 'female respectability', female artists were expected to show divine rather than human love; therefore, their performance should show restrained devotion, rather than demonstrate *sringara rasa* – erotic sentiment, sensual experience, or raw passion. This ideal has been challenged by the experimental singer and composer, Susheela Raman. She uses the Carnatic and Tamil devotional songs she learned growing up in a South Indian family in the U.K. and in Australia in experimental arrangements, and in doing so, she veers away from ideas of South Asian femininity and restrained devotional demeanour. Raman's arrangements of Carnatic songs demonstrate new creativity as she fuses and transforms the pieces far beyond the rule-bound practice of *manodharma sangeetham*. Her performance is controversial amongst the Carnatic music scene because of her unconventional pronunciation and treatment of *raga*, her non-South Indian vocal style and her highly passionate on-stage performance. Provoking a great deal of response, a number of South Indian music enthusiasts credit Raman for her adaptation and spread of Carnatic compositions to a broad audience on the one hand.[1] On the other, her arrangements of Carnatic music and her on-stage movement have come under great scrutiny from some Hindu devotees and *rasika* music lovers. While Raman's style divides the crowd in London's music scene, even amongst the second generation, it demonstrates the highly emotive responses to her creative treatment of Carnatic music, which are based on her being a female artist.

Limits of musical creativity

The esteemed female vocalist, D. K. Pattamal, performed highly virtuosic forms in the face of male occupancy of the Carnatic music scene in the twentieth century. Despite her reverence, she was subjected to 'unjust opposition' as she sang the *pallavi* form and virtuosic *kalpana swaram* – improvised passages using the solfège sargam notes – that were considered male territories. She suggested that many male musicians would not accompany female musicians as 'certain territories are sacrosanct and women must not enter them', while others held the opinion that '[w]omen have sweet mellifluous voices. Let them sing ragas and *kirthanas* and *padams*. Why do the ladies trouble their pretty little heads over things like *kalpana svaras*, which require brainwork!' (D. K. Pattammal cited in Lakshmi, 2000, xxxii). Musically, female artists were not supposed to imitate the creativity and virtuosity of male musicians in concerts but instead to perform *raga alapana*, semi-classical and classical compositions without the virtuosic, complex improvisation that has come to characterise Carnatic music (Weidman 2003, 215). According to this discourse, the extended and competitive *ragam thanam pallavi* form should not be performed by female artists as it is a display of technique and skill. This is largely disregarded by female artists in Chennai now but Weidman argues this musical 'uneventfulness' is part of the aesthetic production; 'nothing out of the ordinary is supposed to happen' (2006, 135). While many high-profile female Carnatic musicians demonstrate great virtuosity and inventiveness, their performances, gestures and on-stage personas are often distinct from the extravagant performances of male artists such as Sanjay Subramaniam, the Mysore Brothers and Shashank Subramanyam.

The London-based organisation Raga Room challenges the conception of non-virtuosic musicality of female artists and British-trained performers more generally, as well as the concert hall context developed in colonial India and is highly innovative in the U.K.'s South Indian music scene. An online concert platform developed by second-generation violinist, Kiruthika Nadarajah, Raga Room is a digital concert series for full-length Carnatic performances by musicians who have learned in diasporic settings (see Raga Room 2018). The concerts are performed at the organiser's house and are broadcast live over YouTube. The platform was crowdfunded in order to give opportunities to musicians to perform full-length Carnatic concerts, including extended forms such as the *Ragam Thanam Pallavi*. After seven broadcasted concerts and one live performance at the South-bank Centre, more female musicians performed the *Ragam Thanam Pallavi* than their male counterparts. The organiser felt that these extended forms, that require high levels of *manodharma sangeetham*, are not prioritised in diasporic performances and so Raga Room provides a space for ambitious second-generation musicians to demonstrate their technical ability, including Kiruthika's own. The *Ragam Thanam Pallavi* form is performed during a music *arangetram* ceremony in London; however, it is widely understood that the music teacher has pre-composed the supposedly improvised variations of the *pallavi* and *swara* passages performed by the music student.

In an increasingly globalised India, Chris Fuller and Haripriya Narasimhan suggest that Chennai's attraction lies in 'its perceived traditionalism, most evident in religion and cultural activity' and in its association as India's 'cultural capital' in the face of cities such as Bangalore and Mumbai, which exude modernity and Westernisation (2014, 163). The musicians discussed here are not based in Chennai; however, strong connections are maintained between diasporic music scenes and the South Indian city. Many continue to receive music lessons from eminent *gurus* in Chennai through annual visits to the city and through online Skype lessons. Through such tuition, migration and the Internet, ideals perpetuated from the Chennai Carnatic music scene are spread, and even challenged in diasporic settings.

New creativity in diasporic settings

To demonstrate new creativity among female musicians, the following discussion focuses on musical examples by two British-Sri Lankan Tamil musicians, both of whom have a

Carnatic musical education having learned to sing and play the *veena*. Both Mithila Sarma and Abi Sampa use their musical foundations in Carnatic music to break into the mainstream music scene whilst also engaging with community-based scenes and the Tamil independent music scene as well as the British Asian music scene. While also highly engaged with the Carnatic musical system and style, the musicians reveal virtuosity, individuality and new creativity. These examples are prominent in the music scene and distinctive in both approach and contribution to female creativity and performance. Sampa's use of Carnatic music is demonstrated in her cultivation of an idiosyncratic popular style that challenges feminine ideals more implicitly through the medium of performance and composition. Sarma's approach is more explicit; she actively seeks to challenge traditions and social issues through creative musical collaboration, composition and performance.

Mithila Sarma and Subduction Zone

The first example, the music and dance production, 'Subduction Zone' by Mithila Sarma, tells the story of growing up in British Tamil culture. 'Subduction Zone' was distinct from the Carnatic concerts organised by the first generation, often in suburban theatres or in temple halls around the capital. The foyer outside the performance space in the East London art centre, Rich Mix, was full of mostly second-generation British-South Asian young adults, aged in their twenties and thirties. The bar was doing good business, and once the doors opened to the performance space, the crowd sat on tiered seating, facing a space with instruments lining the perimeter. Sarma is rare in London's Tamil diaspora in that she makes a living within the arts; many Tamil children are encouraged to pursue careers in medicine, engineering, law or economics while keeping music as a semi-profession or a hobby. Sarma is an active performer, composer and collaborator with artistic directing experience at zerOclassikal – a project developing innovative composition in British South Asian music – and she works at Arts Council England. She is currently receiving tuition from the eminent artist and *guru*, Padmavathy Anandagopalan, in Chennai in order to strengthen her classical technique. Sarma has not had formal music education in any other system, so her new creativity is largely based on her knowledge of the Carnatic music system. She has also been inspired by her involvement with the South Asian Music Youth Orchestra (SAMYO) and Tarang – unique ensembles with musical arrangements reflecting the diversity of South Asian diasporic cultures in the U.K. In an interview, Sarma told me: 'there's no clear direction as to how it all happens [the creative process] … when I think about it [the music], I'm thinking ragams, like 'what ragam is going to go well with this piece'. This scene is perfect for *alairuppu* [dance], I'm going to play this *thirupukkal* beneath it' (personal communication, November 2016). Following experimental Carnatic vocalist, O. S. Arun's model, Sarma gives the example of her thought process behind a scene based on East London life in which she pairs an *alairuppu* (an invocatory dance piece) with a *thirupukkal* (a Tamil devotional temple song for the God Murugan). With both the dance and the song being rhythmic in character, based on complex metres, and mutual in their invocatory and devotional function, the pieces are often paired in classical performances but are re-imagined in this diasporic context.

'Subduction Zone' was the result of a commission by Rich Mix, looking for works to address the social and political issues of East London through music, dance and theatre.

The name of the production gives an indication to both the themes tackled and the musical and dance content; the subduction zone being the place of the convergence and tension of two tectonic plates, with the potential coexistence of both or submergence of one of them over the other. These plates act as metaphors for competing cultural identities and internal conflict in this case, reflected in the musical and choreographed content. The production brought together Carnatic and Hindustani musicians, popular musicians and classical and street dancers, all of whom Sarma previously knew. Influenced by the male-dominated Asian Underground, by Nithin Sawhney and Talvin Singh, and by the American-Tamil singer Sid Sriram, Sarma not only creatively experiments with her Carnatic music background, she also explicitly addresses issues of sexism, feminism, human love and sex in her production through themed and choreographed dance and through a metaphorical choice of songs, contrary to the ideals of Indian nationalist femininity. Sarma also challenges ideas of the standardised concert format and concert rules in her performance, as well as attitudes towards traditional dress. In an interview, Sarma questioned why a *thillana* – a dance piece – has to come at the end of a concert and why she has to wear a sari when she plays Carnatic music (personal communication, November 2016). In Sarma's performance, these questions challenge bigger issues in the music scene through non-conformance to 'traditional' conventions, such as the concert format that came about as a result of colonial influence and representations of sari-clad women.

Carnatic repertoire (which overlaps with Tamil repertoire in complex and contested ways), *raga* melodic frameworks, *talam* beat-cycles, instrumentation and the Sanskrit, Telugu and Tamil languages were at the basis of the production. These musical elements were performed by an ensemble of *veena*, Carnatic voice and Euro-American popular voice (by the same female vocalist), live electronics and synths, cello, bass guitar, cajon, and *mridangam*. Along with the female voice, the *veena* was central to and foregrounded in this instrumentation, and it was used innovatively in building musical layers through ostinatos, chords and arpeggios. The *veena* was also used in its traditional role in *raga* melodic and improvisatory performance. Classical repertoire often heard in traditional concerts was recontextualised in 'Subduction Zone' to reveal the themes of Sarma's story. For example, the second piece, 'Day Break', starts with the *suprabhatam* prayer usually sung in temples to wake the deities, with a backing of the *shruti* drone and with the female dancer on-stage waking up in her East London home, getting ready, and leaving the house after being reminded to complete *pooja*. The piece segues into 'Dance class', where Thyagaraja's highly-classical and devotional composition, 'Entharo Mahanubhavulu', was used to reveal the story of growing up in London and attending classical dance and music classes. Other pieces based on Carnatic music repertory include 'Play Doll', based around Papanasam Sivan's devotional 'Naan Oru Vilayattu'. The song's lyrics ask the Mother Goddess Uma if the singer is a toy doll to her, but Sarma uses this to show the complexity of parental expectations and relationships. Performed in its original melodic form and style, the song is sung above a foundation of a sampled *veena* chord loop, synths and electronics. Further into the piece, a *veena* improvisation in *raga* navarasa kannada is superimposed onto this innovative foundation. The asymmetrical *raga* navarasa kannada is traditionally said to be particularly well suited to *veena* in Carnatic music and Sarma maintains the integrity of the *raga* in her performance, something which she believes cannot be compromised in experimental and 'fusion' arrangements (personal communication, November 2016).

The story featured a piece entitled 'Love', which focused on human, rather than devotional, love. The female voice sings Tamil poetry in the iconic South Indian vocal style, with the cello providing counter melodies over a *veena* ostinato recorded on a loop pedal. After the Tamil verse, Sarma plays a virtuosic solo *veena* improvisation in *raga* behag, an asymmetrical North Indian-derived *raga* associated with romance. The musical setting is combined with *bharatanatyam* and street dancing. While the recontextualisation of Carnatic music here is quite extreme in some ways, the music that is at the heart of the production is unmistakably grounded in the Carnatic music system, repertoire and stylistic delivery of *raga*. Sarma states that 'you stay classical, but you expand those boundaries' rather than claim these experiments are no longer considered as being Carnatic music (personal communication, November 2016). While 'Subduction Zone' was not approached as a classical production, Sarma says that difficulties with the reception of such projects arise when traditional customs surrounding Carnatic music and its performance are challenged:

> Classical [music] for them is traditional, and then once you break tradition it's no longer classical. That's what it is, splitting the words traditional and classical ... classical music is literally what we learn when we grow up, it's got set rules, it's got set characteristics, I'm not talking about performance structure or anything like that, I'm talking from a basic 7 notes ... and you have your 72 melakarta ragas, you've got hundreds of ragas from it, you've got your compositions, you've got your varnams, keerthanams, your swarams. I think that's basically it. For me, its raga and tala, that is what classical music is (personal communication, November 2016).

Sarma argues that it is the musical system, not the performance conventions or instrumentation that determines Carnatic music, and therefore breaking such conventions while maintaining the musical rules of Carnatic music retains its classical aesthetic. This shift in Carnatic music is grounded in the British Asian classical music scene, in finding relevant and accessible means to perform the music to broad audiences, including the large second-generation demographic.

Abi Sampa and *Raag'n'Blues*

The second example is 'Raag'n'Blues' by Abi Sampa. Although her main profession is not within the arts, she regularly performs in various collaborations in venues across the U.K., including London's Rich Mix and Southbank Centre, and on the B.B.C. Asian Network radio station; and she posts her latest musical experiments on social media. Sampa's virtuosic musical style of combining Euro-American songs with her Carnatic music background was revealed to the mainstream with her participation in the B.B.C. broadcast of 'The Voice U.K.' singing competition in 2013. For instance, she uses *raga alapana* – improvisatory unfoldings of a *raga* – as short extemporisations before the start of Euro-American popular songs, such as Oasis' 'Stop Crying your Heart Out' (see BBC 2013), and features the integration of Carnatic *gamaka* ornaments in pop-style melismas and virtuosic *kalpana swaram* solfège passages in bridge sections. Her current projects involve her voice, electric *veena* and harmonium with her band, blending influences of Qawwali, Carnatic and Euro-American popular music. There is a fluidity between the combination of popular song, Carnatic music and the associated stylistic characteristics resulting from Sampa's Carnatic musical education and her listening to Euro-American popular styles while growing up in London. In a similar way, Sarma says her work is 'an amalgamation of everything I have ever listened to and everything I enjoy listening to' (personal communication, November 2016).

Sampa's 'Raag'n'Blues' is a version of Thyagaraja's 'Nagumomu Kanaleni', a virtuosic and newly creative display of the staple Carnatic song. This version is distinct from M. S. Subbulakshmi's rendition described above. The performance of this piece is captured on a video clip posted on Sampa's artist Facebook page, as part of an ongoing series of experimental improvisations and arrangements on the electric *veena*. The video is self-recorded at the artist's house, with the backdrop of her belongings rather than a stage or religious shrine, as is often the case with *veena* performance. This is a solo *veena* performance in Sampa's home, reminiscent of the domesticity of middle-class female *veena* players of the mid-twentieth century. While the video is filmed and posted from her home, Sampa's 'Raag'n'Blues' video received 4.1 million views, with comments on the performance from international followers (see Sampa 2017). In contrast to the colourful silk sari and plaited hair which consist of the usual attire for a female musician playing the *veena* in Tamil community-based performances and Carnatic concerts, Sampa wears black skinny jeans, a navy shoulder-less top, socks, and her hair is untied. Sampa plays 'Nagumomu' on the electric *veena* with a distorted and delayed sound effect through a Marshall guitar amp. Over an ostinato that Sampa pre-recorded on the *veena* and then looped via a loop pedal, Sampa plays the piece's *pallavi* thematic line which is then varied through improvisation. Importantly, and as in much of Sarma's music, there is no *shruti* drone which is otherwise considered as a fundamental of Carnatic musical performance as a point of reference and return. Instead, the ostinato loop functions as the foundation of the piece. Unlike M. S. Subbulakshmi's rendition, Sampa's version of 'Nagumomu' is a solo performance; there is no accompanying violin, *mridangam* or *ghatam*. The video audibly and visually places Sampa in the foreground of the performance.

Sampa plays in the song's original *raga* abheri (Sa, Ga2, Ma1, Pa, Ni2, Sa, Sa Ni2, Dha2, Pa, Ma1, Ga2, Ri2, Sa). *Raga* abheri's *arohana* ascending scale is the same as the minor pentatonic 'blues' scale. Linking the soundworlds of Carnatic music and iconic blues improvisation heard in blues, jazz and various Euro-American popular styles, the overall tone of the *veena* sounds like a solo electric guitar with the characteristic *gamaka* ornaments and treatment of *raga* abheri. Sampa makes use of the blues scale within *raga* abheri, adding some additional 'blues' licks and blues notes, such as the Ma2 in several places and thus completing the full hexatonic blues scale (see the circled notes in Figure 1). The transcription below (Figure 1) shows up to half way through the performance (from 0'00" to 0'59"), showing three distinct sections: first, the blues style '*alapana*' of *raga* abheri (playing only the 'blues scale' *arohana* notes); second, the recitation of the song's main *pallavi* theme which adheres fully to *raga* abheri; and third, the development of the *pallavi* theme into the improvisation based again on only the notes of the 'blues' scale *arohana*.

One of Sampa's Facebook followers referred to this piece as 'veena shredding', linking the ancient Carnatic instrument to the male-dominated practice of rock guitar playing. While the response to the piece was largely positive, some Carnatic musicians and listeners were upset by Sampa's treatment of *raga* abheri and her inclusion of blues, or 'western', notes (Ma2). Such sentiments were expressed even though abheri is considered a '*bhasanga raga*', so that it may include an additional note that is not in its parent scale. Her

Figure 1. A transcribed excerpt in sargam and stave notation from 'Raag'n'Blues'. The transcription places Sa as F# as in the original video. The sargam notation here refers to *raga* abheri (*arohana* ascending, Sa, Ga2, Ma1, Pa, Ni2, Sa, and *avarohana* descending, Sa Ni2, Dha2, Pa, Ma1, Ga2, Ri2, Sa).

clothing also provoked comments, particularly on her wearing socks and non-conformance to the 'Hindu culture of the *veena*': the instrument is strongly associated with Goddess Saraswati and, therefore, with ideals of South Asian feminine appearance. This response, however, reveals ongoing tensions between newly creative treatment of Carnatic music in London and the Carnatic music scene, particularly in Chennai, and ongoing attitudes that emerged during colonialism.

Conclusion

The examples discussed above show female musicians working within and referencing their Carnatic music education, retaining an 'Indian' sound and appropriating Euro-American styles into their new creative projects. Their creative processes show a shift from an aesthetic that was responsive to colonialism in India to highlight the everyday sounds in Britain that influence them. They highlight issues of cultural hybridity in a diasporic community that uses Carnatic music to portray an essentialist sense of Tamil identity. The Carnatic music system, repertoire and style are at the foundation of the work, suggesting that these female artists retain a certain role as 'bearers of tradition'. They are, however, at the forefront of exploring a broader, unrestricted creative practice within the Carnatic music system in relation to expanding its use, and reaching out to become established as artists within London's global music scene.

Bakrania suggests that 'a woman who becomes too British risks being seen by her community as not only inauthentic but also traitorous' (2013, 167). Responses by more conservative Carnatic musicians suggest that new creative projects are considered 'inauthentic' or even 'traitorous'; or, as Sarma suggests, no longer classical if the surrounding traditions are broken. Within London's Tamil diasporic community, these artists have received largely positive responses as their projects are based on a Carnatic music education and maintain connections with the broader Tamil diaspora, particularly the second-generation. Through their experimental styles, these artists challenge ideals of South Asian femininity and break away from rigid notions of the Carnatic music aesthetic.

These musicians represent their senses of British Tamil identities and their creativity reflects cultural hybridity. Their shifts from conventional Carnatic style also shows how they are highly empowered female musicians, a gendered dimension of decolonising processes. Their individual creative processes reflect broader social and cultural movements; postcolonial migration and diasporas, the transnational dimensions of musical practices, the acknowledgement of 'home' as a myriad, complex concept, shifts in gender roles, and current challenges to gender inequality.

In her work on diasporic musical performance in the U.K., Tina K. Ramnarine emphasises that looking at everyday creative decision-making can reveal intricacies beyond population movements, resettlement and culture contact in order to move towards politically articulated readings of social relations and creative processes (2007, 7). Female performance practices are changing to an extent in South India too and these resonate with those in London. New creative projects by female artists in both contexts can be read as revealing distinctly feminist acts of creativity. These acts challenge gender roles, ethnonational identities and cultural expectations. These artists are, therefore, contributing to creative music-making practices in the decolonising era by reconfiguring gender issues in Carnatic music, with the potential for forging new directions in creative expression.

Note

1. YouTube comments on Raman's videos include: 'a new revolution in Tamil devotional songs' (Karthikmein), 'New era for Tamil devotional songs, no words Susheela!!! simply great!!! just do more!!!' (Kayan Velauhtam), 'a very special voice and style. It will take some more years to appreciate her style since in Chennai people are orthodox and conservative. Well done madam' (Thygarajan Srinivasan), 'This is a real prostitution of a noble Karnatic music. Never heard [raga] Shanmukhapriya has been so distorted. Many of the lines are totally out of pitch! God save music from these people' (Jayaprakash Panicker).

Disclosure statement

No potential conflict of interest was reported by the author.

ORCID

Jasmine Hornabrook ⓘ http://orcid.org/0000-0003-0662-9822

References

"Art, Culture Should Help Us De-baggage Our Identities, Says TM Krishna." 2017. *Deccan Chronicle*, November 25, 2017. Accessed September 12, 2018. https://www.deccanchronicle.com/entertainment/music/251117/art-culture-should-help-us-de-baggage-our-identities-says-tm-krishna.html.

Bakrania, Falu P. 2013. *Bhangra and Asian Underground: South Asian Music and the Politics of Belonging in Britain*. Durham: Duke University Press.

BBC. 2013. "The Voice UK 2013 | Abi Sampa Performs 'Stop Crying Your Heart Out' – Blind Auditions 6 – BBC One." Accessed September 12, 2018. https://youtu.be/XqZ6y60ZVNk.

Chatterjee, Partha. 1989. "Colonialism, Nationalism, and Colonialized Women: The Contest in India." *American Ethnologist* 16 (4): 622–633.

Chatterjee, Partha. 1993. *The Nation and Its Fragments: Colonial and Postcolonial Histories*. Princeton, NJ: Princeton University Press.

Daniel, E. Valentine. 1996. *Charred Lullabies: Chapters in an Anthropography of Violence*. Princeton, NJ: Princeton University Press.

Fuller, C. J., and H. Narasimhan. 2014. *Tamil Brahmans: The Making of a Middle-Class Caste*. Chicago: University of Chicago Press.

Hornabrook, Jasmine. 2017. "South Indian Singing, Digital Dissemination and Belonging in London's Tamil Diaspora". *Journal of Interdisciplinary Voice Studies* 2 (2): 119–136.

Kaur, Seetal. 2016. "Review of Subduction Zone." *Pulse*. Winter 2016, 22.

Lakshmi, C. S. 2000. *The Singer and the Song: Conversations with Women Musicians*. New Delhi: Kali for Women.

M. S. Subbulakshmi (uploaded by dartdisah). 2008. "Nagumomu Kanaleni (Abheri)." Accessed September 12, 2018. https://youtu.be/TmZ5U9SfDNk

Murthy, Dhiraj. 2009. "Representing South Asian Alterity? East London's Asian Electronic Music Scene and the Articulation of Globally Mediated Identities." *European Journal of Cultural Studies* 12 (3): 329–348.

Panchapakesa Iyer, A. S. 2008. *Gānāmrutha Bōdhini: Sangeetha Bāla Pādam.* Chennai: Gānāmrutha Prachuram.

Raga Room. 2018. Accessed September 12, 2018. https://www.youtube.com/channel/UCgra7S3AAdoM2Sa9Nj32HKA.

Ramnarine, Tina K. 2007. "Musical Performance in the Diaspora: Introduction." *Ethnomusicology Forum* 16 (1): 1–18.

Reed, Susan A. 2010. *Dance and the Nation: Performance, Ritual, and Politics in Sri Lanka.* Madison: University of Wisconsin Press.

Russell, Jane. 1982. *Communal Politics under the Donoughmore Constitution 1931–1947.* Dehiwala: Tisara Prakasakayo.

Sampa, Abi. 2017. "Raag'n'Blues." Accessed September 12, 2018. https://www.facebook.com/AbiSampa/videos/808353182676137/.

Shukla, Sandhya R. 2003. *India Abroad: Diasporic Cultures of Postwar America and England.* Princeton, NJ: Princeton University Press.

Srinivasan, P. 2012. *Sweating Saris: Indian Dance as Transnational Labor.* Philadelphia: Temple University Press.

Srinivasan, P. 2016. "Becoming Subbulakshmi by Dr Priya Srinivasan – performance based research." Accessed September 12, 2018. https://vimeo.com/235829956.

Subramanian, Lakshmi. 2006. *From the Tanjore Court to the Madras Music Academy: A Social History of Music in South India.* New Delhi: Oxford University Press.

Weidman, Amanda J. 2003. "Gender and the Politics of Voice: Colonial Modernity and Classical Music in South India." *Cultural Anthropology* 18 (2): 194–232.

Weidman, Amanda J. 2006. *Singing the Classical, Voicing the Modern: The Postcolonial Politics of Music in South India.* Durham and London: Duke University Press.

Wilson, A. Jeyaratnam. 2011. "Language, Poetry, Culture, and Tamil Nationalism." In *The Sri Lanka Reader: History, Culture, Politics,* edited by John C. Holt, 459–470. Durham and London: Duke University Press.

Decolonising moves: gestures of reciprocity as feminist intercultural performance

Priya Srinivasan

ABSTRACT
In this article, I think through decolonisation from the place of praxis and cultural artistic exchange in Global South-South encounters. I base my thinking on the concepts of 'neighbouring' by the Argentine theorist, [Savigliano, M. 2009. "Worlding Dance and Dancing Out there in the World." In *Rethinking World Dance Histories*, edited by Susan Foster, 163–191. New York: Palgrave.] and 'the gift' by the French sociologist, [Mauss, M. 2011. *The Gift: Forms and Functions of Exchange in Archaic Societies*. London: Martino Fine Books.]. The paradox of being a 'good neighbour' or 'friend', lies in its offers of help and its implicit demands for a reciprocal counter-gesture. I work with the Melbourne based carnatic singer Uthra Vijay in a dialogic (auto) ethnography that explores our ongoing performance and collaboration since 2016, including our friendship and how we 'neighbour' with various intercultural partners including our ongoing work with Indigenous partners in Australia.

In this article, I think through decolonisation from the place of praxis and cultural artistic exchange. I base my thinking on the concepts of 'neighbouring' by the Argentine theorist, Savigliano (2009) and 'the gift' by the French sociologist, Mauss (2011).[1] I argue that the paradox of being a 'good neighbour' or 'friend' lies in its offers of help and its implicit demands for a reciprocal counter-gesture through the gift, which can be accessed through the intersubjective encounter. While Mauss questions what power lies with the gift that causes its recipient to pay it back, I am interested in attending to feminist praxis in the shared collaborative space of performance where gifts are not products but practices that are constantly shared and being circulated simultaneously. Savigliano's notion of 'neighbouring' as a verb enables the understanding of entanglement of bodies in proximity and in permanent negotiation in encountering others. I use this concept to understand relationships in performance that are based on decisions that are constantly shifting and moving. I work with the Melbourne based carnatic singer Uthra Vijay in a dialogic (auto) ethnography[2] that explores our ongoing performance and collaboration since 2016 including our friendship, how we work together and 'neighbour' with various intercultural partners. I discuss the contradictions of our double histories of colonisation (India and Australia) through our respective performance practices of Indian music and dance. We work towards decolonising our performances, specifically through the nationalist, postcolonial and so called 'traditional' forms we have been trained in (carnatic music for Uthra and my training in Bharatanatyam, a classical dance genre and experimental choreography). We use feminist praxis and performative tools that are both intra- and inter-cultural drawing on subaltern women's voices, texts and subjectivities, including the figure of the hereditary dancer (*devadasi*) as our locus of engagement. Having performed in Australia and several international venues including site specific works in museums, theatres, galleries, and universities[3] and with a host of collaborators from Indigenous Australian, Spanish, Suriname-Dutch, Iranian, Chilean, German-Yiddish, Sri Lankan and Indian artists from UK, USA, India and elsewhere, we have personal experiences of the inherent contradictions and difficulties of this kind of performance work, as well as the utopic possibilities that emerge between women artists who bring together music and movement as a decolonising encounter.

As Harrison (1997) in her remarkable work over twenty years ago proposed, a decolonising praxis would necessitate women of colour to engage with each other without mediation via a white centre. Epistemological beliefs that allow for alternate genealogies of time, the body, space and identity have to be evaluated carefully in negotiating decolonising encounters. For this article, I focus on two encounters. The first is the ongoing intra-cultural collaboration between Uthra Vijay and me since 2016 within which we explore issues facing Indian women through our art forms by unearthing subaltern Tamil female poets, *devadasis* (hereditary female dancers and musicians) and hidden archives present in our Indian forms. The second is the project that premiered in Melbourne in December 2017: 'Serpent Dreaming Women' involving Indian Diaspora/Indian/ Indigenous Australian artists, and which works on understanding ancient and contemporary concerns around water and climate crises through a cosmological exchange between two old cultures sharing common histories and cultural practices such as India and Indigenous Australia.

The method of practice as research has yielded complex alternate visions for intercultural exchange and dialogue. In order to better understand the intersubjective encounter, I focus on embodiment and language, as well as attending keenly to the dialogic encounter between differentially colonised peoples (Indian or Indigenous Australian) and global south feminist ethnography approaches (Mohanty 1996; Narayan 1997). These are illustrated in Part 2, in particular, in investigating 'Serpent Dreaming Women.'

Part 1: talking dance/ singing movement

This section focuses on the partnership and intra-cultural collaboration between singer and composer Uthra Vijay and I as we play with time, texts, movement and ragas.[4] Intrinsic to Indian performance is the intimate relationship between music and dance, and between musicians and dancers. Hereditary artists, for example from the community, *Isai vellalar* (the caste from which many of the *devadasi* community of women and men came) passed on their performance traditions through oral transmission and embodied practices via matrilineal descent in South India. Women known as devadasis undertook a range of cultural work including court and temple dancing. They were present during births, deaths and special life ceremonies as domestic ritual workers. Many were married to a deity of the temple in the town they lived and yet they had human lovers.

They were viewed as ritual workers called '*Nityasumangalis*' – the women who were forever auspicious (because they were married to God so their husband could never die; see Kersenboom 1987). Many of them were the only literate women of their time and could sing, dance, read and write in multiple languages; essentially they were scholar-artists par excellence. The doubleness of their roles as wives of the Gods yet with human lovers (being in non conjugal relationships) became the issue for British law-makers, missionaries and others because the devadasi could only be understood within Victorian concepts of the 'virgin versus the whore' or the 'nun versus the prostitute'. The devadasi did not fit any Victorian models of femininity and thus became the anomalous crux of colonial and nationalist reform (Soneji 2011). During the colonial period, and particularly in the struggle for independence in the late nineteenth- and early twentieth-centuries, the devadasi became part of the reformation and the 'Women's Question' (Chatterjee and Menon 2010).[5] The devadasi system was decimated by the systematic takeover of kingdoms, lack of patronage and increasing polemic around the status of these female performers, which led to the Devadasi Abolition Act of 1947. Devadasi performance was re-imagined through modernist practices by Rukmini Devi Arundale (one of the key founders of modern Bharatanatyam) and by Brahmin male figures, who initially attempted to reinstate the devadasi on formal stages in the city of Madras but failed to do so because of increasing pressures due to the Reform Movement (Meduri 1996). Ultimately, the dance form was transplanted onto middle class and upper caste female bodies and the practice of music onto Brahmin men. Eventually Brahmin women also practiced music. However a distinct divide opened between women dancers and women singers.[6] This divide had not existed in earlier devadasi practices but it soon became cemented in its modern iteration on Brahmin bodies such that women musicians, particularly vocalists, sat very still while women dancers moved but could not sing or speak; they were rendered mute (see Weidman 2006). It is within this history that our work intervenes.

Uthra and I both come from a Tamil Brahmin background. While she was born in Kullithalai in Tamil Nadu and moved to several nearby cities and towns in the first twenty six years of her life, I was born in Chennai and moved to Kolkata for eight years, and then to Melbourne for the next fifteen years of my life. After various journeys to different cities and countries over the next twenty years I returned to Melbourne (16 moves in 20 years). The constant was my dance through all these moves. Uthra had moved to Chennai after her marriage and then to Melbourne where she began her school of music for the last fifteen years. The constant for her was music. Ultimately, what brought us together in July 2016 was the historical /mythological figure of Andal and her songs.

My grandmother, paati as I called her, was from a town called Srivilliputtur in Tamil Nadu which was famous because of an eighth century female poet named Andal, who had resided there. Andal is the only female Alvar among the 12 Alvar saints of South India. The Alvar saints are known for their affiliation to the *Srivaishnava* tradition of Hinduism. The hagiography of Andal was that she had been found abandoned in the temple grounds where the temple priest named Perialwar found her under a tulsi plant and raised her as his own; despite not knowing her caste he thought her to be a gift from the divine lord he worshipped. Andal grew to love the main deity of the temple *Vatapatrasayi* (a form of the God Vishnu) in which her father served. As she grew older, she is believed to have worn the garland she wove herself before dedicating it to the presiding deity of the temple. Perialwar, who later found it, was highly upset and stopped her practise of weaving a garland. It is believed Vishnu appeared in his dream and asked him to dedicate the garland worn by Andal to him daily, which is a practise still followed in various Vaishnavite temples. Andal wrote several large poems dedicated to Vishnu and these are considered to be some of the greatest Tamil works: the *Thiruppavai* and *Nachiar Tirumozhi* (Venkatesan 2010), which are still recited by devotees during the winter festival season of Margazhi. In particular, the poems of the Thiruppavai in their sung form were gifted from mother to daughter and grandmother to granddaughter through a matrilineal female practice of oral transmission for hundreds of years. In hagiography, Andal went to Srirangam, a temple town several hundred kilometres away from Srivilliputtur. Upon seeing the vision of Vishnu in his form as *Ranganatha* she disappeared in the garba griha (the womb centre of the temple in the sanctum sanctorum). A statue of Andal is said to have appeared inside the temple approximately one hundred years later and she is worshipped to this day as one of Vishnu's wives.

Andal arrived for me in my mother's womb. A few weeks before my paati died she told me that when she sang Andal's songs I would kick inside my mother's womb. I asked her why she waited so many years to share this story with me and she gave me her signature toothless grin. She could not clearly see me in her last days. But in her cloudy eyes there was a knowing silence, one we had shared for decades which spoke volumes without actual words exchanged. She then lapsed into incoherence. I had always known Andal through the songs my paati sang. Similarly, Uthra's mother and grandmother had shared these songs with her. As a singer, she frequently sang songs from the *Thirupaavai* but it was not until we met that she began considering setting aspects of the *Nachiar Tirumozhi* to *raga* (melodic framework) and *tala* (rhythmic cycle) structure. These songs are not transmitted by women but rather they remain the purview of men who perform the Arayar Sevai as a form of worship in the temples as chants and in specific ritual clothing at sacred days and hours. While the *Thirupaavai* is seen as a benign text focused on 'Dasya Bhakti' in which the devotee sees her- or him-self as a devotee of God and worships him as a master-figure, the *Nachiar Tirumozhi* is seen as a much more charged text in 'Sringara Bhakti' form in which Andal associates herself with Vishnu in a familiar and intimate way. This aligns with Vaishnavite philosophy, which at its essence, sees the divine in human terms, meaning that God can be equally chided, scolded, loved and worshipped.

Despite her initial misgivings, Uthra agreed to set the music for one verse of the *Nachiar Tirumozhi* and we created a new kind of performance called 'Talking Dance' – something I had been developing earlier but that I worked on much more deeply in my collaboration with her. This form featured her voice alone with no musical accompaniment such as the drum or violin as is common in classical carnatic music. I offered commentaries on the text she sang in Tamil and my body sometimes performed aspects of the text through dance. In essence, to Tamil speaking audiences, we created the ideal framework in which Tamil is supposed to be understood as iyal isai natakam – song, poetry and drama/dance (Kersenboom 1995). An audience could hear her singing Andal's lyrics in Tamil while also hearing my interpretation in colloquial Tamil and in English and witness my bodily interpretation of the text/song. The first time Uthra sang Andal's songs and I embodied them, we both felt electrified, as if an ancient and contemporary connection had been awakened. It was like nothing I had experienced before, an immersion in another universe of vibration, a divine world experienced through the sensorial framework of sound and movement: Uthra said she had experienced it from time to time through attuning herself to her singing and would find herself lost in that world of exquisite emotion. This was the gift that she gave me. She continues to offer it every time she sings, and perhaps it is something that all deeply committed singers offer dancers. But it is not a gift that can be exchanged equally. Initially I believed that this encounter is a one way transaction with power differentials embedded, something Mauss hints at in his theorisation of the gift. However, Uthra disagrees. She suggests that for her the performance we create exists in a reciprocal relationship where my voice speaks, comments and creates different soundscapes for her to respond to and improvise with simultaneously.[7] Therefore, the traditionally mute dancer is now speaking within the framework of the 'talking dance' and can be heard simultaneously, along with the voice of the singer. Additionally, my friend and renowned choreographer Kalpana Raghuraman from the Netherlands points out that the moving body in space creates a subtle but powerful vibration that can be felt by those attuned to the frequency of the body.[8] Musicians such as Uthra are finely tuned to attending to frequencies of different kinds. There is also the sharing of power on stage. In most conventional relationships between music and dance, the musicians are the accompanists who sit on the periphery, while the dancer remains front and centre, taking up most of the stage space. In order to even the relationship and to democratise the practice of the dance form, I have requested Uthra to sit in the centre of the stage while I performed around her, sometimes centrally behind her, mirroring her gestures, and sometimes in the periphery. This move enabled audiences to see both of us at once and to experience the intimacy of the performance without diverting their attention. It also complicates audience perceptions of who is the centre and who is the periphery, who is the main performer and who is the accompanist. Additionally in our site specific work in galleries and museums for example, Uthra also moves while she sings. She has told me repeatedly that it is very difficult for her to move and sing and yet she has risen to the challenge. In some version(s) of our Andal performances she also interacts directly with me through singing, making eye contact, touch, and giving me 'gifts' of flowers, bindi and bangles inside the performance. The form also enables the singer to physically move and improvise, something that is not always possible in the current modern practice when singing for dance. Devadasi practice had a much greater flow between musician and dancer, and it was framed within structures of improvisation where both the dancer and the musicians freely improvised in certain parts of the performance. This is perhaps the strength of our practice. The 'Talking Dance' intervenes in the postcolonial classical forms that exist today to decolonise the fragmentation and dismemberment within our art forms that have split the singer and the dancer. By enabling the singer to move and the dancer to speak, we are asking, in each iteration of rehearsal and performance, how we continuously decolonise by disrupting colonial, nationalist and patriarchal narratives by neighbouring together. I do believe that the reciprocal power of the gift also creates a web of kinship threads beyond the performance encounter which Uthra and I find ourselves negotiating. The gift here is in allowing multiple perspectives to co-exist in the shared collaborative exchange both inside and outside the performance space.

When we performed 'Talking Dance' in public for the first time, the largely Tamil audience found it to be a moving and a unique experience. Audience members said that without the din of the accompanying instruments the female voice could be experienced more clearly and that the female body and voice narration could be felt at a deeply 'affective' level. They felt a unique synergy between the song, text and dance. They also enjoyed the movements through time, the toggling between past and present texts, between the female authors/poets and us. I am left wondering, however, what it means to be friends and to work together artistically inside our form. Sometimes our communication is not always clear and there are different expectations that are not always met. Despite many commonalities we also differ fundamentally in our political leanings. Yet we continue to negotiate the creative space to find a balance that is based on trust. The terrain we navigate is continuously changing, with no clear pathways except our focus on the affection, care and respect we show each other.

The affection between us in the intersubjective, intracultural encounter offers the framework to neighbour in intercultural encounters. Unlike the large, patriarchal intercultural projects by theatre directors such as Peter Brooks and others, we bring a feminist collaborative ideal that collapses the distance between subject/object, between etic/emic, and that disrupts power relations enabling dual or multiple viewpoints (Banerji 2009). We can ask then what happens when knowledge is produced inter-subjectively, when a representation is consciously co-created and subjects/objects are fluid, temporal and dynamic. We used these questions to structure our intercultural performances, often using Andal's text as the core to connect with several women performers in different parts of the world, as a way of decolonising ourselves. Moving away from western feminist texts to Indian Tamil texts allowed us to deconstruct our own past whilst simultaneously create bridges between women. We also created performances based on devadasi women such as Bangalore Nagarathnammal and invoked the poetry of ancient Tamil texts such as the heroine Kannagi of Cilapatikaram fame and writings by women poets like Avvaiyar and stories of contemporary female Tamil war colonels to discuss how Tamil women have dealt with war in very different ways through time.[9] We broke the notion that contemporary performance had to look and be framed a certain way. We worked with an Iranian Australian singer: Tabassom Ostad and a Chilean Australian visual artist: Arun Munoz, who were bemoaning the loss of homeland while simultaneously embracing the opportunities offered in Australia. We also connected Andal to the Yiddish singer and dancer pair: Inge Mandos and Hannah Schwadron in Hamburg and Berlin, who had collected the texts and voices of young Jewish girls lost in the holocaust in Germany. We paired Andal with Romanian visual artists such as Andreea Campaneau, who were working in Sudan with girls living on the border in crisis. We worked with flamenco singers and dancers in Barcelona such as Alba Guerrero and Deborah Torres to meditate on the crisis over female bodies in public spaces. We also worked with Surinamese-Dutch choirs in Amsterdam and a group of visual artists/ scholars and performers from the Moving Matters Collective. In these collaborative intersubjective encounters we play with time in going back and forward between Andal, the figure of the devadasi, and female poets with Romanian, Sudanese, Spanish, Yiddish, Iranian, Chilean and Surinamese performers. The gifts in these encounters are varied and rich and there is a blurring in giving and receiving. Particularly as Andal has formed a central thread in many of these interactions and continues offering her gifts through time even as we offer ourselves to her in return, it becomes increasingly unknowable as to who is the giver and who receives; much like the relationships Vaishnavite devotees have to Vishnu. The experiences generated by these intercultural practices parallel those in the project discussed in the next section.

Part 2: 'Serpent Dreaming Women'[10]

As Uthra and I were walking through the Bunjilaka Aboriginal Museum (a part of the Melbourne Museum) following Gunditjmara Indigenous cultural leader Vicki Couzens in central Melbourne, in October 2017, we heard the ancient chants of the Kulin Nation on the speaker above us.[11] We looked at each other and smiled in recognition as a shiver went through our bodies. It was a chant that seemed deeply familiar to us. Uthra immediately began to hum *raga alapana*, layering her voice underneath the music that descended from above. Vicki grinned widely, watching our pleasure unfold as we continued walking very slowly and pausing at certain moments to allow the music to enter into us further. What we heard were 15,000 year old Indigenous chants that to our ears sounded like the carnatic form of the Revathi *raga*. We continued walking through the exhibit, witnessing the ancient cultures that had survived – 60,000 years of uninterrupted history until colonial settlement and invasion, which had, within 200 years, almost decimated the languages, technologies and knowledges of the Kulin people (in the state of Victoria).[12] By now, Vicki's face had turned grim. The further we walked into the exhibit, the more the decimation and violence became apparent as voice-overs from Kulin Nation elders detailed the wars that had been fought despite the colonial histories that had recorded the land as 'terra nullius' (Connor 2005).[13] By the time we emerged from the exhibits we were overwhelmed and we began a heated conversation with Vicki about what we had seen and heard. Of course we had known the history; but to be guided by Vicki, whose own voice mingled with the Elders, and who was contributing to the reconstruction of Indigenous languages and displaying art work as part of the exhibits we had seen, brought it to us in an embodied way we had not experienced before. The gift of her presence in sharing the story of this decimation was powerful and humbling. This intersubjective encounter of deep encounters allowed us to neighbour and it laid the framework for our collaboration.

What we started then was a collaboration that had begun earlier in smaller performances such as 'honouring country',[14] linking Indian and Indigenous Australian songlines, stories and movement. The more we shared our stories the more we discovered startling connections much like what the Indian dancer and scholar Dr Padma Subrahmanyam had discovered during her visit to Australia in 1979 (Subrahmanyam 2018).[15] We started with the premise of linking mythologies such as Gunditjmara spirits, notably the Goddess Spirit Mountain Gulaga,[16] and Hindu mythologies of the universe that emerges from Ananta Sesha,[17] the serpent on which the great Goddess Lakshmi resides. Our collaboration developed by weaving local understandings of creation from various indigenous perspectives into it, such as the Rainbow Serpent from dream time. I brought together renowned Indian classical dancer Priyadarsini Govind (from Chennai) and The Desire Machine Collective from Assam (comprising two visual arts creatives who worked with us remotely) with Australian-based collaborators, Vicki, Gundijtmara/Yuin creatives, Yaraan Bundle, Gina Bundle, Uthra and myself – all on Wurundjeri and Bunurong land (parts of Melbourne) – we explored commonalities and differences, struggles and challenges. We explored collaborative relationships and partnerships between women of colour in unceded land, as migrant/racialized settler colonials and as Indigenous women. What emerged was the practice of 'neighbouring' which meant to sit, stand, flow, exist, move, sing, talk and listen alongside one another; sometimes in odd juxtapositions of personal, mythological and political fragmented narratives and non-narratives that created an experimental and experiential model of engagement for ourselves and audiences when we all participated in the event at Bunjilaka Aboriginal Cultural Centre at the Melbourne Museum.

This project was supported at the highest state level by the Australia India Council, Department of Foreign Affairs and Trade, Arts Centre Melbourne, and Multicultural Arts Victoria (the latter helped spearhead the project). It built on the ongoing interactions, meetings, collaborations we had initiated for ASIATOPA (an international Asian festival of the arts), extending into more explicitly intercultural performance. The goal of the project was to ask about interculturalism specifically; to question how Indian and Indigenous women can meet through the exchange of stories, visual objects, songs and movement to address issues around land, water and sky using a global south feminist approach. We wanted to find the intersections between the custodians of an unceded land and the migrants who have come to live there. In particular, it offered utopic hope. Art accounts for colonisation and decolonisation, uneven power, women's writing/dancing/ dreaming and it offers us possibilities for futures that are devoid of violence and conflict. Through art we experienced an evening of power between the people that live on this land and neighbour the sea. This latter aspect was vital to the collaborative project. We were asking how oceanic understandings of intersubjectivity might shift if Indian and Indigenous Australian contact pre-dates British colonial settlement, and actually goes back 4000 years as emerging archaeological and linguistic evidence increasingly suggests (Berndt and Berndt 1989; Culhane 1998; Ganter 2006; Macknight 1976; McIntosh 1996, 2003, 2011; Merlan 1986; Stanner 1966; Subrahmanyam 2018; Westrip and Holroyde 2010). The premise for this contact was one of reciprocal exchange not of colonisation since Indian traders and seafarers had visited Australia but not taken it over. How might this kind of intercultural performance offer us insights into the gift? How might we explore decolonisation embodied in a women's project through dance, song and visual arts to channel the past to forge present and future connections, exploring these histories of exchange in such intersubjective encounters?

By accounting for their respective processes of colonisation while attending to new and emergent possibilities, 'Serpent Dreaming Women' also seeks to intervene in current Australia-India trade and diplomacy exchanges (DFAT's Australia India Economic Strategy 2035) and to give an account of how the knowledge of the Indian Diaspora in Australia turns them into key players in these exchanges. The White Paper Australia India Policy Paper released by DFAT (June 2018) stresses the urgency of prioritising the Indian Diaspora in Australia and also of moving towards a more expansive understanding of what Australia-India engagement might look like. 'Serpent Dreaming Women' enables a unique exchange between several key knowledge systems from Indian Australian, Indian and Indigenous Australian sources, including cultural leaders and scholars, framed by the practice of art that is at once political and theoretical. What this project also offers is a different timeline of Australia-India engagement since evidence has emerged that Indians have travelled to Australia many times in the last 4000 years predating white settlement which is just over 200 years old).[18] These early exchanges offer an alternative to the settler colonial model of engagement disrupting the notion that Indian migrants are 'new' to Australia having arrived in large numbers only after the lifting of the White Australia Policy in 1973. What these early records also suggest is the active engagement of 'neighbouring' as a political praxis, as opposed to colonisation as the only narrative for exchange between two different cultures.

As the process unfolded, we experienced some difficulties because of our different senses of time and space, our differentially colonised bodies, and our dis-similar postcolonial experiences. We struggled at times to hear each other. But my writing, movement, energy and speech have changed by being near my Indigenous Australian collaborators and by being educated by them. The 'we' that was Uthra and I expanded to include a larger 'we' with Priyadarsini. They were different to us and also similar. We were vegetarian and they were not. They laughed at our food and we laughed at theirs. Sometimes we shared food, but not often. We all took off our shoes when we moved together in the sacred spaces we created. But Gina made us possum skin cloth to wear; and we gave both her and Yaraan bindis and cottons. We gifted each other many things with implicit promises attached. We shared ochre and the powder and colours of the earth we were all comfortable wearing. We were frustrated by having to wait three of four hours for all the project's members to arrive, and they were upset by how much labour was required in each rehearsal everyday at the Arts Centre leading up to the Bunjilaka presentation, as well as by the demands of the grant awarded by the Department of Foreign Affairs and Trade and MAV. They had to deal with family, work and community commitments, which often took priority over rehearsals. This was hard for us to understand sometimes but slowly we accepted their prioritisation of family over everything and everyone else. We accepted this as we rearranged our work and family commitments to suit the needs of our indigenous collaborators, placing them above ours. We accepted their sovereignty on this land. We improvised, we neighboured; by that, I mean we sat next to one another, we danced and sang next to each other – borrowing, sharing and also ultimately going back to our own homes after the project was over. We worked to learn their time and energy vibrations and to unlearn our colonised approaches to time. Although we experience our own restrictions as migrants of colour in Australia, we are not the same. How can we account for our colonisation by the British when our colonisers left in 1947 and we have had 70 years to rebuild our nation (however problematic that might be and however colonised we remain)? More than 200 years of colonisation here in Australia is yet to end; no reparations have been made, no land has been ceded. Languages and cultures have been systematically destroyed. What does recovery mean to Gunditjmara creative organisations that exist on a completely different scale to Indian Tamil 'recovery'. How do we help their recovery? There were no easy answers or solutions.

Magical moments emerged too; especially when we moved and neighboured alongside one another, sometimes in silence, sometimes through the juxtaposition of haunting music of both our cultural traditions. The 'we' that had been Uthra and I came to include Priyadarsini, Vicki, Gina and Yaraan. Hearing Vicki give thanks before we began rehearsals as we held hands and felt the vibrations together was powerful. We found deep connections to land, water and sky through animal totems, real and mythologised, such as the snake stories that wound together Gunditjmara land, Assam and Tamil forests, creatures and land in India. We explored commonalities between Indian and Indigenous Australian mythologies through 'serpent dreaming.' We brought together several stories from 'dreaming'. This included the 'Whale Dreaming' story passed onto Yaraan Bundle by her ancestral women and which remains a secret that cannot be shared without permission and only hers to give. 'The Churning of the Ocean' story passed onto me by my grandmother was something which Priyadarsini, Uthra and I in turn shared with Vicki, Yaraan and Gina. We realised in both our cultural traditions the importance of listening to animals, living in communion with them, and listening to the ocean – what emerged from its murky depths and blue, seemingly calm flat, surfaces was important to both our communities. Our elders had been guided by the rhythms and fluidity of water, air and land, and the vibrations emerging from all around had to be felt, absorbed, neighboured and weathered with and by our bodies.

We cried tears of joy and sadness knowing that our stories, songs and texts linked us to the pre-colonial, pre-verbal, primordial space, as well as into the present and future. When Uthra wound her ancient *raga* and texts around 4,000 years old around Vicki's even more ancient chants around 15,000 years old not a single body in the space was unmoved or did not feel the vibration. None of us could stop crying when Gina, who had been quiet and reserved for a long time, began accounting for her past as a product of the stolen generation telling her mother's story. I told my story of being a dark migrant child mistaken for an aboriginal girl, who then found herself in identification with dark bodies in the midst of Australia's white policy when I was growing up in Australia.[19] We wound these stories together and shared them in the performance.

When we shared these stories during the workshops and rehearsals in the weeks leading to the performance, we realised the many common threads between us as we wove them together. Our stories led to a water – fire – smoke ceremony, involving the burning of eucalyptus, wattle and Indigenous flowers together with Indian flowers, jasmine and tulsi. A producer within the arts centre that sponsored part of this process commented: 'we could never imagine a smoking ceremony with white artists, which corresponds to Indigenous smoking rituals. This hybrid smoking fire ritual of yours was incredible.'[20] I had been worried that our forms would be seen as exotic, primitive and orientalist, but I realised we had also attempted to productively auto-exoticize ourselves. Knowing that we would be exoticized, no matter what, it felt better to take control of this process. Secondly, I also knew we were working with deep time; an expanded imagination of time that worked in our intersubjective encounter as we toggled back and forth. I responded to the producer saying that smoking and fire and flowers and leaves already existed for Indigenous and Tamil peoples predating white settler engagements in the Australian context. Returning to the water and fire in a performance context was a return to cosmological understandings for both our communities and alien to neither.

I do not have a happy multicultural or neat ending to this story. Neither do I have a conclusion because the project has not ended. I have only questions. We are still talking, texting and emailing each other. We meet to rehearse, continue our creation and perform. We know we will be meeting this coming year and in the years to come. We love and care about each other even though we are not necessarily clear on how we will continue to work together. But we are ready to re-imagine our performance again and again. So perhaps it was not just the sharing of texts, music and stories that was important to us. It was the embodied experience of attending to one another through odd and difficult juxtapositions that simultaneously produced energy, magic and new co-creations by women of colour in the processes of decolonising separately and together as we have continued to 'neighbour.' What has been revealed in this intercultural performance and process as feminist political praxis is that the oppositional structure of 'us' and 'them' shifted, expanding the 'we' of Uthra and I to become the larger encompassing 'we' that represented all of us. The expanded 'we' continued to negotiate with one another to give and receive stories, songs and dances to create common ground through the magical, oceanic, intersubjective encounters that recuperate ties to the past as vibrational energy and synergy in the present.

Notes

1. Many thanks to Uthra Vijay for humoring me in allowing me to write about our work and to represent her, Vicki Couzens for her prompt attention to this article and support of it, Hannah Schwadron for her timely and critical feedback, and also to Tina K. Ramnarine for her patience and deep engagement with this article.
2. I use ethnography and auto-ethnography here as methodologies because of the capacity for intimacy.
3. We have performed in a wide range of venues such as Hermitage in Amsterdam, Melbourne Museum and the Immigration Museum in Melbourne, Showroom, Typografia, and George Paton galleries in London, Bucharest and Melbourne, historical buildings such as the Centre Civic Besos in Barcelona and Treasury Building Melbourne, experimental and classical theatres like Dancehouse Melbourne, Kalakshetra Foundation and Spaces in Chennai, Shoonya Theatre Bangalore, as well as the Indian Council of Cultural Relations-Indian Embassy Theatre, Berlin and universities such as Kings College, Royal Central, and Melbourne University to mention a few.
4. For excerpts of our work see: 'Nagarathnammal's Dream' at https://youtu.be/kcA34OR1alk, 'Reimagining Andal' at https://youtu.be/SjtIRNcm_Xc, and 'Uthra Vijay carnatic Concert' at https://youtu.be/2l-P0cNop4M (all last accessed 31 October 2018).
5. The rationale for British colonisation became the rescue of Indian women from Indian men. The subsequent Indian nationalist independence movement focused on three main issues of the women's question including widow remarriage, sati (bride burning) and the devadasi as the locus for women's reform.
6. This does not discount the fact that many men from the isai *vellalar* communities continued their role as gurus (teachers) and as *nattuvanars* and mridangam players (percussionists).
7. After reading the initial draft of this article, Uthra suggested that she would not be performing if there were not reciprocal and powerful exchanges occurring inside the practice. Therefore I modified my argument to incorporate her perspective (personal discussions with Uthra Vijay, 29-30 October 2018).
8. Personal discussions Raghuraman, 30 October 2018.
9. While I created the dance and text through structured improvisation and from research, Uthra strung together a repertoire of songs from the composer Thyagaraja for 'Nagarathnammal's Dream.' For Kannagi and Avvaiyar she used the ancient Tamil poetry and composed music almost effortlessly shifting and changing *ragas* and the material every time we performed, using structured improvisation. She also painstakingly created the music that had not been done previously for a section of the text from the 'Radhika Santwanamu' written by the devadasi Muddupalani in the 18th century (Mulchandani 2011).
10. See 'Serpent Dreaming Women' at https://youtu.be/ciPk6d_oq8k (last accessed 31 October 2018).
11. 'First Peoples' was co-curated by the Yulendj Group of Elders, community representatives from across Victoria, and Museum Victoria staff. Yulendj is a Kulin word for knowledge, which describes the deep cultural and historical knowledge that the Yulendj group brought to the exhibition. See https://museumsvictoria.com.au/bunjilaka/whats-on/first-peoples/ (last accessed 31 October 2018).

12. Before British colonisation, there were five population groups in South Eastern Australia speaking five related languages. These languages were spoken in two groups: the Eastern Kulin group of Woiwurrung, Boonwurrung, Taungurong and Ngurai-illam-wurrung; and the western language group of just Wathaurung. The chants we were hearing were in the Boonwurrung language.
13. Terra nullius – 'Nobody's land' was the justification by the colonial government used to colonise Australia despite the presence of at least 20,000 people of the Kulin population alone in the area of Victoria. This is also a debate about land being settled versus being conquered, culminating in the history wars in the Mabo case in 1992. In 1982, Eddie Mabo and four other Torres Strait Islanders from Mer (Murray Island) started legal proceedings to establish their traditional land ownership. This led to Mabo versus Queensland. In 1992, after ten years of hearings before the Queensland Supreme Court and the High Court of Australia, the latter court found that the Mer people had owned their land prior to annexation by Queensland. The ruling thus had far-reaching significance for the land claims of Indigenous Australians.
14. Honouring Country is a way to acknowledge Mother Earth and her contribution to all our lives. It can be done verbally or through song and movement. It is a form of welcome performed by Indigenous people from neighbouring regions. It is only the tribes who are on their own land who can perform an 'Acknowledgement to Country'.
15. Dr Padma Subrahmanyam a renowned dancer and scholar visited Australia in 1979 for an Indian Ocean festival in Perth and encountered an indigenous tribe called Gugudja from the Balgo Hills. They found music and words in common but were not allowed to pursue further connections. We were able to pursue these connections much further.
16. Gina shared the story of the Mountain Gulaga from her region with us during the creative development period: 20-30 November 2017.
17. We in turn shared the story of Ananta Sesha the giant serpent upon whom the God Vishnu resides.
18. Creagh (2013); Curnoe (2016); Goodall, Ghosh, and Todd (2008); Macdonald (2013); McRae (2013); Morris (2017); Phillips (2016); Pascoe (2016); and Subrahmanyam (2018).
19. The White Australia Policy known as the Immigration Restriction Act are various historical policies that barred people of non-European descent from immigrating to Australia from 1901 until 1973.
20. Discussion with a former producer Arts Centre Melbourne, 7 December 2017.

Disclosure statement

No potential conflict of interest was reported by the author.

References

Banerji, A. 2009. "An Intimate Ethnography." *Women & Performance: A Journal of Feminist Theory* 19 (1): 35–60.

Berndt, R. M., and C. H. Berndt. 1989. *The Speaking Land: Myth and Story in Aboriginal Australia*. Ringwood, Vic.: Penguin Books.

Chatterjee, Partha, and Nivedita Menon. 2010. "The Nationalist Resolution of the Women's Question (1989)." In *Empire and Nation: Selected Essays*, 116–135. New York: Columbia University Press.

Connor, Michael. 2005. *The Invention of Terra Nullius*. Sydney: Macleay Press.

Creagh, S. 2013. "Study Links Ancient Indian Visitors to Australia's First Dingoes." http://theconversation.com/study-links-ancient-indian-visitors-to-australias-first-dingoes-11593.

Culhane, Dara. 1998. *The Pleasure of the Crown: Anthropology, Law, and the First Nations*. Vancouver: Talon Books.

Curnoe, D. 2016. "An Ancient Australia Connection to India." https://theconversation.com/an-ancient-australian-connection-to-india-55935.

Ganter, R. 2006. *Mixed Relations: Histories and Stories of Asian/Aboriginal Contact in North Australia*. Perth: University of Western Australia Press.

Goodall, H., D. Ghosh, and L. Todd. 2008. "Jumping Ship, Skirting Empire: Indians, Aborigines, and Australians Across the Ocean." *Transforming Cultures eJournal* 3 (1). http://epress.lib.uts.edu.au/journals/TfC.

Harrison, F. 1997. *Decolonizing Anthropology: Moving Further Toward an Anthropology of Liberation*. Virginia: American Anthropology Association.

Kersenboom, Saskia. 1987. *Nityasumangali. Devadasi Tradition in South India*. Delhi: Motilal Banarsidass.

Kersenboom, Saskia. 1995. *Word, Sound, Image: The Life of the Tamil Text*. Washington: Berg Publications.

Macdonald, A. 2013. "Research Shows Ancient Indian Migration to Australia." https://www.abc.net.au/news/2013-01-15/research-shows-ancient-indian-migration-to-australia/4466382.

Macknight, C. C. 1976. *The Voyage to Marege: Macassan Traders in Northern Australia*. Carlton, Vic.: Melbourne University Press.

Mauss, M. 2011. *The Gift: Forms and Functions of Exchange in Archaic Societies*. London: Martino Fine Books.

McIntosh, Ian S. 1996. "Islam and Australia's Aborigines? A Perspective from North-East Arnhem Land." *Journal of Religious History* 20 (1): 53–77.

McIntosh, Ian S. 2003. *Macassan History and Heritage: Unbirris Pre-Macassan Legacy, or How the Yolngu Became Black*. Canberra: ANU Press.

McIntosh, Ian S. 2011. "Missing the Revolution! Negotiating Disclosure on the Pre-Macasasans (Bayini) in North-East Arnhem Land." In *Exploring the Legacy of the 1948 Arnhem Land Expedition*, edited by M. Thomas and M. Neale, 337–354. Canberra: ANU E-Press.

McRae, A. 2013. "Aboriginal Genes Suggest Indian Migration." https://www.australiangeographic.com.au/news/2013/01/aboriginal-genes-suggest-indian-migration/.

Meduri, Avanthi. 1996. "Nation Woman Represented: The Sutured History of the Devadasi." (PhD Thesis). New York University.

Merlan, F. 1986. "Australian Aboriginal Conception Beliefs Revisited." *Man* 21 (3): 474–493.

Mohanty, C. P. 1996. *Feminism Without Borders: Decolonize Theory, Practicing Solidarity*. Durham: Duke University Press.

Morris, L. 2017. "Four Thousand Years Ago Indians Landed in Australia." https://www.nationalgeographic.com.au/australia/four-thousand-years-ago-indians-landed-in-australia.aspx.

Mulchandani, S. 2011. *The Appeasement of Radhika: Radhika Santawanam*. New Delhi: Penguin.

Narayan, U. 1997. *Dislocating Cultures: Identities, Traditions and Third World Feminisms*. New York: Routledge.

Pascoe, Bruce. 2016. *Dark Emu*. Sydney, Australia: Penguin.

Phillips, N. 2016. "Ancestors of Modern May Have Come to Australia Before Europeans, Genetic Study Shows". https://www.smh.com.au/world/ancestors-of-modern-indians-may-have-come-to-australia-before-europeans-genetic-study-shows-20130115-2crk9.html.

Savigliano, M. 2009. "Worlding Dance and Dancing Out there in the World." In *Rethinking World Dance Histories*, edited by Susan Foster, 163–191. New York: Palgrave.

Soneji, Davesh. 2011. *Unfinished Gestures: Devadasis, Memory, and Modernity in South India.* Chicago: University of Chicago Press.

Stanner, W. E. H. 1966. *On Aboriginal Religion* (Oceania Monograph 11). Sydney: University of Sydney Press.

Subrahmanyam, P. 2018. *Kanchi Maha Swami's Vision of Asian Culture.* Chennai: Vanathi Pathippakam.

Venkatesan, A. 2010. *The Secret Garland: Antal's Tiruppavai and Nacciyar Tirumoli.* New York: Oxford University Press.

Weidman, Amanda. 2006. *Singing the Classical, Voicing the Modern: The Postcolonial Politics of Music in South India.* Durham: Duke University Press.

Westrip, J. P., and P. Holroyde. 2010. *Colonial Cousins: A Surprising History of Connections between India and Australia.* Kent: Wakefield Press.

Decolonising human exhibits: dance, re-enactment and historical fiction

Prarthana Purkayastha

ABSTRACT
This article focuses on decolonising exhibition practices and colonial archives. It begins with a survey of literature on nineteenth-century colonial exhibitions and world's fairs as a cultural practice and the complicity of academic disciplines such as anthropology and ethnology in promoting violent forms of pedagogy. Next, the article examines the failed Liberty's 1885 exhibition in London, specifically analyzing the *nautch* dancers whose moving bodies both engaged and disrupted the scopophilia framing such live human exhibits. In the final section, the article examines how re-imagining the Liberty's *nautch* experiences by embodying archival slippages might be a usefully anarchic way of exhuming the memories of those dancers forgotten by both British and Indian nationalist history. The article delineates the structural limitations of reenactments, a current trend in contemporary Euro-American dance, and it argues that historical fiction as a corporeal methodology might be a viable decolonising strategy for dance studies.

In September 2014, *Exhibit B*, a live performance installation featuring black performers and curated by the white South African director Brett Bailey, was forced to close down following a social media campaign and a large public protest outside The Barbican Theatre in London. Bailey's anti-imperial reenactment of colonial exhibitions was designed to offer a critique of nineteenth-century 'human zoos' where colonised bodies were displayed as objects, connecting that deeply racist past with the plight of present-day asylum seekers and immigrants around the Mediterranean basin who were installed as 'found objects'. The show backfired badly in London amidst questions of unequal representation, covert power and 'complicit racism', which in turn prompted The Barbican to accuse protestors of censoring artistic freedom (Muir 2014).

As Katrin Sieg suggests, the event clearly signalled the urgent need for 'more differentiated engagements with the ethics of confronting a violent, racist history, the dramaturgy of interracial encounter and the politics of decolonizing cultural institutions' (2015, 250). I often bring this controversial performance event and its attendant debates to my classroom when I ask British students of theatre and dance studies to debate the politics of race and positionality in performance. Such politically charged material within a pedagogical context inevitably introduces an affective charge to the space of learning: the horror of my students as they encounter the phenomenon of the 'human zoos' for the first time is matched by the horror I feel upon learning that a majority of my students have little to no knowledge of Britain's deeply racist and violent colonial past. The erasure from the national school curriculum of the knowledge of Britain's colonisation of lands and its systematic loot, plunder and genocide in its colonies in recent history – its inglorious past, to use popular historian Shashi Tharoor's (2017) words – is indicative of a crafting of British nationalist history that has little regard for the collective memory of several diasporic constituencies.

This article, following Sieg's prompt to decolonise cultural institutions, focuses on decolonising exhibition practices and the colonial archives. It notices how traditions of display and curation in the Euro-American exhibition model are framed by unequal colonial power structures, and argues that an embodied and creative encounter with such violent pasts may provide an ethical step towards decolonisation. The article begins with a survey of literature on nineteenth-century colonial exhibitions and world's fairs as a cultural practice and the complicity of academic disciplines such as anthropology and ethnology in promoting violent forms of pedagogy. Next, the article examines one particular colonial exhibition, the failed Liberty's 1885 exhibition in London, and specifically analyzes the *nautch* dancers whose moving bodies both engaged and disrupted the scopophilia framing such live human exhibits. In the final section, the article examines how re-imagining the Liberty's *nautch* experience by embodying archival silences and slippages might be a usefully anarchic way of exhuming the memories of those dancers forgotten by both British and Indian nationalist history. By locating my own performance lecture on the Liberty *nautch* dancers within the current trend of reenactments in contemporary Euro-American dance, the article delineates the structural limitations of such reenactments and argues that historical fiction as a corporeal methodology might be a viable decolonising strategy for dance studies.

Race on display: human exhibits and pedagogical violence

In the past few decades, colonial Euro-American museum and exhibition practices have been carefully scrutinised in multiple fields, including history and art history, anthropology, ethnology and cultural studies. Some of the earliest research on colonial exhibitions by Allwood (1977) and Altick (1978) focused on the British Empire's insatiable hunger for objects and products collected from its colonies and on the importance of displaying these in Britain as spectacles for a curious public with little access to global travel. In the 1980s, a number of important studies further highlighted the direct relationship between European and US colonial expansion and exhibiting practices. Rydell explored the US empire and its dominion over lands and peoples, noting how, to organisers such as George Brown Goode of the Smithsonian, the world's fair illustrated 'the steps of progress of civilization and its arts in successive centuries, and in all lands up to the present time'; it would become, 'in fact, an illustrated encyclopedia of humanity of civilization' (1984, 45).

Rydell's study explored how fairs such as the Chicago World's Columbia Exposition of 1893 featured ethnographic exhibits curated by the Smithsonian and Peabody museums, and noticed how they were necessary to educate and 'formulate the Modern' (1984, 45). The Smithsonian exhibit of 1893, according to Rydell, 'provided the cement for integrating ideas about progress and race into an ideological whole' (1984, 27). However, cementing this ideology occurred much earlier in Britain and in other parts of Europe such as France, Germany and Spain. Europe's perceived racial and civilizational superiority over other 'savage races' resulted in the practice of putting 'natives' on display in public fairs from the fifteenth century onwards, but the Industrial Revolution and advancements in technology took exhibition practices to an international level in the mid-nineteenth century. Greenhalgh (1988) and Hoffenberg (2001) put Britain's 1851 Great Exhibition of the Industry of all Nations at a watershed moment in the history of international exhibitions, ushering in an era of heated competition between European colonial empires, mainly between the French, German, Dutch and the British, and the new US empire. The Great Exhibition of 1851, also known as the Crystal Palace exhibition (named after the vast building covering nineteen acres and erected in London's Hyde Park for the sole purpose of housing it), set a standard template for other international ones in terms of creating four categories of exhibits: Manufactures, Machinery, Raw Materials and Fine Arts; and Greenhalgh noted how themes such as international peace, education, trade and progress were at their theoretical core (1988, see chapter one). Later studies on exhibition practices focused on the importance of visual representation to empire's progress. Breckenridge studied how objects from India were taken out of their everyday contexts and turned into a 'spectacle of the ocular' (1989, 196), and how the systematically categorised displays maintained a visual illusion of order and control that provided an antidote to an otherwise disturbing and chaotic colonial experience. Corbey wrote that in human ethnological exhibits, 'the citizen's gaze on alien people was determined to a considerable degree by stories and stereotypes in his or her mind' (1993, 361), and that the motto 'To see is to know' became the 'underlying ideology that is at work in a range of seemingly disparate practices in colonial times: photography, colonialist discourse, missionary discourse, anthropometry, collecting and exhibiting' (1993, 360). By the mid-1990s, Tony Bennett had coined 'exhibitionary complex' to include along with art museums, history and natural science museums, dioramas and panoramas, national and international exhibitions, and department stores, 'which served as linked sites for the development and circulation of new disciplines (history, biology, art history, anthropology) and their discursive formations (the past, evolution, aesthetics, man) as well as for the development of new technologies of vision' (1995, 59).

Bennett argued that the 'exhibitionary complex' ran parallel and in juxtaposition to Foucault's notion of the 'carceral archipelago', in which objects and bodies were transferred from private spaces and collections to public displays for the masses. The spectacles offered by objects in museums were intended for individuals to know themselves as the subject of knowledge and to engage in a 'voluntarily self-regulating citizenry' (1995, 63).

This literature points to the encyclopedic nature of colonial expositions and fairs, including inventories of all cultures of the world and a crafting of a history of the 'human race', with some peoples considered superior (morally, intellectually, technologically, and economically) and others primitive or barbaric on a linear scale of progress. This spectacular narrative, which legitimised colonial rule and appropriation in Europe, was paralleled by the huge efforts of the colonial state apparatus to justify the cost and hardship associated with colonial conquest abroad (Auerbach 2002, 3). Alongside focusing on the taxonomic impulse to categorise races and their cultural products, the studies mentioned above pay attention to the relationship between colonial exhibitions and pedagogy on a mass-scale. The consensus amongst writers is that the most vicious yet acceptable form of nineteenth-century imperialist ideology and contemporary social Darwinism framed the human exhibits. 'Savages' were displayed for Euro-American citizens for what we today call 'edutainment', with the supply of 'natives' to exhibits following close on the heels of a colonial conquest. Moreover, as Coombes (1994) has found, conflicting representations of exhibited peoples or cultures, for instance of Africa, were circulated often in the exhibitions, depending on political or disciplinary imperatives.

The display of exotic people in colonial exhibitions ran parallel to nineteenth century circuses and freak shows run by producers such as Phineas Taylor Barnum (1810–1891), which mainly focused on entertaining the masses. From 1874 until World War I, the animal trainer and trader Carl Hagenbeck (1844–1913) of Hamburg exhibited nomadic Sámi ('Laplanders'), Nubians from Egyptian Sudan, North American Indians, people from India, Inuits and Zulus across several German and other European cities in his *Volkerschau* (ethnic or folk shows). These were framed as 'anthropological-zoological exhibitions' or *Anthropologisch-Zoologische Ausstellung*. Not all human exhibits were treated the same by curators of exhibitions. As Thode-Arora (2014, 79) notes, the ethnic shows were a complex phenomenon, sometimes featuring people who were abducted or kept under poor conditions and sometimes, as with the Hagenbeck company, with professional contracts that formalised food and accommodation, medical care, fees and performance schedules. Roslyn Poignant notes how Indigenous Australians transformed themselves into accomplished performers in order to survive the brutal tours, in the process becoming 'professional "savages"' (2004, 4). Jensen (2018) notes that certain cultures, such as those of India's, could not be easily labelled 'primitive' or 'savage' within the exhibitionary complex, as it was deemed to be an ancient (albeit pre-modern) civilisation. Despite some differences in experiences, human labour in ethnic shows and exhibits was extremely profitable for producers, although human lives were dispensable. Many natives travelling for human exhibits lost their lives and never made it back to their homelands. The violence that informed and underpinned Europe and USA's pedagogical drive to understand the world's cultures remained implicit and covert.

World's fairs and exhibitions would include laboratories where visitors could see or even take part in scientific research on racial features of various human population groups. Corbey finds that 'anthropologists used to be represented on the committees heading the anthropological sections of world fairs, often quarrelling with those who wished to cater more to commercial than to scientific or educational interests' (1993, 354). Parezo and Fowler (2007) examine the intricate relationship between anthropological research at US fairs and the promotion and advertising of both the nation state and the academic discipline. Sadiah Qureshi (2011) notes how museums of ethnography or colonial museums were often the direct offshoot of a world's fair or exhibition. Some of the shows gained immense popularity in the academic community: for example, Buffalo Bill's Wild West Show in US world fairs, which would feature Native Americans on display. Some of those exhibited also became popular amongst anthropologists, such as Saartjie Baartmann, the 'Hottentot Venus' who was put on show when alive and dissected when dead. A similar clinical and educational approach framed the display of Ota Benga, a Pygmy man, caged along with chimpanzees and orangutans (Putnam 2012).

In 2013, the term 'human zoo' was coined by Blanchard et al to encompass French expositions, the Swiss and German *Volkerschau*, British exhibitions featuring live human displays and freak shows. The term has remained in circulation ever since. It highlights the lasting significance of human displays in exhibitions in studies of empire, race and colonialism. I would argue, however, that with the exception of Priya Srinivasan's groundbreaking discussion of the fate of *nautch* dancers in Coney Island (2012), dance history has paid little attention to the minefield of acts and performances that populated human exhibits. Second, attending to the narratives of dancers in colonial exhibitions opens up a violent relationship that dance shared with visual art and exhibition practices. This is a point that recent Euro-American conceptual experimentations with dance in museums and galleries never reference or acknowledge. Third, most of the literature outlined above privileges ocular experiences and histories over embodied or corporeal ones. This emphasis on spectacle and gaze, on the visual grammar of the display, undermines the bodily experiences, sensations and corporeal politics of those on display, rendering them as passive individuals lacking agency. As Munro suggests, historians have focused mainly on a top-down approach to studying colonial exhibitions, focusing on archival materials such as committee reports, newspaper accounts, catalogues and visual images, and revealing little about the experiences of those exhibited (2010, 84). Following Munro's prompt, the discussion below applies a bottom-up approach to the history of human exhibits, focusing on a re-imagining of the corporeal experiences of *nautch* dancers in the Liberty's exhibit of 1885 when faced with archival anomalies on these individuals.

Please don't touch: *nautch* in Liberty's exhibition of 1885

In the winter of 1885, a group of 'natives' were shipped from India to London by Liberty's, the luxury department store in London, to be installed as human exhibits in a 'living Indian village' at the Albert Palace in Battersea Park. Available visual records suggested that the exhibition arena was a lavish architectural show in itself, with newspapers highlighting the splendour of the site. *The Graphic* (1885, 591) reported:

> The building is a handsome structure of glass and iron, and consists of a nave 60 feet high, 473 feet long, and 84 feet wide, with a gallery running round, and an apse at the centre of the nave, 50 feet long by 84 feet wide. There is also an annexe, known as the Connaught Hall, 60 feet high, 157 feet long, and a 118 feet wide, which has a double gallery all round, admirably adapted for musical entertainments.

As the image and the text in Figure 1 show, the 1885 exhibition followed the logic of grand Victorian exhibitions, established by the Great Exhibition of 1851, with the purpose of advertising trade, commerce and colonial power. The Liberty's exhibit was designed to promote and advertise the store and to hike up sales in the Oriental Antiques and Curios Department. The British weather, however, altered this plan. Day and night-time temperatures plummeted to a record low: it was the coldest winter in Britain in thirty years. As the historian Saloni Mathur (2000) noted, the exhibition was a disaster, financially as well as in terms of Indian and British relations. The bitter cold caused a break-down of hot water pipes at Albert Palace, causing freezing conditions for the Indians on show. The spectacle of 'native' authenticity failed as the Indians were given European winter-wear to fight off the cold, much to the disappointment of British spectators. Moreover, the Indians who were shipped in to become live exhibits were deceived

Figure 1. 'Opening of the Albert Palace, Battersea.' Image reproduced with the permission of Westminster City Archives and Liberty Ltd.

by their recruiting agent who ignored contractual obligations around suitable board, fees, accommodation and clothing. The group turned to Nandalal Ghosh, a Cambridge-educated Bengali barrister living in London, who chaired a committee that began legal proceedings on their behalf. The case received wide publicity in Britain and in India, and a relief fund was set up in India to help raise funds for their return passage. By the time the Indians returned home, one had died, and the group had been starving for a week.

DANCE, MUSIC AND CULTURES OF DECOLONISATION

The failed Liberty's exhibit has fittingly attracted attention from scholars such as Mathur for the backlash against colonial power that it exhibited and the impact of 'popular, commercial, or "low" cultural practices on the history of anthropological production' (2000, 516). A detailed archival search reveals the journalistic reporting of the event and other important details of the legal case led by Nandalal Ghosh (see Jensen 2018). The archives expose several fascinating details about this particular colonial exhibition (as discussed in the aforementioned studies by Mathur and Jensen), revealing a complex tapestry of 'native' bodies, colonial law, and anti-colonial agency from seemingly oppressed constituencies of people in Britain. Yet, if we attend closely to the dancers who were part of the Liberty's exhibit and re-trace their movements, the picture becomes further complicated. I will open up, therefore, a different set of archival remains: those from a slim file housed in the Westminster City Archives, to suggest that by focusing on the dancing bodies, a more nuanced view of colonial history is afforded.

Most of the available primary records of the Liberty's exhibit cited by Mathur (2000), mainly in the form of newspaper records, concur that among the 'natives' exhibited were two women, a pair of *nautch* dancers who had travelled with a group of forty Indian men.[1] Mathur reported that these dancers were described as '"bewitching" objects of sexual curiosity', and by quoting *The Indian Mirror* newspaper from 6 April 1886, highlighted how visitors to the exhibit tried to '"touch the nautch girls ... in doubt as to whether they are the real article"' (2000, 503). The fact that the dancers were subjected to unsolicited physical touching by visitors to the living display at Battersea Park is not surprising. Most studies on human exhibits have found that despite clearly demarcated zones for spectator and those exhibited, regulations for contact between bodies were often breached. One of the first striking points about a newspaper article attributed to *Illustrated London News* in the Westminster City Archives file is the relegation of dance labour to non-work. The article announces:

> The Indian village at the Albert Palace, Battersea, was opened on Saturday afternoon. It presents in a small space a variety of typical Hindoo industries, and is peopled by forty-five natives from different districts of India, of different castes and creeds. The natives are divided in to two classes – the entertainers and the workers. The former give performances illustrative of Hindoo juggling, dancing, and snake charming; the latter are employed in their respective trades. (*Illustrated London News*, Nov. 21, 1885a, 524)

This paragraph reveals the Victorian anthropological and taxonomic impulse to not only categorise people of colour, but also to place different values on their class of work. There is no hesitation here to curate the 'different castes and creeds' of India. The caste system was a matter of great curiosity, generating attitudes of superior moral indignation and marking out differences from Euro-Americans. On the other hand, the taxonomy of labour swiftly classifies the work of the Indians into the binary categories of 'entertainers' and 'workers.' Dancing, along with juggling and snake charming, is not considered work, and dancers are not 'employed' in a trade. A similar absenting of dance labour occurs in the captions of the visual document from the *Illustrated London News* (1885b, 527; see Figure 2).

The dancer is at Number 2, labelled 'Nautch dancing'. She is not given a profession or trade, and is not labelled a Nautch *dancer*, as the rest of her colleagues. She and the

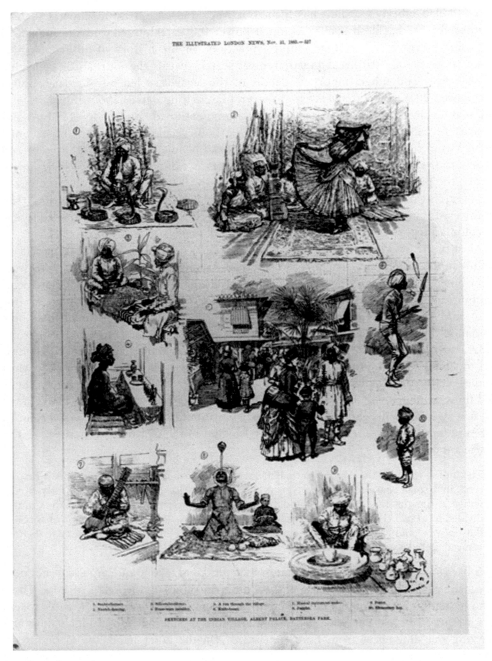

Figure 2. 'Sketches at the Indian Village, Albert Palace, Battersea Park.' Image reproduced with the permission of Westminster City Archives and Liberty Ltd.

'Elementary Boy' are stripped of any identity pertaining to trade or work. The second piece of information of note is a short paragraph in the same newspaper article on the dancers:

> The entertainment provided by the jugglers and dancers attracted a large number of spectators, who were much interested in the exhibition of sleight-of-hand. The nautch dancers, of whom there are three, go through a series of graceful evolutions to the accompaniment of strange and monotonous music. Throughout the performance both dancers and jugglers keep up a continuous song or conversation in Hindustani, explanatory of the entertainment. The snake-charming forms an important part of the performances. (*Illustrated London News*, Nov. 21, 1885a, 524)

The article above suggests that there were three dancers, not two as found in the archival records consulted by Mathur (2000). Who was the third dancer? Is this an error in reporting, along with the fact that the first excerpt reports forty-five natives, instead of forty-two? The archival reportage on the dancers becomes further complicated when we learn, through Mathur (2000), that the pair of *nautch* dancers was a mother and daughter duo. The pithy file at Westminster City Archives tells a different story. In a document (see Figure 3) titled 'List of Indian Natives', forty-five 'natives' are listed, and three people are named as dancers: Dancing Boy Sheik Ameer Sheik Mohideen from Delhi (age 14), Dancing Girl Sahina Jayabanoo from Delhi (age 16) and Dancing Girl Sheeta Thayi from 'Carnatic' (age 20).

This document is significant for manifold reasons. First, it reveals discrepancies and inconsistencies in the archives relating to those exhibited in colonial displays. Second, the list includes a 9-year old boy, Bala Balaya, the 'Elementary Boy' here listed as

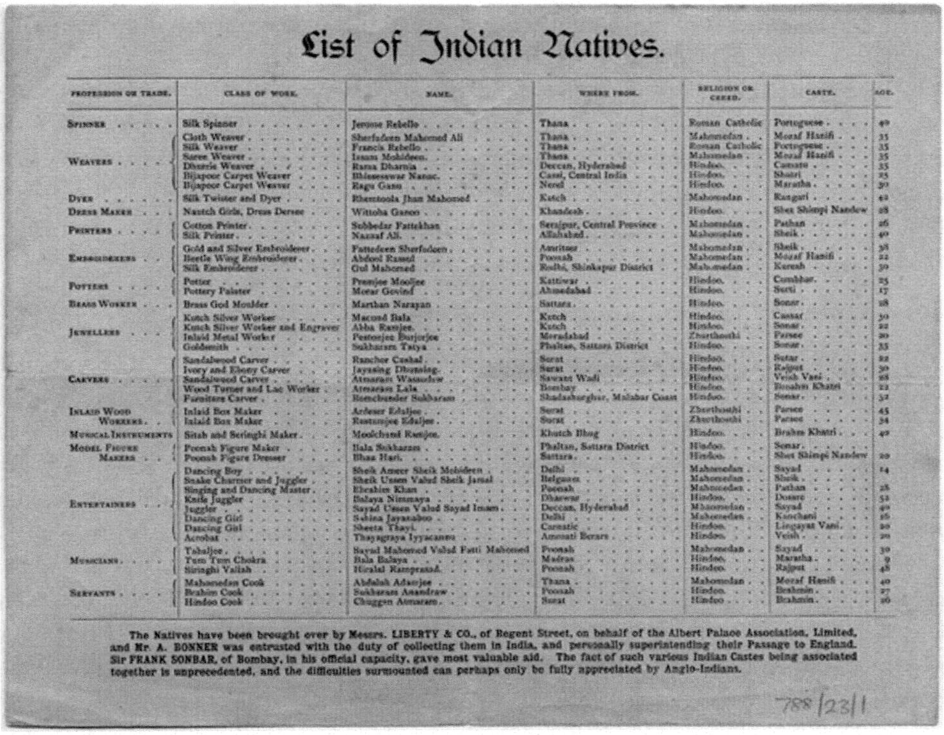

List of Indian Natives.

PROFESSION OR TRADE.	CLASS OF WORK.	NAME.	WHERE FROM.	RELIGION OR CREED.	CASTE.	AGE.
Spinner	Silk Spinner	Jerome Rebello	Thana	Roman Catholic	Portuguese	40
Weavers	Cloth Weaver	Sherfudeen Mahomed Ali	Thana	Mahomedan	Moraf Hanifi	35
	Silk Weaver	Francis Rebello	Thana	Roman Catholic	Portuguese	35
	Saree Weaver	Issam Mohideen	Thana	Mahomedan	Moraf Hanifi	35
	Dhurrie Weaver	Rama Dharnia	Deccan, Hyderabad	Hindoo	Camatu	35
	Bijapoor Carpet Weaver	Bhissesswar Nanac	Cassi, Central India	Hindoo	Shatri	25
	Bijapoor Carpet Weaver	Ragu Gano	Nerul	Hindoo	Maratha	30
Dyer	Silk Twister and Dyer	Rhemtoola Jhan Mahomed	Kutch	Mahomedan	Rangari	42
Dress Maker	Nautch Girls, Dress Dersee	Wittoba Ganoo	Khandesh	Hindoo	Shet Shimpi Nandew	28
Printers	Cotton Printer	Subbedar Fattekhan	Serajpur, Central Province	Mahomedan	Pathan	26
	Silk Printer	Nazraf Ali	Allahabad	Mahomedan	Sheik	40
Embroiderers	Gold and Silver Embroiderer	Fattedeen Sherfudeen	Amritsur	Mahomedan	Sheik	38
	Beetle Wing Embroiderer	Abdool Rasool	Poonah	Mahomedan	Moraf Hanifi	22
	Silk Embroiderer	Gul Mahomed	Rodhi, Shinkapur District	Mahomedan	Kureshi	30
Potters	Potter	Premjee Mooljee	Kattiwar	Hindoo	Cumbhar	25
	Pottery Painter	Morar Govind	Ahmedabad	Hindoo	Surti	17
Brass Worker	Brass God Moulder	Marthan Narayan	Sattara	Hindoo	Sonar	28
Jewellers	Kutch Silver Worker	Macund Bala	Kutch	Hindoo	Cassar	30
	Kutch Silver Worker and Engraver	Abba Ramjee	Kutch	Hindoo	Sonar	22
	Inlaid Metal Worker	Pestonjee Burjorjee	Moradabad	Zhurthoshti	Parsee	20
	Goldsmith	Sukharam Tatya	Phaltan, Sattara District	Hindoo	Sonar	35
Carvers	Sandalwood Carver	Rancher Cushal	Surat	Hindoo	Sutar	22
	Ivory and Ebony Carver	Jaysing Dhunsing	Surat	Hindoo	Rajput	30
	Sandalwood Carver	Atmaram Wassudew	Sawant Wadi	Hindoo	Veish Vani	28
	Wood Turner and Lac Worker	Atmaram Lala	Bombay	Hindoo	Bonahm Khatri	22
	Furniture Carver	Romchunder Sukharam	Shadashurghur, Malabar Coast	Hindoo	Sonar	32
Inlaid Wood Workers	Inlaid Box Maker	Ardeser Edaljee	Surat	Zhurthoshti	Parsee	45
	Inlaid Box Maker	Rustumjee Edaljee	Surat	Zhurthoshti	Parsee	34
Musical Instruments	Sitah and Seringhi Maker	Moolchand Ramjee	Khutch Bhog	Hindoo	Brahm Khatri	42
Model Figure Makers	Poonah Figure Maker	Bala Sukharam	Phaltan, Sattara District	Hindoo	Sonar	
	Poonah Figure Dresser	Bhau Hari	Sattara	Hindoo	Shet Shimpi Nandew	20
Entertainers	Dancing Boy	Sheik Ameer Sheik Mohideen	Delhi	Mahomedan	Sayad	14
	Snake Charmer and Juggler	Sheik Usmn Valud Sheik Jamal	Belgaum	Mahomedan	Sheik	
	Singing and Dancing Master	Ebrahim Khan	Poonah	Mahomedan	Pathan	28
	Knife Juggler	Balaya Nimmaya	Dharwar	Hindoo	Dosare	52
	Juggler	Sayad Usmn Valud Sayad Imam	Deccan, Hyderabad	Mahomedan	Sayad	40
	Dancing Girl	Sahina Jayanaboo	Delhi	Mahomedan	Kanchani	16
	Dancing Girl	Sheeta Thayi	Carnatic	Hindoo	Lingayat Vani	20
	Acrobat	Thayagraya Iyyacanno	Amraoti Berars	Hindoo	Veish	20
Musicians	Tabaljee	Sayad Mahomed Valud Fatti Mahomed	Poonah	Mahomedan	Sayad	30
	Tum Tum Chokra	Bala Balaya	Madras	Hindoo	Maratha	9
	Siringhi Valiah	Hiralal Ramprasad	Poonah	Hindoo	Rajput	48
Servants	Mahomedan Cook	Abdulah Adamjee	Thana	Mahomedan	Moraf Hanifi	40
	Brahim Cook	Sukharam Anandraw	Poonah	Hindoo	Brahmin	27
	Hindoo Cook	Chuggen Atmaram	Surat	Hindoo	Brahmin	26

The Natives have been brought over by Messrs. LIBERTY & CO., of Regent Street, on behalf of the Albert Palace Association, Limited, and Mr. A. BONNER was entrusted with the duty of collecting them in India, and personally superintending their Passage to England. Sir FRANK SONBAR, of Bombay, in his official capacity, gave most valuable aid. The fact of such various Indian Castes being associated together is unprecedented, and the difficulties surmounted can perhaps only be fully appreciated by Anglo-Indians.

788/23/1

Figure 3. 'List of Indian Natives.' Image reproduced with the permission of Westminster City Archives and Liberty Ltd.

'Tum Tum Chokra', showing that for exhibit curators such Mr. A. Bonner and Sir Frank Sonbar of Bombay (named at the bottom of the document), child labour was not an issue. Third, attending to the entries for the dancers reveals the chaotic and haphazard way in which dances were curated and presented for the spectacles at the exhibition. Not only were the two women dancers not a mother and daughter, they also came from opposite sides of India: Sahina from Delhi, and Sheeta from the vaguely labelled 'Carnatic' region, probably meaning from South India. The two dancers would have hailed from very different movement traditions: a close inspection of the image in Figure 2, especially the garments that the dancers seem to be wearing, suggests that Sahina trained in a north Indian dance form (she is wearing a *churidar*, a long skirt, a blouse and a veil), whereas Sheeta, seated and playing a musical instrument, seems to be wearing a *sari*. Sheik Ameer Sheik Mohideen, the Dancing Boy, has left no visual trace of his dancing. The reportage of the performance from the extract above suggests that snake charming was an 'important part of the performances.' Not only were the live *nautch* performances a complete mish-mash of north and south Indian movement idioms, they also collapsed animal and human performances. The dancers apparently kept up a conversation in Hindustani while dancing. What was this 'Hindustani' language, spoken by a Carnatic dancer and two performers from Delhi, hailing from different linguistic territories? The spectators who thronged the exhibitions were desperate for an 'authentic' taste of the exotic. Instead, they were served a chaotic and disorderly South Asian aesthetic in the name of authenticity. On the other hand, the chaotic framework of the performance may have allowed for new forms of creativity as dancers adapted to each other's movement vocabularies through improvisation, and thus brought about new hybrid dance aesthetics.

The layered up bodies of the *nautch* dancers were a visual oddity for spectators and of no value to anthropologists. These dancing bodies disrupted both the scopophilic gaze that attempted to consume them, and the violent anthropological/pedagogic/taxonomic drive that may have wanted to study and visually dissect them. The corporeality of the dancers butted against the ocular hegemony of the exhibition.

'Dance Remains': reenactments and historical fictions

Confronted with archival fake news, inconsistencies, and the failure of textual and visual records in adequately capturing the lived experiences of the dancers in Liberty's exhibit, I ask: in what ways can a creative, performative and corporeal engagement with the archives, with history, offer a valuable methodology for research? From the nearly vanished remains of dancing bodies in the colonial archive, what form could a re-imagining of *nautch* dancers, their dancing and their histories take? To attempt a reconstruction, to give Sahina, Sheeta and Sheik Ameer a 'true voice' to speak back to history seems to be a fair way forward but Spivak whispers that I, the privileged academic and 'native informant' would then be ventriloquising for the subaltern (1993, 79). I therefore turn to performance reenactments in order to seek a viable methodology to make sense of a violent colonial history. The performance studies scholar, Rebecca Schneider wrote a seminal essay, 'Performance Remains', probing the ephemeral nature of performance within the logic of the archive, according to which performance is 'that which does not remain' (2001, 100). Schneider argues against this tendency of the archive to make performance vanish,

DANCE, MUSIC AND CULTURES OF DECOLONISATION

suggesting that archives themselves perform the institution of disappearance. Schneider writes:

> When we approach performance not as that which disappears (as the archive expects), but as both the act of remaining and a means of reappearance (though not a metaphysics of presence) we almost immediately are forced to admit that remains do not have to be isolated to the document, to the object, to bone versus flesh (2001, 103).

Schneider warns that we should not treat 'performative remains as a metaphysic of presence that privileges an original or singular authenticity' (2001, 104). She suggests that 'it is not *presence* that appears in performance but precisely the missed encounter – the reverberations of the overlooked, the missed, the repressed, the seemingly forgotten' (2001, emphasis in original). This rejection of authentic pasts in reenactments is also echoed in contemporary dance reenactments, and in scholarship on such reenactments. Andre Lepecki proposes that a choreographic 'will to archive' in current dance reenactments gives dancers 'the capacity to identify in a past work still non-exhausted creative fields of "impalpable possibilities"' (2010, 31). In re-enacting dances, Lepecki suggests, 'we turn back, and in this return we find in past dances a will to keep inventing' (2010, 46). A concern with the 'economies of authorship' (2010) also appears in Ramsay Burt's essay on dance reenactments, which highlights the political potential of an active rather than a 'reactive use of history' (2003, 37), exploring how contemporary dances butt against the imposed hegemony of codified dance vocabularies and techniques as methods of regulating bodies. He suggests that in dance work where the use of historical citations emphasises the present experience of the performer and her relationship to the past, it is possible to 'short-circuit the power relations through which dancing bodies are disciplined and controlled' (2003, 41). In such reenactments, 'history is no longer seen as a source of transcendent, aesthetic values' (2003) and the spectators, through partial access to memory acts, engage in a new relationship with the past.

In Mark Franko's recently edited volume of essays on dance and reenactment (2017), the increasing significance of reenactment as a methodology in dance studies is made clear. Franko carefully delineates the difference between reconstruction as a 'method of recovery' and reenactment as a 'dramaturgy of presentation' (2017, 8), highlighting, like Schenider (2001) the rejection of authenticity within the reenactment process. Discussing reenactment as a methodology, Franko suggests:

> In reversing the ideological premises of reconstruction while conserving its methodology, re-enactive dancers have taken the representation of the past into their own hands, and accordingly have transformed it. This appropriation of the historical function can be interpreted in a number of ways: (1) as the "right of return" to earlier work; (2) the use of performance as a historiographical medium with discursive dimension; and (3) self-staging as an contemporary agent in confrontation with this project, hence a wilful theatricalization of the entire situation (2017, 11).

In attempting to re-narrate creatively the history of the *nautch* dancers in the Liberty's exhibit, I could see myself, a historian-dancer, as agreeing to the features outlined above: exercising my 'right to return' to the past; using my own dance as a historiographical medium with a discursive element; and staging my own self in confrontation with the historiographical project. I could not agree more with Franko that '[i]n many ways, reenactments tell us the past is not over: the past is unfinished business' (2017, 7). Yet,

Bret Bailey did all the above in *Exhibit B*, a reenactment which, according to Chikha and Arnaut engaged mostly white bourgeois audiences, in 'bourgeois ventriloquism' (2013, 679), which failed disastrously in London, a city with politically conscious diasporic constituencies. I would argue that there are ideological underpinnings within current contemporary Euro-American dance reenactments, which fail certain kinds of archival traces, certain violent histories, and certain types of dance remains. Most of the Euro-American dance reenactments are overwhelmingly concerned with the politics of authorship, as noted by Lepecki (2010) and Burt (2003). The choreographers involved in many of the reenactments discussed in Franko's volume remain tethered to a mostly white, self-referential history. Most, if not all of the reenactments, rely methodologically on the idea of notations or other written records of dance, on the presence of recoverable materials, as Anna Pakes points out (2017). Neither authorship as a conceptual drive nor notation as a methodological tool can help us re-imagine the *nautch*. So I picked up the threads of Pakes's wonderful but tentative proposal. While my re-imagining of the Liberty *nautch* dancers has very little in common with the three dance works Pakes cites as examples of historical fictions (Fabian Barba's *A Mary Wigman Dance* Evening, 2009; Philippe Decouffle's *Panorama*, 2012; and Kirov Ballet's *Sleeping Beauty*, 1999), the idea that the function of these fictions 'is to test how things might have been without necessarily committing to the claim that this is how they were' (2017, 98) is appealing. So I ask, for my project of reimagining the lived experiences of the *nautch* dancers: how does historical fiction as a corporeal methodology enable a more ethical recovery of subaltern voices muffled by the colonial archive?

When I first encountered the history of Liberty's human exhibit through Mathur's (2000) essay, I was struck by a gap in the historical narrative, between the written text and the visual archive. Mathur wonderfully captured the bitterly cold winter of London in 1885, when the human exhibit opened. This icy history crept inside me and began to settle as I began to wonder about the displayed Indians, shivering and trembling, their breath freezing. In sub-zero conditions, the motley group of South Asians, in their cotton *dhotis*, *kurtas*, *churidars* and *saris*, still managed to find a voice – they complained about a lack of adequate clothing, and were given winter clothes. Instead of the warm brown skin of exotic bodies, spectators witnessed the 'natives' covered in layers of European woollens and left the exhibit disappointed. There was no spectacle of coloured human flesh for the voyeuristic white gaze.

The visual records however, do not tell the story of the cold. In the image reproduced in Figure 2, and on the pages of the *Illustrated London News*, the 'natives' are all sketched as wearing their usual attire, without any signs of winter wear. Was this a lie, a bit of 'fake news', to rope in audiences through false publicity? Or was the sketch made once the displayed Indians were asked to remove their warm clothing to pose for the sketching artist, despite the cold? I kept thinking of the dancers. What would they have looked like in a woollen coat, hat, gloves and scarf and shoes, layered on top of their Indian clothes? How did they move, pirouette, gesture, with the weight of the garments, the burden of empire? To understand their bodily, kinaesthetic experience, I decided to corporealize history. I wore a long skirt, a blouse, a *dupatta* as a veil, and on top of these I wore a long coat, hat, gloves, scarf and shoes. I tried to dance. I moved awkwardly, clumsily, unable to pirouette at speed, to traverse space fluidly. My hand gestures were muffled by the gloves. My neck and head movements were buried under the hat. My footwork vanished under the cover of shoes.

Theirs was a clumsy, awkward dance. A dance muffled, buried, vanished in the cold, in the archives. Yet, I had to return this awkward and clumsy dance to the pages of history. I wrote a keynote on the *nautch* dancers in the Liberty's exhibit for the 'Dance in the Age of Forgetfulness' conference organised by the Society of Dance Research in 2018, and I performed my reenactment. I walked on to the performance space wearing layers of clothing, European woollens on top of layers of mismatched Indian articles, carrying a suitcase. I tried to briefly reenact the frozen moment of dancing in Figure 2, turning slowly while holding the veil, and then abandoned the pirouette, the gesture. As my performance lecture progressed, I began to take off the articles of clothing. I bit one glove with my teeth, pulled it out of my hands and spat it. I shook off the other glove. I flung my hat at the audience, threw my coat and cast off my *dupatta*. I undid my blouse, unhooked my skirt. By the end of my lecture, the space was strewn with overthrown clothes. I gathered these strewn garments, packed them in the suitcase and wheeled it away, leaving an empty space. When I re-performed the lecture at the opening plenary of the Dance Studies Association annual conference in 2018, I added another layer. I imagined what the dancers would have muttered under their breath when their buttocks were groped or their breasts pinched by spectators of the Liberty's display. I wrote a fiction in which the *nautch* dancers swore back. Along with my dance colleagues Melissa Blanco Borelli and Ann Cooper Albright, I performed a choreography of choral swearing, in which the filthiest of expletives were uttered, echoed, and repeated loudly.

In the absence of notations, reliable visual records or other forms of documentation, a reenactment of the material conditions in which the Liberty *nautch* dancers may have moved was a useful starting point to imagining their corporeality. However, the limits of reenactment as a methodology in this context lay mainly in the impossibility of returning to a violent history without repeating or reifying its violence. Hence, in my own corporeal engagement with the *nautch* dancer's history, only one gesture – that of holding the veil and turning slowly – is attempted and then it is abandoned. The rest of the movement mainly arises from the fictional overthrowing of garments. It is historical fiction which affords a new set of corporeal acts – flinging, shaking and straining take the place of any plausible or recognisable South Asian movements that might lend an air of 'authenticity' to the reimagined colonial past. The lack of any written historical materials on movement leads to the potential for subverting representations of the exotic oriental dancer.

A letter to liberty's *nautch* dancers

Dear Sahina, Sheeta and Sheik Ameer: yours is a dance I can never claim to reenact. I cannot. Yours is voice I can never claim to recover. I need not. You had a voice and you used it. But in fictionalising your history, I have in my body felt the tiniest fraction of the enormous weight and burden of empire that you did. I have overthrown, cast off and shed that burden, as you managed to do, even if partially. I swore back, as you may or may not have. I took some liberties. I appropriated your history by performing your story. But I also bit, pulled, spat at, shook off, flung, threw, cast off, undid and unhooked the part written for you by the archive. Dancing is a doing, and my dance allowed me to do this. And I hope that your traces have allowed me, in an anarchic way perhaps, to decolonise the archive.

Note

1. It is important to examine briefly here the multiplicity of meanings that the term '*nautch*' evoked for people in South Asia and for those in Europe. As Rosie Jensen (2018) suggests, one meaning pointed to the dramatised and fictional character of an exotic South Asian dancer, which was popularised on the European stage through ballets such as *La Bayadère* (1877) and productions such as *The Nautch Girl* (1891). These were played by white performers. The other versions of *nautch* were the real South Asian dancers who Euro-Americans encountered in India, or who travelled to Europe and North America from India. The term *nautch* is an anglicised version of the word '*naach*', which translates simply as 'dance'. It was an umbrella term used by Europeans to collapse a range of different practices of dance from across the South Asian sub-continent. The *nautch* body, along with the bodies of *devadasis* (temple dancers) became the centre of fierce debates on South Asian dancing women's sexual promiscuity, public sexual health, property and inheritance rights for women, etc. under colonial rule. Simultaneously attractive and fearsome, beautiful and dangerous, skilled but disreputable – the *nautch* embodied ambivalent attitudes to the idea of Indian exotic femininity. An anti-*nautch* campaign was launched by British Christian missionaries and urban Indians, including nationalists and professionals, in 1892, a few years after *nautch* dancers were brought over for the Liberty's exhibit. It ultimately led to the suppression of the *devadasi* (temple dancer) system in India. See Pallabi Chakravorty (2008) for a more detailed discussion of *nautch*.

Acknowledgements

This work was supported by the British Academy/Leverhulme Trust under the Small Research Grants Scheme (SRG2016).

Disclosure statement

No potential conflict of interest was reported by the author.

Funding

This work was supported by the British Academy/Leverhulme Trust under the Small Research Grants Scheme [grant number SG161464].

References

Allwood, John. 1977. *The Great Exhibitions*. London: Studio Vista.

Altick, Richard D. 1978. *The Shows of London*. Cambridge: The Belknap Press of the Harvard University Press.

Auerbach, Jeffrey. 2002. "Art, Advertising, and the Legacy of Empire." *The Journal of Popular Culture* 35 (4): 1–23.

Bennett, Tony. 1995. *The Birth of the Museum: History, Theory, Politics*. London: Routledge.

Blanchard, Pascal, Nicolas Bancel, Gilles Boëtsch, Éric Deroo, Sandrine Lemaire (eds), and Teresa Bridgeman (trans.). 2013. *Human Zoos: Science and Spectacle in the age of Colonial Empires*. Liverpool: Liverpool University Press.

Breckenridge, Carol A. 1989. "The Aesthetics and Politics of Colonial Collecting: India at World Fairs." *Comparative Studies in Society and History* 31 (2): 195–216.

Burt, Ramsay. 2003. "Memory, Repetition and Critical Intervention: The Politics of Historical Reference in Recent European Dance Performance." *Performance Research* 8 (2): 34–41.

Chakravorty, Pallabi. 2008. *Bells of Change: Kathak Dance, Women and Modernity in India*. Calcutta: Seagull Books.

Chikha, Chokri Ben, and Karel Arnaut. 2013. "Staging/Caging 'Otherness' in the Postcolony: Spectres of the Human Zoo." *Critical Arts* 27 (6): 661–683.

Coombes, Annie E. 1994. *Reinventing Africa: Museums, Material Culture and Popular Imagination in Late Victorian and Edwardian England*. New Haven and London: Yale University Press.

Corbey, Raymond. 1993. "Ethnographic Showcases, 1870–1930." *Cultural Anthropology* 8 (3): 338–369.

Franko, Mark. 2017. "Introduction: The Power of Recall in a Post-Ephemeral Era." In *The Oxford Handbook of Dance and Reenactment*, edited by Mark Franko, 1–18. New York: Oxford University Press.

Greenhalgh, Paul. 1988. *Ephemeral Vistas: The Expositions Universelles, Great Exhibitions and World's Fairs, 1851–1939*. Manchester: Manchester University Press.

Hoffenberg, Peter H. 2001. *An Empire on Display: English, Indian, and Australian Exhibitions rom the Crystal Palace to the Great War*. Berkeley and London: University of California Press.

Jensen, Rosie. 2018. "India in London: Performing India on the Exhibition Stage 1851–1914." PhD dissertation. University of Exeter.

Lepecki, Andre. 2010. "The Body as Archive: Will to Re-Enact and the Afterlives of Dances." *Dance Research Journal* 42 (2): 28–48.

Mathur, Saloni. 2000. "Living Ethnological Exhibits: The Case of 1886." *Cultural Anthropology* 15 (4): 492–524.

Muir, Hugh. 2014. "Barbican Criticises Protesters Who Forced Exhibit B Cancellation." *The Guardian*. 24 September. Accessed 9 September, 2018. https://www.theguardian.com/culture/2014/sep/24/barbican-criticise-protesters-who-forced-exhibit-b-cancellation.

Munro, Lisa. 2010. "Investigating World's Fairs: An Historiography." *Studies in Latin American Popular Culture* 28: 80–94.

Pakes, Anna. 2017. "Reenactment, Dance Identity, and Historical Fictions." In *The Oxford Handbook of Dance and Reenactment*, edited by Mark Franko, 79–100. New York: Oxford University Press.

Parezo, Nancy J., and Don D. Fowler. 2007. *Anthropology Goes to the Fair: The 1904 Louisiana Purchase Exposition*. Lincoln: University of Nebraska Press.

Poignant, Roslyn. 2004. *Professional Savages: Captive Lives and Western Spectacle*. New Haven and London: Yale University Press.

Putnam, Walter. 2012. "'Please Don't Feed the Natives': Human Zoos, Colonial Desire, and Bodies on Display." In *The Environment in French and Francophone Literature and Film Volume 39*, edited by Jeff Persels, 55–68. Amsterdam and New York: Rodopi.

Qureshi, Sadiah. 2011. *Peoples on Parade: Exhibitions, Empire, and Anthropology in Nineteenth-Century Britain*. Chicago and London: University of Chicago Press.

Rydell, Robert W. 1984. *All the World's a Fair: Visions of Empire at American International Expositions 1876–1916*. Chicago: University of Chicago.

Schenider, Rebecca. 2001. "Performance Remains." *Performance Research* 6 (2): 100–108.

Sieg, Katrin. 2015. "Towards a Civic Contract of Performance: Pitfalls of Decolonizing the Exhibitionary Complex at Brett Bailey's Exhibit B." *Theatre Research International* 40 (3): 250–271.

Spivak, Gayatri Chakravorty. 1993. "Can the Subaltern Speak?" In *Colonial Discourse and Postcolonial Theory: A Reader*, edited by Patrick Williams and Laura Chrisman, 66–111. New York: Columbia University Press.

Srinivasan, Priya. 2012. *Sweating Saris: Indian Dance as Transnational Labor*. Philadelphia: Temple University Press.

Tharoor, Shashi. 2017. *Inglorious Empire: What the British Did To India*. London: Penguin Books.

Thode-Arora, Hilke, ed. 2014. *From Samoa With Love? Samoan Travellers in Germany 1895–1911. Retracing the Footsteps*. Munich: Hirmer Verlag.

Newspaper sources

1885. *The Graphic*. June 13: 592.

1885a. *Illustrated London News*, November 21:524.

1885b. Illustrated London News November 21: 527.

Index

Note: *Italic* page numbers refer to figures and page numbers followed by "n" denote endnotes.

abhinaya 53, 66n1
African National Congress party 21
African Trinidadian musical style 45
alairuppu 91
Albright, Ann Cooper 125
Allwood, John 114
Altick, Richard D. 114
Ambedkar, Bhimrao Ramji 3, 4
Anandagopalan, Padmavathy 91
anthropological-zoological exhibitions 116
Anthropologisch-Zoologische Ausstellung 116
anti-indenture songs 3
anti-nautch campaign 126n1
arangetram 86–87, 90
Arun, O. S. 91
Ashta Nayika 77
assimilationism 60

Baartmann, Saartjie 116
Bahadur, Gaiutra 11
Bailey, Brett 113, 124
Bakrania, Falu 84
Balchandran-Gokul, Mira 55–56, 58
Ballengee, Christopher L. 13
Barnum, Phineas Taylor 116
Basu, Urbi 59, 66n14
Battle of Karbala 42
BBC *see* British Broadcasting Corporation (BBC)
BBC Young Classical Musician 55
BBC *Young Dancer* 13, 54, 55; South Asian dance category, inclusion of (*see* South Asian dance category, inclusion of)
BBC Young Musician 55
The Beatles 8
Bèlè 49n4
Bennett, Tony 115
bharatanatyam 85, 86
Birdsong Academy model 40
Birdsong Steel Orchestra 39, 40
Black Power Movement 40, 41
Blanco Borelli, Melissa 125
Bonner, A. 122

bourgeois ventriloquism 124
Brereton, Bridget 38
British Broadcasting Corporation (BBC) 53
Brooks, Peter 104
Brown, Ismene 58, 61, 67n20
Buckland, Theresa 58
Buffalo Bill 116
Bunjilaka Aboriginal Museum 105
Burt, Ramsay 124

Camilleri, Peter 61
Campaneau, Andreea 104
Carnatic music, in London 84–88; musical creativity, limits of 89–90; new creativity, in diasporic settings 90–91; voice, devotion and ideal femininity 88–89
Carnatic South Indian classical music 83
Carnival Development Committee (CDC) 38
Carroll, Noel 57
CDC *see* Carnival Development Committee (CDC)
Chakravorty, Pallabi 126n1
Chatterjee, Partha 2, 7, 87
Clegg, Johnny 19
colonial matrix of power 18, 20
Coney Island 117
Conquergood, Dwight 60
contemporary dance 62–64
Contemporary South Asian dance 70–72, 76, 77, 79, 80n3
Cook, Emory 49n3
Coombes, Annie E. 116
Corbey, Raymond 115–116
Couzens, Vicki 105
creole culture: nationalising 37–38
Creole culture 36
Crystal Palace exhibition 115
cultural competency 73

Dance Studies Association 125
Dāsa, Purandara 86
Davis, Basil 40

INDEX

decolonial aesthesis 21
decoloniality 54
decolonisation: definition of 1; scholarship 4–6
decolonising exhibition practices: human
    exhibits and pedagogical violence 114–117;
    Liberty's exhibition 117–122, *118, 120, 121*;
    liberty's nautch dancers, letter to 125–126;
    reenactments and historical fictions 122–125
Department of Foreign Affairs and Trade
    (DFAT) 106
De Sousa Santos, Boaventura 5, 6
Devadasi Abolition Act (1947) 101
devadasi system 101
Devar, Siva 23
D'Evergreen Tassa Group 46
DFAT *see* Department of Foreign Affairs and
    Trade (DFAT)
dhol-tasha 42
dialogic pedagogies 6–9
dingolay 45, 49n3
Dyke, Greg 54

Edwards, Leon 47
Empire Windrush 7
Euro-American exhibition model 114
European colonialism 38
Exhibit B 113, 124

Fanon, Frantz 2, 7, 13
Farrell, Gerry 8
feminist intercultural performance 99–100;
    'Serpent Dreaming Women' 105–109; talking
    dance/ singing movement 100–105
'First Peoples' 109n11
Fowke, Francis 8
Fowler, Don D. 116
Franko, Mark 123
Freire, Paulo 9, 13
Fuller, Chris 90

Gandhi, Mahatma 3, 4, 6, 10–12
Gandhi, Mohandas 20
Garvey, Marcus 6
Gorringe, Magdalen 13
Govender, Suria 19–22, 25, 27–28, 30, 33;
    biography 21; choreography 21, 23; work
    with Surialanga 29; Zulu-Indian model,
    commitment to 22
Govind, Priyadarsini 105
The Graphic 117
grassroots educational programmes 40
Grau, Andrée 59
Greenhalgh, Paul 115
Group Areas Act 20–21
Guerrero, Alba 104
gumboot dance 23

Hackett, Jane 55–57
Hagenbeck, Carl 116
Hagenbeck company 116
Harrison, F. 100
Harrison, George 9
Higgins, Charlotte 59–60
Hill, Amelia 66n7
History of the People of Trinidad and Tobago
    (Williams) 38
Hoffenberg, Peter H. 115
Holst, Gustav 9
Hornabrook, Jasmine 14
human zoo 116

*The Ignorant Schoolmaster: Five Lessons in
    Intellectual Emancipation* (Rancière) 7
Illustrated London News 119
Immigration Restriction Act 110n19
In Akbar's Palace 61
Indian classical dance, nationalist reconstruction
    of: development, history of 70; ethnic dance
    par excellence 76–80; multicultural politicsof
    69–70, 80n1; overview of 69–72; postcolonial
    and multicultural forms 70; transnational
    present, dance and identity in 72–76
The Indian Cultural Pageant 41
Indian Diaspora 1, 2
Indian Home Rule (Gandhi) 12
The Indian Mirror 119
Indian Music and the West (Farrell) 8
Indian Trinidadian cultural renaissance 40–41
Indian Trinidadian drumming terminology 42
intellectual emancipation 6–9
International Conference Centre in Durban 27
Isai vellalar 100

Jagan, Cheddi 10
Jensen, Rosie 116, 126n1

Kaladeen, Maria del Pilar 7
kalpana swaram 89, 93
Kanneh Mason, Sheku 66n10
kapitha 53, 66n2
Kathak Company 81n5
Kaur, Seetal 83, 85
Kaushik, Mira 55, 62
Keali'inohomoku, Joann 58
Kesavan, Piriyanga 55
Khan, Akram 57, 61
Korom, Frank 49n3
Krishna, T. M. 89
Kuch Kuch Hota Hai film 23
Kumar, Lenny 44, 46, 47, *48*

Lakshmi, C. S. 84, 88
Lenin, Vladimir Ilyich 3, 7

INDEX

131

Lepecki, Andre 123, 124
Letter to a Hindu: The Subjection of India – Its Cause and Cure (Tolstoy) 11
Local Classical Singing 42
London, Carnatic music in 84–88

McFee, Graham 62
Mandela, Nelson 18, 19; African National Congress party 21; historic inauguration of 19; inauguration 32–33; vision 26–29
manodharma sangeetham 84, 85, 89
Manormani Dance Academy 29
Manuel, Peter 49n3
'Many Cultures, One Nation' 19
Marriott, Bruce 58, 66n9
Mathur, Saloni 117, 119, 121, 124
matriarchal aesthetics, counter-culture of 84
Maturana, Humberto 54
Mauss, M. 99, 103
Mbeki, Thabo 26
Menuhin, Yehudi 8, 9
Mignolo, Walter 2, 13, 18, 21, 29, 54
Ministry of Community Development, Arts, and Culture 40
multicultural politics 69
Munoz, Arun 104
Munro, Lisa 117
musical creativity, limits of 89–90

Nachiar Tirumozhi 102
Nadarajah, Kiruthika 90
'Nagumomu Kanaleni' 88
Naidoo, T. P. 22
Naipaul, V. S. 4
Narasimhan, Haripriya 90
Narell, Andy 39
National Gas Company of Trinidad and Tobago 47
National Science Museum 39
Natyashastra 77
nautch 71
The Nautch Girl 126n1
Ndlovu-Gatsheni, Sabelo 18
Ngema, Mbogeni 26
Nityasumangalis 101
non-Indian/white dancers 75

orientalism 60
Orientalist fantasies 72
O'Shea, Janet 63
Ostad, Tabassom 104

Panday, Basdeo 49n5
Parezo, Nancy J. 116
Parmanand 10, 11
participatory research 4–6

Patel, Seeta 57, 64–65
Pattamal, D. K. 89
People's National Movement (PNM) 37–39
Persad-Bissessar, Kamla 49n5
PNM *see* People's National Movement (PNM)
Poignant, Roslyn 116
A Portrait of the Maestro of the Sitar film 8
post-apartheid Durban, Indianness and coloniality in 20–22
Purkayastha, Prarthana 14–15

Quijano, Anibal 54
Qureshi, Sadiah 116

'Raag'n'Blues' (Sampa) 93–96, *95*
Radhakrishnan, Smitha 13
raga abheri 94
ragam thanam pallavi 90
Raga Room 90
'Raghupathy Raghava' song 23
Raghuraman, Kalpana 103
rainbow nation 18
Rajarani, Nina 56
Raman, Susheela 89
Ramsumair, Donna 46
Rancière, Jacques 7
Reform Movement 101
regularly funded organisation (RFO) 61
Reith, John 56
Republic Bank of Trinidad and Tobago (RBTT) 43
Rydell, Robert W. 114

Sabri, Sonia 63
Sampa, Abi 84, 88, 91, 94
Sampson, Vicky 28
SAMYO *see* South Asian Music Youth Orchestra (SAMYO)
Sarma, Mithila 84, 86, 88, 91, 94; Subduction Zone 91–93
satyagraha 3
Savigliano, M. 99
Sawhney, Nithin 92
Schenider, Rebecca 123
Schneider, Rebecca 122–123
Selvon, Sam 6
'Serpent Dreaming Women' 105–109
Shah, Jiwan 8
Shankar, Ravi 8, 9
Sharma, Lalbihari 11
Shay, Anthony 60
Sheik Mohideen, Sheik Ameer 122
Shikara 53, 66n2
Sieg, Katrin 113, 114
The Singer and the Song (Lakshmi) 88
Singh, Talvin 92

INDEX

Society of Dance Research 125
Somasundaram, Nisha 58, 66n14
Sonbar, Frank 122
South Africa, Surialanga Dance Company in *see* Surialanga Dance Company, in post-apartheid South Africa
South Asian dance category, inclusion of 55–56; in Britain 61–62; category confusion and 'contemporary' dance 62–64; dialogic representation 60–61; education 56–58; equal representation 58–59; institutional endorsement 59–60
South Asian Music Youth Orchestra (SAMYO) 91
spatial segregation 21
sringara rasa 89
Srinivasan, Priya 14, 86, 89, 117
Sriram, Sid 92
Sristhi Dance Creations 56
Srivastava, Anita 63
Subbulakshmi, M. S. 88–89, 94
'Subduction Zone' 83, 84; by Mithila Sarma 91–93
Subrahmanyam, P. 105, 110n15
Subramanian, Lakshmi 88
Surialanga Dance Company, in post-apartheid South Africa: Bharatanatyam 21–23; decolonial project, growth of 22–27, *24, 26*; Indianness and coloniality in 20–22; overview of 18–19; transforming selves 29–32

talking dance/singing movement 100–105
tamil cultural nationalism 85
Tamil Diaspora 14
tassa: competitions and public pedagogy projects 43–48, *46, 47*; contextualising 41–43
Tassa Association of Trinidad and Tobago (TATT) 43
Tassa Monarch Competition 43
Tassa Taal 43
'terra nullius' 105, 110n13
Tharoor, Shashi 114
Tharp, Kenneth 56, 66n13
The Graphic 117

Thiong'o, Ngũgĩ wa 7
Thiruppavai 102
thirupukkal 91
Thobani, Sitara 5, 14
Thode-Arora, Hilke 116
Tolstoy, Leo 3, 11–12
Torres, Deborah 104
Trinidad All Steel Percussion Orchestra 39
Trinidad and Tobago 36–37; Carnival, calypso and steel pan 38–40; contextualising tassa 41–43; Indian Trinidadian cultural renaissance 40–41; nationalising creole culture 37–38
Trinidadian tassa 41–43
Trinidad & Tobago Sweet Tassa Academy *46, 47*
Trini, Mighty 47–48
truth force 3

Uthra Vijay 14, 99–101, 103, 105, 107, 109, 109n1, 109n7, 109n9

Vaishnavite philosophy 102
Vatuk, Ved Prakash 10

Wajid Ali Shah 11
Walsh, Catherine E. 2
Watts, Graham 62, 67n26
Weibye, Hanna 66n15
Weidman, Amanda 88, 90
Western aesthetic hegemony 62
Western Contemporary dance 76, 78
Western epistemic trap 21
White Australia Policy 107, 110n19
Wignakumar, Anjelli 55
Williams, Eric 37, 41
The Wretched of the Earth (Fanon) 2–3

zerOclassikal project 91
Žižek, Slavoj 67n22
Zulu dance 23, 25
Zulu-Indian intercultural dance 28
Zulu-Indian interculturalism *26*
Zulu song 19
Zuma, Jacob 28